THE GREEKS
AND THE MAKING OF
MODERN EGYPT

THE GREEKS
AND THE MAKING OF
MODERN EGYPT

ALEXANDER KITROEFF

The American University in Cairo Press

Cairo New York

First published in 2019 by
The American University in Cairo Press
113 Sharia Kasr el Aini, Cairo, Egypt
200 Park Ave., Suite 1700, New York, NY 10166
www.aucpress.com

Dar el Kutub No. 11307/17
ISBN 978 977 416 858 1

Dar el Kutub Cataloging-in-Publication Data

Kitroeff, Alexander
        The Greeks and the Making of Modern Egypt / Alexander Kitroeff.—Cairo: The American
University in Cairo Press, 2019.
        p. cm.
        ISBN 978 977 416 858 1
        1. Egypt—History—1952—1970
        2. Greeks—Egypt
        962

    2 3 4 5   23 22 21 20

Designed by Rafik Abousoliman
Printed in the United States of America

Contents

Introduction

There are presently about three thousand Greeks living in Egypt, most of them in Cairo, the rest in Alexandria. They are a pale reminder of a glorious past. In the period between the two world wars, a century after they began arriving, the Greeks in Egypt were about one hundred thousand. They were the largest and most diverse of the foreign communities in Egypt and played a prominent role in the country's banking, cotton, and commercial sectors. This book tells the story of how the Greeks first settled in Egypt in the early nineteenth century, how their numbers and influence steadily grew, how a slow decline set in as Egypt began eliminating the privileges that benefited the Greeks and other foreigners, and concludes with the nationalization of most of Egypt's economy in the 1960s, prompting an exodus that left only a few thousand Greeks who chose to remain. The book concludes with a discussion of the affection for Egypt and their past lives there that most of those who left still feel.

My connection with the history of the Greeks in Egypt is both personal and academic. My great-grandfather Alexander Theodore Kitroeff was one of the many Greeks who left their islands in the Aegean, in his case Chios, and settled in Alexandria in the late nineteenth century. He is buried there, next to his wife Polyxeni, in the Greek Orthodox Cemetery. Both my paternal grandparents were born in Alexandria in the early twentieth century, and my father was also born there. He left Egypt after the Second World War and eventually settled in Athens, where he married my mother. My grandmother also left Egypt around the same time, with her second husband, a Greek naval officer who was stationed in Egypt during the war. My grandfather stayed on until he had to reluctantly leave

1

Egypt and go to Athens after the company he worked for, the Associated Cotton Ginners, was nationalized in 1961.

By that time most of my father's relatives had moved from Egypt to Greece, and I grew up hearing stories about life in Egypt: the size of my great-grandfather's house in Ramla, how he forced my grandfather to go into the cotton business and limit his interest in classical music to playing chamber music in his free time, his brother's love of clay pigeon shooting and shooting real pigeons in the Nile Delta, my grandmother's experiences at the French lycée before she eloped with my grandfather, and my father's pre-Second World War childhood, which involved the freedom of swimming in the harbor of Alexandria to enduring the disciplined routines of the British Boys' School and Victoria College. All those stories were told in English or in Greek interspersed with generous helpings of Arabic, French, and a few Italian words.

My first academic encounter with the study of the Greeks of Egypt was in writing my master's thesis at Keele University. I chose to write about the Greek microcosm created in British-controlled Egypt during the Second World War—the Greek government-in-exile that was based in Cairo, the military units that managed to escape before the Axis occupied Greece, and the Greek residents in Egypt. This topic reflected the great interest in the Greek 1940s that shaped Greek historiography in the late 1970s. My supervisor was Professor Paul Rolo, who was a descendant of one of Alexandria's most influential Anglo-Jewish families, and through his guidance I became familiar with the wider context of the events I was studying, including the lives of Greek and European communities in Egypt. Moreover, during my research I received a great deal of help and advice from the author Stratis Tsirkas (the nom de plume of Giannis Hadjiandreas), who spent most of his life in Egypt as a left-wing activist and writer. His two most important and influential studies were one which placed the poet Constantine Cavafy in Egypt's sociohistorical context and the other was a three-part novel about the left-wing uprising in wartime Egypt, written in a style that echoed but also challenged Lawrence Durrell's own literary evocation of wartime Alexandria.

It should therefore come as no surprise that I chose to study the Greeks of Egypt when at St. Antony's College at Oxford University it came time to pick a subject for my doctoral dissertation, which appeared in book form in 1989.[1] At the time, the study of Greek diaspora communities was a major concern for many historians of Greece. The thinking in the late 1970s was that the relative weakness of the bourgeoisie within Greece, coupled with a wealthier diaspora bourgeoisie that played a middleman or 'comprador' role, contributed to Greece's allegedly distorted capitalist development. This entailed focusing on the Greek merchant communities abroad, primarily in terms of their relationship to the Greek homeland. In deciding to examine the Greeks in Egypt it made sense for me to break with that approach and place the Greeks in their Egyptian context during the period immediately preceding the Second World War, a time that witnessed the rise of the Egyptian nationalist movement. Thus, I treated the Greeks both as a cohesive ethnic group with ties to Greece but also as an entity divided along class lines depending on their social position in Egypt, thus generating different responses to the rise of Egyptian nationalism. This approach was encouraged and immeasurably enriched thanks to the guidance of three leading scholars of the Middle East: my thesis supervisor Roger Owen, my second reader Albert Hourani, and the Alexandria-born economist Robert Mabro—all fellows at St. Antony's Middle East Centre.

When I started writing this book I thought that producing a concise history of the Greek presence in modern Egypt would be relatively easy. A few years ago I had the opportunity to revisit the subject of the Greek role in Egypt when the Cultural Foundation of the Piraeus Bank Group in Greece asked me to edit contributions by an international team of scholars on aspects of the history of the cotton sector in Egypt. These were destined to form the academic blueprint of a cotton museum the Group planned to establish in Egypt, along the lines of several 'technological museums' the Group set up in several areas in Greece. Unfortunately the outbreak of the Greek economic crisis forced the Group to shelve the plan for a cotton museum in Egypt, but hopefully such an undertaking might materialize in the future. At any rate, I believed that my task would be a smooth one in distilling the knowledge I gained working toward my master's thesis and my doctoral dissertation, reworking part of my book to relieve the cumbersome theoretical apparatus, deploying what I had learned doing the cotton museum project, and taking into account the substantial number of excellent studies on foreigners and Greeks in Egypt. Presenting an overview of a historical trajectory that spanned over a century and a half is not easy for any subject. In practice, the job of presenting the Greek role in Egypt—from the era of Muhammad Ali to the nationalizations of private industry that took place under President Gamal Abd al-Nasser—is challenging. The Greeks did not have merely a superficial, colonial-type of presence in the country but instead penetrated deep into its fabric, its economy, and its cities and provincial towns. They developed a complex network of ethnic institutions that fostered their identity, strengthened their ties to each other, and formed a strong bond to their homeland. Finally, the Greeks in Egypt saw themselves as having a special relationship with Egypt and the Egyptians. This sense was built by invoking the relations between the ancient Egyptian and Greek civilizations, and in the modern era, the idea that Greeks were contributing to Egypt's development more as partners rather than foreign residents.

These four aspects of the Greek presence in Egypt—the geographical spread, the varied socioeconomic profile, the strong sense of nationality, and the special relationship between Greeks and Egyptians—are threads that run through this study and, woven together, show how the Greeks adapted and played a role in Egypt's development. The geographical dispersion of the Greeks throughout Egypt was remarkable. Several British observers noted with a mixture of admiration and surprise that they found Greek traders or grocers operating in the most remote parts of the Egyptian provinces. The biggest concentration of Greeks was in Alexandria; the wealthiest resided in the Quartier Grec and may also have had houses in the Ramla district, where many middle-class Greeks lived. A little further out the suburb of Ibrahimiya was home to thousands of middle- and lower-middle-class Greeks. Out of the approximately one hundred thousand foreigners resident in Alexandria, according to the Egyptian census of 1927, over thirty-seven thousand were Greek and their number remained as high and began to dip only after the Second World War. Compared to their fellow Greeks in Cairo, the Alexandrians were wealthier overall and more 'cosmopolitan' because Alexandria had a larger percentage of foreign residents and was oriented toward Europe economically and culturally. By the same token, the Cairo Greeks were able to adapt a little bit better to the Egyptianization measures. After the Greek exodus in the early 1960s in the wake of the nationalization measures, more Greeks remained in Cairo than in Alexandria.

Outside Egypt's two major cities there were large numbers of Greeks in the towns along the Canal Zone. They had arrived to work on the opening of the Suez Canal and stayed to work in the company that ran the operations, ancillary jobs, or in white-collar or retail positions. There were also many Greeks working in a range of jobs in the Delta and towns in Upper Egypt. The Greek grocer, *baqqal* in Arabic, was ubiquitous. Baedeker's guide to Egypt published in 1898 informs its readers that for expeditions off the railway track between Cairo and Luxor one used a donkey and could rest assured that "in most towns the Greek bakkal keeper will provide a simple sleeping room."[2] Very often, and certainly in the smaller towns, the Greeks were the only Europeans. By the same token, when the Egyptians began to play a greater role in their country's economy in the 1930s onward, many Greeks left the provincial towns and resettled in Cairo and Alexandria. The conflicts in the Canal Zone in the 1950s meant the steady diminution of the Greeks in that area. Until the late 1950s and early 1960s, there was a significant demographic presence of Greeks in Alexandria and Cairo, all the more noticeable because almost all the other Europeans had left Egypt.

Next to considering the geographical spread of the Greeks throughout Egypt it behooves one to take into account the class divisions that divided them horizontally based on their wealth and social status. The elite was made up of the major bankers and cotton merchants at the very top, and others in finance, import–export, and owners of major manufacturing firms a little further down the pecking order. The Greek middle class consisted of senior- and middle-level employees in the major banks and commercial and manufacturing enterprises, doctors, lawyers, accountants, and owners of retail shops, cafés, cinemas, and restaurants. What we could call the intellectuals, the writers, literary critics, journalists, and teachers were significant in that they shaped the contours and the content of the identity of the Greeks of Egypt. Among them were philosophical and political differences, and differences in the way they regarded Egypt, with some adopting a superior vantage point but others considering themselves and other Greeks as part of Egyptian society.[3] The lower-middle class, the petty bourgeoisie, included owners of small businesses and shops, and middle- and lower-level employees. There were also Greek workers in manufacturing and jobs associated with the Suez Canal. One of the earliest strikes in the history of labor in Egypt was in the cigarette manufacturing sector and pitted Greek craft workers against Greek capitalists.[4] By the 1950s the Greek grocers had left the provinces but could be found in Alexandria, and during the Suez Crisis-induced blackout in the city, a young André Aciman and his mother sheltered in a Greek grocery.[5] Finally, a small but not insignificant number of Greeks were in the margins of society and legality, involved in the sex trade, smuggling, and selling drugs. In the early twentieth century, when there was a wave of emigration from Greece to Egypt, "Many Greek girls for instance were said to be lured on the promise of a job or a marriage match and welcomed upon their arrival by local intermediaries disguised as the groom's relatives."[6]

Aside from identifying the class stratification of the Greek entity, the challenge is to understand whether their motivations stemmed from their class interests, their national identity, or both. In seeking to understand those motivations I have not assumed that either class or national interests were consistently dominant. Instead I have tried to show how the specific historical context shaped those motivations. I have found that even though the Greeks were divided into distinct classes, they only sometimes operated based on their class interests, and at other times based on national identity, and in some instances even tried to combine both. If there is anything that clearly emerges from the study of the Greeks of Egypt, from the wealthiest entrepreneurs to the smallest grocers, it is that they were alert to their changing environment and tried to adapt to new circumstances as best they could.

The Greeks themselves did not use the term 'ethnicity' because they considered themselves a national group and the same was true of the way Egypt classified them. The definition of who was Greek was blurred because some had Ottoman and later Egyptian citizenship, others British or Italian because they came from islands such as Cyprus or Rhodes that had been ruled by Britain and Italy. But in practice, despite the primacy of those with Greek citizenship, there was a sense of a culturally defined entity who were Greeks—they spoke Greek and were Greek Orthodox Christians—with a small minority of them being Jewish. There were also a few Greek-speaking Muslims from Crete who considered themselves Greek. Those common cultural bonds produced a sense of cohesion and solidarity expressed by informal family ties and preferences about whom to employ, whom to work for, and where to shop. The Benachis, the Choremis, and the Salvagos, the three most prominent Alexandrian families, cemented their economic and social ties through marriages among themselves and with members of other important families, such as the Mitarachis and the Sinadinos. Prior to the First World War there were even instances of marriages between first cousins. There was a strict division of labor between the sexes in these prominent families: the men ran the family business and sat on the boards of the Greek community organizations, and the women ran the household as well as Greek philanthropic projects. Formally, those common cultural connections were manifested in the establishment of Greek social and cultural organizations, many of which had the term 'Hellenic' in their English and French titles because that, rather than the word 'Greek,' served as a reminder that modern Greeks claimed continuity with the ancient Hellenes.

The principal organization was the 'community' (Κοινότητα in Greek), which was modeled on the self-governing local administrative bodies Greeks had formed back in the Ottoman era. The community organization was run by the wealthy Greeks and thanks to their contributions it administered Greek schools and in larger cities Greek hospitals, programs to assist the poor, orphanages, and old people's homes. These were often named after their benefactor; for example the Benachi Orphanage, the Kaniskeris Orphanage, the Antoniades Old People's Home in Alexandria, and Achilopouleos Girls' School and the Melachrino School in Cairo. Despite the existence of the Greek Orthodox Patriarchate in Alexandria—one of the oldest churches in the eastern Mediterranean—it was the local community organizations that ran the Greek Orthodox churches that Greeks established throughout the country. This enabled the community organizations to claim that they were the body that spoke for all the Greeks in each town. Their leaders had left for Egypt from places which were under Ottoman rule and where the local notables exercised considerable power. In Egypt their powers were relatively circumscribed, but that did not prevent them from assuming a leadership role. The dependence on the patronage offered by the community institutions to most of their fellow Greeks cemented their hegemonic role.[7] In contrast, there was no single institution claiming to represent the entire local Italian population.[8] Beyond those core institutions, Greeks established a broad range of cultural, social, and sports organizations. Another strong bond was their connection with their places of origin, their allegiance to Greece and its political parties, and their dependence on Greek consular authorities for protection and confirmation of their privileged status in Egypt. That status was based on the Capitulations, the extraterritorial rights foreigners enjoyed in Egypt. After they were abolished in 1937 and 'Egyptianization' policies began to increase, the Greeks still relied on Greece's diplomatic representatives and the Greek government, hoping optimistically that the special relationship with Egypt would protect them from the worst of those measures. Their responses were different because the Greeks were not a single cohesive entity. The differences notwithstanding, among the Greek responses, there is a common denominator in the way the Greeks of Egypt reacted if we compare them with other foreign minorities, each of which had its own particular connection to Egypt. In placing the Greeks in their Egyptian context, I examine the ways other foreigners reacted to change, and not surprisingly there were differences and similarities at every turn.

The Greeks may have exaggerated the contemporary significance of the ancient ties between Greece and Egypt, and they conveniently overlooked the significance of the privileges they enjoyed when they proclaimed their contribution to Egypt's development. But there is no denying that the Greeks played a significant role in the making of modern Egypt. The original settlement was the result of Muhammad Ali's invitation to a group of merchants, and they and the thousands who followed them over the next century came across the Mediterranean as settlers not conquerors. For most of the period, Egypt was under Britain's sway. The Greeks, even the most Anglophile, never fully identified with the colonial rulers and many times they saw things differently. The Greeks brought know-how and commercial skills, along with the ability to network with the British and French, gaining their trust, if not their respect. They brought with them the innovative drive of the immigrant and were responsible for introducing many new things to Egypt, from different varieties of cotton to new industries, as well as the latest European fashions and consumer goods. The Aegean Island Greeks went to Egypt to dig the Suez Canal and settled in the towns that sprouted along the waterway, becoming an integral part of the functioning of the Canal Zone economy. It was the Greeks that went far into the Egyptian hinterland and set up shop as grocers, conferring the mixed blessing of a steady stream of supplies but also the sale of alcohol and, until the banks arrived, moneylending at high interest rates. All those Greeks seemed to love Egypt. A sign of their attachment to Egypt was that they described themselves in Greek as Αιγυπτιώτες, an invented term that can be translated as 'Egyptiots,' a concept I have rendered here as 'Greeks of Egypt.' In a formal context the name appeared as Αιγυπτιώτες Έλληνες, Egyptian-Greeks, but most frequently it stood on its own as Αιγυπτιώτες—a unique term that describes a special relationship.

The thousands who had to leave in the 1950s and 1960s still cherish their experiences and maintain a strong affection for the Egyptian people. Their lively association, based in Athens, organizes activities designed to preserve the memory of the Greek experiences in Egypt and works closely with the few Greek organizations that exist in Egypt today. The honorary president of the Greek community organization in Alexandria, Stefanos Tamvakis, eloquently expresses the common view that there is a 'Greeks of Egypt' identity—shared both by those few who remain in Egypt and those who moved to Greece but never forgot their origins—that is well worth preserving.[9]

All this makes for a rich and complex experience, which I have tried to do justice to while using the wide lens of a historical overview. Many of the works on the Greeks of Egypt that have appeared during the past two decades in Greece consist of detailed compilations of the history of the various Greek institutions or about Greek life in Egypt that mention as many events, names, and place names as possible in an admirable collection of many-sided activities of the Greeks. This is not such a book, neither is the bibliography. In the same way I eschewed an explicitly theoretical approach, I have also by necessity produced a representative rather than an exhaustive narrative. This study loosely unfolds along its four main threads—geographical spread, socioeconomic diversity, national cohesion, and attachment to Egypt—and tells the story of the Greeks in Egypt from their arrival in the early nineteenth century through their exodus in the early 1960s. It considers the Greeks as a complex, diverse social entity that played multiple and changing roles in the course of the nineteenth and twentieth centuries and examines their many guises: as a diaspora with ties to Greece and the international economy; as part of Egyptian society with vested interests in its wellbeing; a group that enjoyed considerable advantages compared to the native population; and one that enabled the country's dependency on the West but also helped the emergence of a domestic economy. To the end, as dramatically demonstrated by the support of many Greeks to Egypt during the Suez Crisis of 1956, the Greeks were integral to the changing economic, social, and cultural landscape of Egypt even after the Free Officers' Revolution in 1952. This book shows how their relationship with Egypt unfolded and played out over the course of the nineteenth and twentieth centuries. Overall, it suggests that one constant quality characterized the Greek experience in Egypt from Muhammad Ali to Nasser: the ability to adapt to changing circumstances and to navigate successfully between their ties to their Greek homeland and their Egyptian home.

The story told in this book is organized chronologically. The eight chapters correspond to the specific periods of modern Egyptian history that shaped the Greek presence in the country: the Muhammad Ali era and beyond, which witnessed the foundations of modernization; Britain's control over Egypt from the bombardment of Alexandria in 1882 until the First World War; the rise of the nationalist movement and the erosion of foreign privileges until 1952; Greek responses to economic change and Egyptianization; Greek cultural and social life; the Greeks in-between the cosmopolitan world of the foreigners and Egyptian society; the Greeks in the wake of the 1952 revolution until the exodus of the early 1960s; and a final chapter considers the passionate ways the Greeks of Egypt who resettled in Greece have promoted their history in Egypt, kept the memories of that past alive, and demonstrated a profound sense of nostalgia and affection for both Egypt and the Egyptian people.

Acknowledgments

I remain indebted to all those who helped me embark on my scholarly engagement with the Greeks in Egypt thirty years ago, but these acknowledgments also recognize those who assisted me during the planning and writing of this book. Details, stories, and personal memories furnish the reader with a better sense of the events and people that inhabit the narrative, and I benefited from the information shared with me by several of my relatives, especially my uncle, Micky Capaitzis, as well as Yorgos Avgeropoulos, Irene Chrysocheri, Petros Haritatos, Nick Markettos, and Aris Tsaravopoulos. Angelos Dalachanis kindly shared material he had gathered for his study on the Greek exodus from Egypt, and Maria Adamantidis, who researches the history of the Greeks in Cairo, generously allowed me to review and choose photographs from her personal archive.

Maria Dimitriadi and Tassos Sakelaropoulos helped me to obtain photographs from the historical archive of the Benaki Museum, and Mathilde Pyrli provided photographs from the Hellenic Literary and Historical Archive. A Faculty Research Fund Grant and the Provost's Book Fund from Haverford College covered some of my research expenses and copyright permissions for the photographs used.

I wish to thank everyone at the American University in Cairo Press, especially Nadia Naqib, for her confidence in my work, and Katie Holland, for carefully and patiently overseeing the transformation of the manuscript into this book. Finally, I am grateful to all those who made me feel welcome during the twelve-month period I spent writing this book in Kifisiá, in northern Athens, where I was, coincidentally, staying only a fifteen-minute walk away from the old Benachi family mansion.

Chronology

1805 Muhammad Ali becomes governor of Egypt and will soon invite foreign merchants, including Greeks, to settle in the country

1833 Greece establishes a Consulate in Alexandria, and Michael Tossizza is named consul general

1843 The Greek community organization is formed in Alexandria on April 25, with Michael Tossizza as president

1854 Greece signs a Capitulations treaty with the Ottoman Empire, which extends to Egypt

1856 The Greek Orthodox Church Evanghelismos (Annunciation) is inaugurated in Alexandria on March 25

1860 The Greek Orthodox community organization is established in Cairo; it is reorganized in 1904
The cotton export firm C.M. Salvago Company is established in Alexandria

1865 The Greek community organization is formed in Port Said and, six years later, in Suez

1869 The Suez Canal opens in November; hundreds of Greeks from Kasos and other Aegean islands participate in its decade-long construction

1875 The Khedive Ismail establishes the Mixed Courts of Egypt

1876 The cotton export firm Choremi Benachi & Company is established in Alexandria

1880 The Greek-language *Tachydromos* newspaper begins publication in Alexandria, and thanks to the leadership of its owners and editors, Sotirios Latsis and Georgios Tinios, quickly becomes one of the most important Greek-language newspapers in Egypt

Greek community organizations are established in Beheira, al-Mahalla al-Kubra, Tanta, and Zifta

1882   As nationalism is on the rise in Egypt, ships sent from Greece temporarily evacuate Greek inhabitants of Alexandria prior to the riots that lead to the city's bombardment and occupation by Britain

1889   Between 1889 and 1905 Greek community organizations are formed in Ibrahimiya, Mansura, and the Upper Egypt towns of Beni Suef, Asyut, Minya, Fayum, and Aswan

1895   Ioannis Antoniades, director of the Commercial Bank of Alexandria and who was knighted by Queen Victoria, dies in Alexandria

1898   The National Bank of Egypt is established, with Constantine Salvago as one of the four founding partners

1899   Georgios Averoff dies in Alexandria on July 15
The Union of Greek cigarette makers, one of the earliest Greek labor unions in Egypt, is formed in Alexandria

1901   The Greek Chamber of Commerce in Alexandria is established on January 20

1907   Egypt's census records 62,973 Greek citizens resident in the country

1911   Mikés Sinadino replaces Emmanuel Benachi as president of the Alexandria community organization. Benachi moves to Athens, where he goes on to play an active role in politics on the side of Eleftherios Venizelos

1912   The Greek Hospital in Cairo is inaugurated in January

1914   Following the outbreak of the First World War, Britain declares a protectorate over Egypt

1915   After he was forced to resign as prime minister of Greece following a dispute with the king over the country's stance on the First World War, Eleftherios Venizelos visits Egypt and is warmly welcomed by the Greeks

1917   Egypt's census records 82,658 people of Greek descent, of whom 56,731 have Greek citizenship

1919   Nationalist demonstrations in Alexandria in March spread to other Egyptian cities, involving riots that cost a number of Greek lives and cause damage to Greek shops. Similar events affecting Greeks would take place in 1921

Following Mikés Sinadino's death, Mikés Salvago becomes president of the Greek community organization of Alexandria

1923   The Greek Chamber of Commerce in Cairo is established

1925   Following the death of Patriarch Photios, Metropolitan and former Ecumenical patriarch Meletios is elected patriarch of Alexandria, ushering in a decade of changes that modernize the Church's life in Egypt

1927   Egypt's census records 99,793 people of Greek descent, of whom 76,264 are Greek citizens, an increase compared to the census a decade earlier. There are 37,106 Greek citizens resident in Alexandria, 20,115 in Cairo, and 5,395 in Port Said

1930   Greece's Minister of Foreign Affairs Andreas Michalakopoulos visits Egypt in February to discuss Greco–Egyptian relations and the future of the Capitulations

1932   The foundation stone for the Kotsikion Hospital is laid in Alexandria on December 23

1933   The poet C.P. Cavafy dies in Alexandria on April 29, on his 70th birthday

The Association of Greeks from Egypt is established in Athens

1936   The Anglo–Egyptian Treaty requires Britain to withdraw its troops in Egypt to the Suez Canal, but it falls short of granting Egypt full independence

1937   Egypt abolishes the Capitulations at an international conference held at Montreux, Switzerland, in May

Egypt's census records 80,466 people of Greek descent, of whom 68,559 have Greek citizenship, an overall decrease compared to the census a decade earlier

1940   The king and the Greek government, along with Greek army and navy units, leave Greece when it is occupied by the Axis forces and arrive in Egypt, which is under British control because of the outbreak of the Second World War

1944   The British put down a left-wing uprising within the Greek army and navy units stationed in Egypt in April

The government and military units move back to Greece following its liberation in October

1947	Egypt introduces the Company Law, a measure designed to bring about the 'Egyptianization' of the country's economy Egypt's census records 57,427 people with Greek citizenship
1948	Egypt abolishes the Mixed Courts
1951	Left-wing Greeks supportive of Egypt's anticolonial struggle form the Greek–Egyptian Cooperation Committee
1952	The Free Officers overthrow King Faruq and take power; the Greek community organizations declare their loyalty to the new government
1954	Gamal Abd al-Nasser becomes president of Egypt
1956	The Suez Crisis begins when Nasser nationalizes the Suez Canal and Britain, France, and Israel launch a short-lived attack on Egypt. Greek maritime pilots, unlike other foreigners, continue to work for the nationalized Canal Company during the events
1957	Egypt's government issues laws designed to Egyptianize the country's banking, commercial, and insurance sectors on January 29 Greek Prime Minister Constaninos Karamanlis and Minister of Foreign Affairs Evangelos Averoff visit Egypt between August 17–21
1958	The Greek community organization of Alexandria estimates that the number of Greek businesses in the city has decreased by 60 percent compared to 1936
1959	Egypt's Law 19/1959, introduced in October and implemented a year later, obliges all foreigners to obtain a work permit
1960	Nasser visits Greece for official talks and visits to tourist sites with his family in June Egypt's census records 47,673 people with Greek citizenship in the country
1961	The Egyptian government nationalizes the economy and places all private firms under varying degrees of state control in July Greece's Minister of Foreign Affairs Evangelos Averoff makes a five-day visit to Cairo in August
1964	In the three-and-a-half years that elapsed since the initiation of the nationalization laws, official figures show that

about fourteen thousand Greeks left Alexandria and Cairo to settle in Greece or another country

1967 The number of Greeks remaining in Egypt is estimated at seventeen thousand

1970 The day after Nasser's death on September 28, the front page of Alexandria's *Tachydromos* newspaper announces "The Hero Died Yesterday"

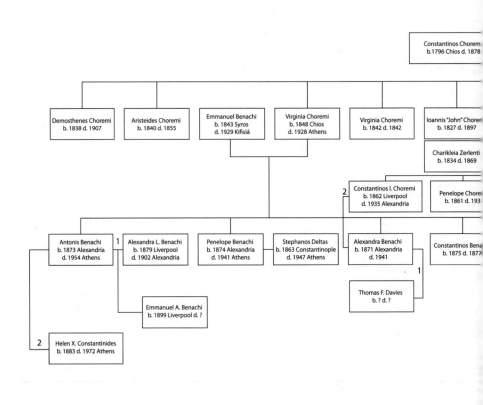

Constantinos Choremi
b.1796 Chios d. 1878

Demosthenes Choremi
b. 1838 d. 1907

Aristeides Choremi
b. 1840 d. 1855

Emmanuel Benachi
b. 1843 Syros
d. 1929 Kifisiá

Virginia Choremi
b. 1848 Chios
d. 1928 Athens

Virginia Choremi
b. 1842 d. 1842

Ioannis "John" Choremi
b. 1827 d. 1897

Charikleia Zerlenti
b. 1834 d. 1869

2 Constantinos I. Choremi
b. 1862 Liverpool
d. 1935 Alexandria

Penelope Choremi
b. 1861 d. 1931

Antonis Benachi
b. 1873 Alexandria
d. 1954 Athens

1 Alexandra L. Benachi
b. 1879 Liverpool
d. 1902 Alexandria

Penelope Benachi
b. 1874 Alexandria
d. 1941 Athens

Stephanos Deltas
b. 1863 Constantinople
d. 1947 Athens

Alexandra Benachi
b. 1871 Alexandria
d. 1941

Constantinos Benachi
b. 1875 d. 1877

1

Thomas F. Davies
b. ? d. ?

Emmanuel A. Benachi
b. 1899 Liverpool d. ?

2 Helen X. Constantinides
b. 1883 d. 1972 Athens

The Choremi–Benachi–Salvago Family Tree

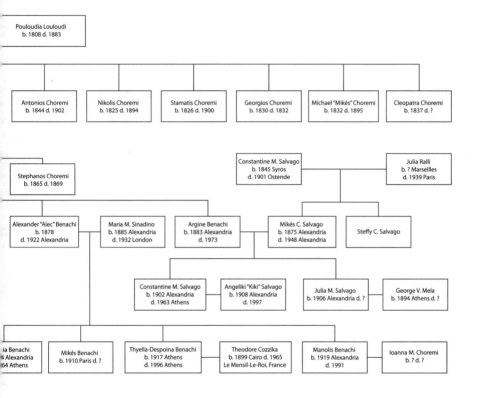

Pouloudia Louloudi
b. 1808 d. 1883

Antonios Choremi
b. 1844 d. 1902

Nikolis Choremi
b. 1825 d. 1894

Stamatis Choremi
b. 1826 d. 1900

Georgios Choremi
b. 1830 d. 1832

Michael "Mikés" Choremi
b. 1832 d. 1895

Cleopatra Choremi
b. 1837 d. ?

Stephanos Choremi
b. 1865 d. 1869

Constantine M. Salvago
b. 1845 Syros
d. 1901 Ostende

Julia Ralli
b. ? Marseilles
d. 1939 Paris

Alexander "Alec" Benachi
b. 1878
d. 1922 Alexandria

Maria M. Sinadino
b. 1885 Alexandria
d. 1932 London

Argine Benachi
b. 1883 Alexandria
d. 1973

Mikés C. Salvago
b. 1875 Alexandria
d. 1948 Alexandria

Steffy C. Salvago

Constantine M. Salvago
b. 1902 Alexandria
d. 1963 Athens

Angeliki "Kiki" Salvago
b. 1908 Alexandria
d. 1997

Julia M. Salvago
b. 1906 Alexandria d. ?

George V. Mela
b. 1894 Athens d. ?

ia Benachi
Alexandria
4 Athens

Mikés Benachi
b. 1910 Paris d. ?

Thyella-Despoina Benachi
b. 1917 Athens
d. 1996 Athens

Theodore Cozzika
b. 1899 Cairo d. 1965
Le Mensil-Le-Roi, France

Manolis Benachi
b. 1919 Alexandria
d. 1991

Ioanna M. Choremi
b. ? d. ?

The numbers 1 and 2 refer to first and second marriages.

Note on the Family Tree

In the period that began with the British occupation of Egypt in 1882 and ended with the Egyptian revolution of 1952, the Benachi, Choremi, and Salvago families were at the center of Egypt's economic life and the communal life of the Greeks in Alexandria. In 1876 the creation of the Choremi Benachi Company, one of the largest firms in Egypt, and the establishment of the Egyptian Salt & Soda Company with the participation of all three families, cemented their economic ties, which would continue to grow stronger over the next few decades. Six years prior to the establishment of the Choremi Benachi Company, the future partners had become linked when Emmanuel Benachi married Ioannis "John" Choremi's younger sister, Virginia. Their youngest daughter, Argine, later married Mikés Salvago in Alexandria in 1901. Argine's sister, Alexandra Benachi (1871–1941), was first married to Thomas F. Davies, a business partner of her father; her second marriage was to Constantinos, the son of Ioannis "John" Choremi. Between these three families the practice of marrying cousins was also adopted or at least condoned. For example, the first marriage of Antonis Benachi, the eldest son of Emmanuel and Virginia, was to his first cousin Alexandra Benachi (1879–1902), the daughter of Emmanuel's brother Loucas. Likewise, Mikés Salvago's son Constantine married his second cousin Angeliki "Kiki" Salvago.

In at least two cases, the family tree shows marriages between members of one of these families and those from two other important Greek families in Egypt, the Sinadinos and the Cozzikas. It also indicates two more important details. The first is the large number of children Greek merchant families had in the nineteenth century, and how that number diminished in the twentieth century. The second is geographical mobility: in the earlier generations, the locations of births and deaths are recorded as the Aegean islands of Chios and Syros, while those of the next generation are in Alexandria, and which

21

by the mid-twentieth century are given as Athens or its northern suburb of Kifisiá; in a few cases births and deaths were recorded in Europe. However, the main purpose of the genealogical data shown here is to demonstrate the presence of these three families in Egypt.

In compiling this family tree I relied on information from several sources, primarily Christopher Long's genealogical information on Greek families, which is available online, the Benachi family photo albums in the Benaki Museum's historical archive, a detailed Benachi family tree compiled by Junior V. Waldo and also available online, and Matoula Tomara-Sideris's *Αλεξανδρινές Οικογένειες Χωρέμη – Μπενάκη – Σαλβάγου (Alexandrian Families Choremi–Benachi–Salvago)* (Athens: Kerkyra, 3rd edition, 2013).

1

The Muhammad Ali Era
and Beyond

I n 1873, the advertising section of the *Elpis*, a Greek-language daily newspaper in Alexandria, bore witness to the diversity of occupations of the city's Greek population, which numbered about 25,500, meaning that one in four of Alexandria's foreign residents was Greek.[1] The advertisements were for the Hotel Bosphorus owned by D. Dilaras, which had recently been refurbished; Georgios Lekkas's bakery, next to the Greek-owned Café Paradeisos on Rue des Soeurs, which sold quality breads and flour; P. Sarandis's Phoenix bookshop, which sold instructional books at reasonable prices and also carried Greek newspapers published in Trieste. The advertisements also showed Alexandria's close connection with Europe. K. Fardoulis's Grand Restaurant et Brasserie Universelle Entresol, located opposite the public gardens, served Viennese beer and quality wines from France, Germany, Hungary, and Greece; a young woman of Christian morals who had been educated at the Hill School and graduated from the Arsakeion (among the best schools in Athens) offered private lessons in Greek, French, and English as well as piano lessons; and the newspaper informed its readers it could offer translation services for Greek, French, Italian, English, German, and Arabic. The "well-known merchant" Constantinos Peleides, who was from the Greek town of Volos, informed the public he had recently returned from Paris bringing a large collection of clothes of the latest fashion.[2]

The *Elpis*, a newspaper of commerce and one of the first Greek-language newspapers to appear in Egypt—the first was the *Egyptos* that appeared in 1862—reported the prices of the different cultivars of cotton and cottonseed at the Alexandria cotton exchange and markets in towns in the Nile Delta region on its front page. It was the prospective wealth in the cotton business that had brought Greek merchants to Egypt in the early 1800s. Their presence grew steadily over the years despite several political

23

and diplomatic upheavals, and they soon branched out from purchasing, exporting, and shipping cotton to investing in banking, cotton ginning, real estate, and transport. Hoping they could also make money, thousands of other Greeks also began arriving in Alexandria. They did not have the capital to invest in cotton but they willingly became employees of the exporters and bankers or took up jobs in the service industries and retail trade that flourished in Alexandria, Cairo, and Egypt's smaller towns.

Arrival

It all began when Muhammad Ali, Egypt's *wali* (ruler) from 1805 to 1849 invited several Greek merchants to work with him to support his plan to push Egypt toward economic modernization, albeit with himself as a main beneficiary. When Muhammad Ali took power Egypt was a province of the Ottoman Empire, but during his rule he managed to carve out significant administrative autonomy for himself and gained the right to hand down power to his descendants who were recognized as Egypt's khedives, an Ottoman title akin to viceroy. Initially a small group that functioned as the *wali*'s commercial agents in the eastern Mediterranean, the Greeks grew in number as others also came to staff Egypt's fleet as captains or offer other services in maritime trade. The Greek presence in Alexandria began to expand as Egypt's economic needs grew and the opportunities it offered foreigners began to increase. Throughout the period that Muhammad Ali and his successors ruled Egypt until 1882 when the British arrived to assume—informally—the reigns of power, the Greeks were the largest and most socially diverse of all the Europeans who came to assist as well as profit from Egypt's drive toward modernization. If the 'pull' factors in this process were Muhammad Ali's invitation and the encouragement of his successors, especially Sa'id, who ruled between 1854 and 1863, and Ismail, who succeeded him and ruled through 1879, the 'push' factors were as important. They included Egypt's geographical proximity to Greece, the existence of Greek merchant networks throughout the Mediterranean, always eager to pursue new commercial projects, and the lack of economic opportunity on many Aegean islands. Those Greeks fleeing the poverty of barren windswept islands were prepared to endure the difficult conditions in small rural towns.

Another attraction Egypt held for the Greeks was the privileges they enjoyed. Muhammad Ali maintained the Ottoman approach to non-Muslim minorities, the so-called millet system that allowed confessional communities to rule themselves in matters of personal law. Greeks could also seek and receive official protection from one of the European powers. From the mid-nineteenth century onward, Greeks were able to benefit from the Capitulations. These were bilateral agreements between the Ottoman Empire and foreign governments granting extraterritorial rights and privileges to foreign subjects resident or doing business in Ottoman domains. Greece became one of those governments in 1856. By virtue of Egypt's nominal status as a province of the Ottoman Empire, notwithstanding its considerable autonomy, the Capitulatory regime was transferred to Egypt, where it functioned with even greater force than it did in the Ottoman Empire. In Egypt, foreigners enjoyed almost complete tax immunity, along with freedom of movement and commerce and freedom from any legal or judicial control. In those cases when the litigants were from the same nationality, their own Consular Court adjudicated. In 1875 the creation of the Mixed Courts of Egypt brought some consistency to judging disputes between foreigners of different nationalities and foreigners and Egyptians.

There was already a small Greek presence in Egypt before Muhammad Ali took power in the early 1800s. Much later on, in the 1920s and 1930s, when the Greeks felt threatened by the rise of Egyptian nationalism, several writers produced studies claiming there had been a continuous close contact between Egypt and Greece that went back to antiquity and flourished during the Hellenistic era. The most comprehensive defense of the continuity thesis came in a well-documented and comprehensive two-volume study of the Greeks in Egypt through the ages and since the rule of Muhammad Ali, authored by Athanasios Politis and entitled *Ο Ελληνισμός και η Νεωτέρα Αίγυπτος (Hellenism and Modern Egypt)*, published in the late 1920s in Alexandria and appearing in both Greek and French.[3] Politis, who was a diplomat serving at the Greek general consulate in Alexandria at the time, purposely chose the term "Hellenism" rather than "the Greeks" in order to allude to the ties between ancient and modern Greece. The evidence of a Greek presence in Egypt during the Ottoman era, which began in the fifteenth century, is thin if we don't count those who converted to Islam. It was sporadic at best and connected with maritime trade. The big exception was the existence of the Christian Church, established by Mark the Evangelist in AD 49 according to church sources. In its formative period the church, known as the Patriarchate of Alexandria, produced two of the major thinkers of early Christianity—known as 'fathers'—Athanasius and Cyril, who were both Patriarchs of Alexandria. After an important meeting of the Christian Church, the Council of Chalcedon in 451, the Church of Alexandria split in two over a doctrinal dispute over the nature of Jesus Christ. This led to the creation of the Coptic Orthodox Church of Alexandria, which represented the majority of Christians in Egypt, and the Greek Orthodox Church of Alexandria. The Greek Orthodox Church used Greek as its liturgical language and remained in communion with the Ecumenical Patriarchate of Constantinople. It is considered one of the four 'historic' patriarchates of Eastern Orthodox Christianity along with those of Constantinople, Antioch, and Jerusalem.

After the Arab conquest of North Africa in the seventh century—which permanently separated the region from the Byzantine Empire—the Greek Orthodox became an isolated minority in Egypt, even among Christians, and the church remained small for many centuries. On several occasions its patriarchs had been forced to move away from Egypt temporarily. The two oldest Greek Orthodox churches in Egypt are the monasteries of St. Savva in Alexandria and St. George in Cairo. Out in the Sinai Desert was the monastery of St. Catherine, built in the sixth century.

After Egypt fell under Ottoman rule, the predominance of Greeks in the Ottoman navy brought small numbers of Greeks to Egypt. The Mamluks, the military caste that continued to rule Egypt in the Ottoman era, enlisted the help of Greeks to develop and operate a navy. Craftsmen also began making their way to Egypt from the Greek lands, especially the islands. When the French landed in Egypt in 1798, the Patriarch of Alexandria reported at the time that his flock amounted to two hundred families. A good estimate of the number of Greeks in Cairo would be around two thousand; one of the streets they lived on was known as Haret al-Rum, the street of the Greeks. The presence of a Greek Orthodox bishop in the small port of Damietta suggests there was a small number of Greeks there as well. The Greeks welcomed the French and the prospect of the end of Mamluk rule, and many joined the French forces so that Napoleon created a Greek regiment, although his treatment of them was uneven. He had to be dissuaded from pulling down the Greek Orthodox Church of St. Savva—supposedly to build military fortifications in its place—and, along with the other indigenous Christians, the French authorities taxed the Greeks fairly heavily.[4]

Muhammad Ali emerged as ruler in Egypt in the wake of the departure of the French after his Albanian troops, who were in the service of the Ottomans, eliminated the Mamluks—who had earlier survived an attempt by Ottoman Turkish troops to dislodge them from power. The Ottoman Sultan reluctantly recognized Muhammad Ali as the ruler of Egypt, who, intent on building his economic base, quickly enlisted the services of for- eign merchants operating in the eastern Mediterranean who would act as his commercial and maritime agents because he was "a pragmatist who made use of whatever talent was available; also he had no racial or religious prejudice." Thus he wasted no time in making use of the skills of Greek and Armenian merchants as well as French and British technocrats and Italian physicians.[5] By patronizing them, as well as Arab and Egyptian merchants, "Muhammad Ali received important financial services, and tied into a net- work of commercial and diplomatic intelligence."[6] Before 'modern' state banking and diplomatic structures appeared, such associates would provide him with these functions. The flow of information permitted the pasha to manipulate exports and export prices to his advantage, and to devise policies—including agrarian policies—in light of international conditions. An attempted British invasion in 1807 had shown him how vulnerable the Egyptian coastline was and led him to develop a navy. A war he waged in the Hijaz was another reminder he needed to expand his fleet. His wish to enhance his and the state's income from trade, meanwhile, led to the expan- sion of a merchant marine. The *wali* encouraged his friends and relations to invest in arms and shipping for him. Skilled foreigners were employed to establish or improve the production of silk, indigo, and opium. Land was granted tax free in order to encourage the cultivation of food crops and other traditional crops such as flax and oil seeds, which remained important for internal consumption, industry, and export. In addition, large new tracts of olives and vines were planted, opium culture was revived, and merino sheep were imported to supply a new wool industry. The Greeks would play a big part in this process.

Greek merchants had spread throughout the Mediterranean by 1800, and their arrival in Alexandria would be a part of a broader pattern. The eastern Mediterranean was under Ottoman rule, but trade across the Empire and beyond was in the hands of its non-Muslim subjects, the Arme- nians, the Greeks, and the Jews. The Greek islanders were also a dominant presence in the Ottoman navy. The upsurge in trade between the Ottoman Empire and the West from the middle of the eighteenth century onward led to the creation of networks of Greek trading communities, one stretch- ing from the Black Sea all the way to the western Mediterranean, and another overland from the Balkans into central and western Europe. The integration of the Ottoman Empire in the world economy only served to strengthen the role of the Greek merchants who acted as middlemen in East–West trade thanks to the growing demand for grain and other goods. Anglo-French competition, moreover, contributed to the increase of Greek maritime trading because many of the English and French ships plying the Mediterranean reverted to naval warfare. Greek maritime trade spread outward from the islands of Hydra, Spezzes, Psara, and Chios. The rudimentary commercial practices of the era required merchants to rely on relatives or friends as their commercial agents along the trade routes. Thus, as Greek-borne trade expanded across the Mediterranean, so did the settlements of Greek merchants. By the late 1700s there were Greek mercantile communities in the ports of Ancona, Livorno, Marseilles, Minorca, Trieste, Venice, and the Black Sea port of Odessa.[7]

To speak of 'Greek' merchants and 'Greek' shipping in this era may sound somewhat anachronistic especially to the ears of anyone familiar with the voluminous scholarship on the modernity and the 'imagined' nature of nationhood. After the Ottomans conquered the Byzantine lands in the Balkans and Asia Minor, the Greeks who were Greek-speaking members of the Eastern (Greek) Orthodox Church became Ottoman subjects. Visions of a modern Greek nation, defined by language, religion, and continuity with Classical Greece gathered momentum in the wake of the French Revolution of 1789, and in 1821 armed uprisings against the Ottoman overlords called upon the Greeks to take up arms to gain freedom and independence. Yet prior to the emergence of a modern idea of Greek nationhood, one can argue there existed a sense of Greekness, though by no means as clearly defined or cohesive. The Ottomans had granted a degree of self-administration to the Greek Orthodox, the Armenians, and the Jews through the millet system. Russian interest in the Mediterranean in the late eighteenth century came with pledges to protect their fellow Orthodox who were under Ottoman rule. Moreover, the rise of commerce in the Balkans and the eastern Mediterranean at the same time had used the Greek language as its lingua franca. Last but not least, European travelers in the eastern Mediterranean, keen to recognize non-Muslim populations and especially the Greeks, whom they assumed were descendants of the Classical Greeks, also contributed to a conventional wisdom that saw a distinctly Greek population present throughout the region.

Following the creation of an independent Greek state in 1830, the elaboration of a Greekness more akin to a modern national identity began

to gain ground thanks to the government's policies, the growth of an educational system, and the cultural output of intellectuals and artists keen
to contribute to the nation's self-awareness. A significant dimension of
those efforts was directed toward the Greeks living in areas under Ottoman rule, which Greece considered as historically Greek and rightfully part
of a greater Greece. Greece also courted the allegiance of the Greeks in
the diaspora, whom it considered as a valuable asset for the nation and its
expansionist program.

Before all this happened, the French Revolutionary Wars and the
Napoleonic Wars between 1792 and 1815 had brought increased prosperity to the Greek mercantile marine and maritime diaspora. The sea
and maritime trade were an outlet to the Greeks who inhabited the many
islands of the Aegean. It insulated them from Ottoman rule and offered
them freedom and often prosperity. Moreover, lacking the guarantees a
powerful government could offer them, the Greeks relied upon themselves
and used kinship and local ties to build their networks. Indirectly, that
mode of operation served to strengthen the ties among the Greeks. The
outbreak of the French Revolution caused the diminution of French trading in the Mediterranean. The French were never to return to their former
strength on the seas and their naval defeats by Britain sealed the decline of
French trading in the Mediterranean. The continental system imposed by
Napoleon in 1806, the embargo on British ships and trade, meant that the
British had to rely on neutral or private shipping in order to trade with the
European ports under French control. Greek shippers and merchants were
prepared to run the risk of breaking the embargo, because local officials
were susceptible to bribes and turned a blind eye to what was, in effect,
Greek smuggling activity, and both the Habsburgs and the Ottomans welcomed trade with Britain. Inevitably, with the end of the Napoleonic Wars
and the restoration of peace throughout Europe in 1815, the economic
boom the Greek middlemen had enjoyed throughout the Mediterranean
came to an end. But they remained in place because yet again they adapted
to the new reality.[8] A series of economic and technological developments
and innovations consolidated Britain's commercial dominance internationally: the establishment of free trade between 1832 and 1849 and the
consequent growth of British shipping and commerce; Britain's ability to
negotiate extremely beneficial trade agreements with the weak governments in the eastern Mediterranean region; the technological advantages
accruing to Britain's merchant marine through its reliance on steamships;

and the rise of the joint-stock company in Britain and France. The newly founded joint-stock companies were much stronger financially than the non-corporate, family-run firms the Greeks operated. Meanwhile steam, coupled with the use of the telegraph—available initially to the British and French but not to the Greeks—shrunk the size of the Mediterranean and the Black Sea, eliminating the isolation of many ports which had been connected to Europe through a network of local, mainly Greek, merchants and shippers. The response of the Greek merchants varied; some relocated to London, in an if-you-can't-beat-them-join-them move. There, they were able to tap the lucrative source of capital on which British overseas superiority was built. Having established a toehold in London, the Greeks were able to show the business sense of the pre-1815 period. They outflanked British houses by daring to reach out to untapped markets—or as one British observer put it, "distant and semi-barbaric regions where Manchester fabrics were before as unknown as the very name itself in England." Greeks also inaugurated the practice of selling bills of landing before the arrival of a vessel, and purchasing return cargoes, thus "operating on relatively small capitals and at the same time earning a reputation for prompt cash payments."[9] Next to London, Cairo and Alexandria also became likely destinations for Greek merchants thanks to Muhammad Ali's timely invitation.

A young Greek who went to Egypt a few decades later, as so many did riding on the coattails of those who became wealthy, observed that both the elite but also the small shopkeepers in the provincial towns were fiercely patriotic. While they had left Greece, they would invest there or remit money to their relatives who stayed behind only when the moment was propitious. They also appeared to be well ensconced in Egypt, quite able to operate in its big cities and rural towns.[10] What that newly arrived Greek was noticing was part of a bigger picture, the adaptability of the Greeks who had settled in Egypt. We can think of it as a continuity of the agility and flexibility that earlier generations of Greeks had demonstrated in their maritime activities in the Mediterranean. It has been argued that the functions of the Greek diaspora merchants of the eighteenth and nineteenth centuries defy any narrow categorization. For example, they were based abroad but attached to Greece and driven by the profit motive. They were middlemen but in no way deracinated compradors, able and ready to switch roles according to prevailing circumstances.[11] In the case of the Greeks in Egypt, we could add, they were developing a deep attachment to that country as well. The adaptability of the maritime trader was about to be transformed into that of the cotton merchant.

Muhammad Ali and the Greeks

Muhammad Ali was already familiar with the Greeks before arriving in Egypt. Of Albanian origin, he was born in Kavala, a busy seaport in Ottoman Macedonia that became part of Greece in 1913 and where his house is preserved as a museum. Kavala, populated mostly by Greeks and Turks as well as Albanians and Jews (all of them Ottoman subjects), was one of the outlets for the export of tobacco from its hinterland, a business in which the Greeks were prominent, and something the young Muhammad Ali would dabble in, and that was how, according to one source, he got to know Theodore Tossizza. He was one of the four sons of Anastasios Tossizza, a fur merchant from Metsovo, a village in the Pindus mountain range, in present-day northwestern Greece. Another source claims that it was Theodore's brother Constantinos who knew Muhammad Ali in Kavala and had lent him some money. Their father, Anastasis, was based in Salonica, the region's wealthy commercial center, and the business was eventually taken over by his four sons. The eldest, Michael, was in charge. With their business feeling the effects of the Continental Blockade imposed by Britain on France, the Tossizzas were glad to respond to Muhammad Ali's invitation to Theodore to move to Alexandria. In 1812 the other two brothers also went and settled in Cairo, and in 1820 Michael also moved to Alexandria.

Soon the Tossizza commercial network based in Egypt had acquired branches in Damascus, Livorno, and Malta. In 1833 newly independent Greece appointed Michael as its consul in Egypt, and two years later he was promoted to general consul. The Greek merchants who were invited by the *wali* were Ioannis d'Anastasi, whose business in Malta was not doing well but he prospered in Egypt and eventually became consul of Sweden, and Athanasios Casulli from Rhodes, whom the ruler placed in charge of Egypt's mint. In 1818 his Greek agents Tossizza and Anastasi built three ships, which would trade in the waters of the Greek archipelago for Muhammad Ali. Tossizza was made director of a glass factory and later became Greek consul. Stephanos Zizinia, whose family-based merchant house included his brother, who was based in Marseilles, also settled in Alexandria. He bought and outfitted a ship to expand the *wali*'s merchant navy, and provided him with his first frigates. A number of Greeks from the islands became the captains of the new fleet and some of them converted to Islam. From 1812, ships bearing Greek laborers and tradesmen had come yearly from the maritime islands of Hydra and Spezzes. In return for his services, Zizinia received a large tract of land, which was later to become Alexandria's Ramla section. Decades later, when the first pieces of the machinery for the tramline to Ramla arrived in Alexandria, it was passed by Zizinia's house in celebration. In what would be a permanent feature in Egypt, the presence of wealthy merchants functioned as a magnet for other Greeks. Very soon craftsmen, farmers, and traders from mainland Greece and the Aegean Islands began settling in Alexandria, Cairo, and the port cities of Rosetta and Damietta.[12]

The most telling sign that Muhammad Ali understood the usefulness of the Greeks came when he became involved in putting down a revolt on mainland Greece at the sultan's request, but he did not let that become an obstacle in continuing his close relations with the Greek merchants in his country. Early on, he had turned a blind eye to their support of the Greek war of independence against the Ottomans, even when the sultan enlisted the help of his son Ibrahim and the Egyptian navy to quell the revolt on the Greek mainland. The planning phase had begun in 1815 and involved Greek merchants based in Odessa in the Black Sea but also elsewhere, including Alexandria. There were Greek uprisings in several places in 1821, the most sustained was in the Peloponnese (the Morea, as it was called at the time), where the Greeks made considerable gains and overran several Ottoman garrisons. The support of the uprisings most Greeks in Egypt openly expressed underscores the fact many 'Greeks' at the time were not merely Greek-speaking members of the Eastern or Greek Orthodox Church, but were also developing a national Greek consciousness. Muhammad Ali observed those events with "benevolent detachment," as one of his biographers put it. After all, any weakening of the Ottoman Porte would likely be to his advantage. The *wali* did not prevent the collection of funds to aid the uprising, which took place in Alexandria in 1820, or even the departure of about 150 Greek volunteers from Alexandria. He set free a group of enslaved Greek captives sent to him during the early phases of Greek–Ottoman clashes. But in 1822 the Sultan offered Muhammad Ali the island of Crete in return for his help in putting down the revolt, which had taken root there as well. It took two years, but Muhammad Ali's forces were successful and this led to further demands from the Porte.

In 1824, the Sultan offered him the *pashalik* (governorship) of Morea, which given the strengthening Greek rebel positions, could have been a poisoned chalice. The *wali* accepted the challenge most probably because, according to an admiring biographer, "the subjugation of the Greeks would mark him out as the leader of the age, enable him, if he pleased, to defy the orders of the Sultan, and (if he fancied) entitle him to the respect, the friendship, even the alliance of one or other of the Great Powers."[13] And the risk of alienating the Greek merchants in Alexandria was negligible. Some of them even helped the *wali* with funds. Michael Tossizza outwardly at least adopted a neutral attitude, so much so that legend has it that the rebel Greeks sent someone to assassinate him. But he literally and metaphorically disarmed the man when they met privately, and explained that he was biding his time so he could help the Greeks after they gained independence. Muhammad Ali's son Ibrahim led the Egyptian forces and after several bloody encounters he was able to end the Greek revolt. But at the eleventh hour the Great Powers intervened on Greece's side and in 1827 at Navarino, on the western coast of the Peloponnese, their combined fleet sunk the entire Egyptian fleet, paving the way for Greek independence.

Muhammad Ali chose not to dwell too much on the disaster—he blamed the Porte for the defeat and studiously avoided alienating the Great Powers or the resident Greeks. It was a setback but nothing was going to prevent him from pursuing his plan for modernizing Egypt, and the Greek merchants, many of whom would declare their allegiance to the new independent Greece established in 1830, would continue to play a role in the process. The Greek government, very much aware of the differences between their Ottoman enemy and the ruler of Egypt, appointed Michael Tossizza as consul in Alexandria in 1833. It was the beginning of a long and close diplomatic relationship between the two neighboring countries, which enabled the Greeks in Egypt to see no contradiction in expressing formal allegiance to Greece and their loyalty to Egypt.[14]

The Greeks who received the *wali*'s favors were the equivalent of the immigrant pioneers who became the founders of the Greek entity in Egypt, but Pavlos Pavlides was somewhat of an exception. He was born in Cyprus and arrived in Egypt as a young boy in the mid-1820s with his father, whose friend, a Greek merchant named Nicolaides, realizing the young Pavlos was very gifted, introduced the child to Muhammad Ali, with whom he was doing business. Recognizing the boy's potential, Muhammad Ali saw to his education and then sent him to Paris to study medicine as long as he would return and serve him as his physician and dentist. The offer was accepted, and in Paris, Pavlos, impressed by one of his professors Louis Jacques Thénard, out of respect changed his last name to Draneht, an anagram of Thénard. He remained in Muhammad Ali's service and received a large tract of cultivable land and took the title Draneht Pasha. He maintained close relations with the Greeks but was not involved in community affairs because he remained a member of the court, serving Muhammad Ali's successors in several positions, including commissioner of the royal theater. It was in that capacity that he became involved in the establishment of the Cairo Opera House.

Early Economic Liberalization and Cotton

Even as his forces continued their engagement with the uprising on the Greek mainland, Muhammad Ali was busy introducing measures designed to make Egypt more welcoming to foreigners, including Greeks. He decreed a greater tolerance for Christian religious practices, and in order to encourage their trading activities the *wali* established a tribunal of commerce in Cairo in 1826, giving it the authority to settle all commercial disputes between native Christians and Europeans. It examined all questions of disputed accounts, even those of debtors to the government. The members of the tribunal were chosen "from among the different nations who are fixed in Egypt" and included

> two Turkish merchants, three Egyptians, two Mogrebis, two Greek Levantines, two Schismatic [non-Greek Orthodox] Greeks, two Armenians, two Jews. A Turkish merchant presides. It holds its sittings three times a-week for the dispatch of business. The president has the right to arrest and imprison an insolvent debtor. No doubt the decision is often influenced by the interference of the wealthy and by the powerful, and the claims of the poor do not receive a due attention; intrigue and corruption are not without their polluting influences.[15]

There was a similar tribunal that was set up in Alexandria. As it befited a multi-ethnic city, the large cemetery area established just outside its walls included separate sections for Muslims, Armenian Christians, Catholics, Copts, Greeks, Jews, and Protestants. All these measures to accommodate non-Egyptians clearly had their intended effect: "The motley population of Greeks, Maltese, and Franks which are found in the principal cities of Egypt, particularly Alexandria and Cairo, have nothing to distinguish them from similar classes of settlers in the different places of traffic in the Mediterranean," wrote John Bowring, a British official entrusted with reporting on the situation in Egypt to the British government. His tone was somewhat condescending, but that made Bowring's observation no less interesting. "Shopkeepers, artisans, and domestic servants," he wrote, "with multitudes of wanderers less respectably and less usefully occupied, crowd the Levantine ports, but they offer no particular topic for observation. The number of such strangers in Alexandria alone is estimated at from 8,000 to 10,000."[16]

Cairo, the seat of power in Egypt, also acquired a growing number of foreigners. A British diplomat and author of travel books, who visited the capital at the time, noted, "the wealthier Greeks were considered as Franks and resided in the Mousky or Franc quarter," where the houses were "mostly in the Greco-Constantinopolitan style, with French furniture inside, Lyons damask hangings and divans, Aubusson carpets, and pier glasses." Around that neighborhood there were also Greek artisans who had come from the Greek mainland or the islands. The older Greek quarter was in the "upper or northeastern" part of Cairo around the Greek Orthodox monastery.[17]

The sudden increase in the role of cotton production and export gave a renewed impetus to Egypt's economic development. It came with the discovery of a new type of cotton when one of the foreign experts that the *wali* had invited to Egypt, Louis Alexis Jumel, identified and developed a type of cotton that was superior in length and strength of fiber. The *wali*, who possessed a keen commercial instinct, quickly realized the potential of cotton to provide income through exportation, especially at a time when Egyptian wheat was facing competition from higher-quality grain produced by Russia. By 1830 Muhammad Ali had issued a law that detailed the ways both local officials and the fellahin should be engaged in the cultivation and gathering of the crop. Although he maintained a strict monopoly control on the overall process of production, export, and income from cotton, Muhammad Ali depended on domestic and foreign merchants for its transportation from the fields to Alexandria and then on to its international buyers. By the late 1830s he began loosening his control and it is no coincidence that as the cotton production and export expanded, so did the numbers of foreign merchants doing business in Egypt. The *wali*'s welcome had prompted the first arrivals of foreign merchants but now "the real magnet was cotton and the large profits that could be made from its sale," and the larger their numbers, the more they began to be aware of their own power.[18]

The relaxation of Muhammad Ali's control and the growing power of the merchants often led to a tense symbiosis between the *wali* and the foreigners and consuls, but in the case of the Greeks the situation was a little different. Greece had relatively little leverage over Egypt and was itself under the 'protection' of Britain, France, and Russia. Thus the Greeks could not afford to displease the Egyptian government. When potential disputes arose, Athens, its consul, and the Greek merchants had to tread carefully. One of the earliest tasks of Tossizza, Greece's diplomatic representative in Egypt, was to try and secure the freedom of hundreds of Greek captives that Ibrahim's army had sent back to Egypt as slaves during the military operations on Crete and the Peloponnese. Significantly, the instructions the Greek Ministry of Foreign Affairs sent Tossizza were to do his utmost to secure as many Greeks as possible be freed, but also to make sure the pressure he applied would not damage the close relations between Greece and Egypt. It is unlikely that a country like Britain or France trying to free their citizens would have exercised such a cautious approach. Aware that their government was not in a position to force Muhammad Ali's hand, the Greek merchants knew they had to behave accordingly and not like their European counterparts who became "a bridgehead in Egypt of the assertive, self-confident, intolerant spirit of European commercial expansion which came inevitably to regard the country as just another market to be invaded."[19]

Some of the Greeks chose to become protégés of one of the European powers rather than rely on their connections to Greece. According to Bowring's report, out of the fourteen most important Greek merchant companies operating in Alexandria in 1837 only four (P.S. Mavrogordato, Proi & Company, Tossizza Brothers, and N. Zaccali) were under Greek protection; four (S. Avierino, G. Popolani, A. Riga Giro, and G. Scaramanga) had English protection; three (G. Braggiotti & Company, G. Sevastopoulo, and G. Vuro) had Austrian protection; one (D. Casdagli) had Russian protection; Zizinia had French protection; and d'Anastasi was the consul of Sweden.[20]

Greek merchants also looked to secure their status in Egypt by relying on building interpersonal relations with officials and, especially, ingratiating themselves with Muhammad Ali along with the time-tested method of falling back on family ties and networks among fellow Greeks. Unlike other Europeans in Egypt, the Greeks did not have a powerful government in their homeland that could intervene effectively on their behalf. They had to establish a relationship of trust with the Egyptian government if they were to remain and continue to prosper. Michael Tossizza, for one, managed to gain the *wali*'s confidence. In 1834 he began accompanying Muhammad Ali on his trips, domestic as well as outside Egypt. Tossizza, along with d'Anastasi and Zizinia, were the three Greeks who were among the *wali*'s closest advisors. When Tossizza was trying to free the Greek captives that had been brought from the mainland by Ibrahim's troops, the Ministry of Foreign Affairs in Athens tempered its praise by reminding him that he should not push too hard and antagonize Muhammad Ali.

Community Life
Another way the Greek merchants looked to acquire greater security in Egypt was to take advantage of their growing numbers and establish community organizations that would create social bonds and solidarity among the Greeks. The new economic conditions in the 1840s brought an increase in trading between Egypt and Greece and the arrival of more Greeks. In 1848 Tossizza reported to Athens that there were 544 Greek subjects living in Alexandria, and thirty-seven of them were merchants. With the Greeks growing in numbers, especially in Alexandria, the wealthiest began taking the initiative to create communal institutions. The first was a hospital to cater to the Greeks to replace the care offered by the monastery of St. Savva, which had been funded by contributions from the Greek ships arriving in Alexandria by order of Consul Tossizza. The Tossizzas, Michael and Theodore, along with their nephew Nikolaos Stournaras, funded a small school that was housed in a private home. In 1843 came the establishment of the Greek community organization. Significantly, it was modeled on similar local self-governing bodies that Greeks established as part of their mercantile activities in the diaspora, rather than the more hierarchical bodies ruled by elders and the clergy that the Greek subjects of the Ottoman Empire had known. It was called the Greco-Egyptian Orthodox Community, a name that sought to balance its secular character with an acknowledgment of the significance of religion in the definition of Greekness. The term 'Egyptian' was an early sign of the pervasive sense the Greeks in Egypt had that they were from Greece but also connected to Egypt.

Similar community organizations would appear throughout Egypt wherever there was a significant Greek presence and they would assume responsibility for administering local Greek cultural, social, and religious institutions. These were essentially voluntary associations run and funded by the wealthiest Greeks. The inaugural meeting in Alexandria, with thirty-eight persons present, was held in April 1843 at the monastery of St. Savva under the chairmanship of Michael Tossizza, who was also elected the new organization's president. It was open to all Greeks, including those under the protection of foreign consuls. For example, Dimitrios Casdaglis, a merchant who was a Russian protégé. On the agenda were the ways the hospital and schools could be better funded and organized. The gathering also discussed the regulations of those two fledgling institutions. The schools would be free and offer Greek-language classes as well as French and Italian for Greeks interested in learning those languages. The hospital would accept with no charge Greek men and women who were poor and had an infirmity, in addition to Greeks and non-Greeks who had the means to pay between 3 and 6 piasters a day for their stay and medicines. The hospital also accepted with no charge those who were blind or otherwise incapacitated, those of advanced old age, and those who were mentally unstable.

A church named Evanghelismos (Annunciation), which was to become the Greek Orthodox Cathedral of Alexandria, was the third institution the community organization created, symbolizing the significance of religion for the identity of Greeks. The Patriarchate of Alexandria was in no position to take the lead and fund such a project, so it was the wealthy leaders of the community organization, and Michael Tossizza in particular, who took the initiative. The Monastery of St. Savva was outside the city of Alexandria and the trip there was not always considered safe, so there were thoughts about establishing a Greek Orthodox Church inside the city. But more than that, Tossizza wished for a grandiose church in the city center that would symbolize and enhance the standing of Alexandrian Greeks. The plan was discussed for the first time in 1844 at a meeting held in Tossizza's house with d'Anastasi and Zizinia. It took a series of campaigns over several years to raise the funds, even after the cornerstone was placed in 1847. The Ecumenical Patriarchate of Constantinople—the mother church of Greek Orthodoxy—and Tossizza donated the land on which it was built. There were several fundraising efforts required before the building could be completed. Its total cost ran at LE17,000. To those who remarked it was far too big for the number of Greeks in Alexandria, Tossizza responded that one day the Annunciation Church would be too small to serve as the Greek Orthodox Cathedral in Alexandria, and he was proven right within a few decades. But he would not be present for the formal inauguration that took place on March 25, 1856, Greek Independence Day and the date of the Annunciation of the Virgin Mary in the Orthodox calendar.

Tossizza had been forced to leave Alexandria in May 1854 because of a brief rupture in the diplomatic relations between Greece and the Ottoman Empire. The two countries were on opposite sides in the Crimean War. Stephanos Zizinia, who replaced Tossizza as president of the community organization, sent him a message informing him of the church's inauguration, adding that the Greeks of Alexandria sent their deepest thanks and warmest wishes. Tossizza died in Athens six months later at the age of sixty-nine. Honoring his generous donations to his hometown Metsovo, the cities of Athens and Thessaloniki where he had begun his business career, and to Alexandria, the Greek government proclaimed him as a "national benefactor."[21]

Whether the Alexandria community organization would be primarily secular or religious in character was the subject of ongoing disputes in that early period. During the Ottoman era, most community notables had to share power with the Greek Orthodox Church, which derived its authority from the millet system. But in mid-nineteenth century Egypt, the confessional basis of the millet system had been replaced by the Capitulations that afforded rights according to citizenship, not membership in the Orthodox Church. Yet because Greek Orthodoxy played such a big part in the way the majority of Greek citizens defined their identity, the Patriarchate of Alexandria and many of the city's Greeks believed that it should hold sway over the community organization, even though it had been established by wealthy merchants working closely with Greek diplomatic authorities, which were actively involved in the community organization's affairs. In 1862 a group of members accused its president and Greece's general consul, Dimitrios Rizos, of corruption and mismanagement of community funds. Those making the complaint favored greater control of the organization by the Greek Orthodox Church. Indeed, the Patriarchate of Constantinople was proposing the reorganization of the Patriarchate of Alexandria in ways that would give it authority over the community organization. But in this case the church came up against the objections of the most influential merchants who had too much at stake to simply hand over the organization to the patriarch. After a year of upheavals, and a contentious meeting attended by 1,500 persons, the Ecumenical Patriarch of Constantinople eventually recognized the community organization's autonomy and the new consul general of Greece became its president. The election of Sofronios as Patriarch of Alexandria in 1870 with the support of both the Alexandria and Cairo community organizations signaled the restoration of peaceful relations and confirmed the community organization's independence from the

Church.[22] Sofronios remained patriarch until his death in 1899 and was buried in Cairo. The troubles had been as much of a turf war between the patriarchate and the Greek government, and the victory of the 'secularists' also meant greater control from Athens, in a sense the 'Hellenization' of the community organization.

Following the establishment of the community organization in Alexandria, other such organizations began appearing wherever there was a significant number of Greeks. The Greek Orthodox in Cairo established a community organization in 1856, which was somewhat unique because its executive committee included representatives of the tradesmen's guilds that existed there, and it was only in 1904 that the organization was restructured and governed by elected members. Even before the community organization was originally established, George Abet, a Greek-speaking Syrian Orthodox merchant in Cairo, bequeathed a large sum in his will for the establishment of a Greek-language school. His brothers Ananias and Raphael offered a house to the community organization for the creation of such a school, and it opened its doors in 1861. In 1876 the school began including Arabic language instruction in its curriculum.

Economic Liberalization and the Cotton Boom
The Khedive Sa'id, Muhammad Ali's fourth son, who ruled between 1854 and 1863, took important steps to jumpstart Egypt's economy and restored the economic liberalization measures that the Khedive Abbas had reversed during his rule from the time of Muhammad Ali's death until 1854. Sa'id's policies included opening irrigation canals, improving the domestic transport network, and abolishing all obstacles to free trade. Alexandria was connected to Cairo with a railway line in 1856 and three years later Cairo was connected by rail to Suez. More tracks were laid southward from Cairo and the line was completed in 1874 as far down as Asyut in Upper Egypt. A Greek mercantile company originally based in London, Cassavetis Brothers, established a branch in Alexandria and in 1854, with Sa'id's encouragement, founded the Nile Transport Company under the name Compagnie Egyptienne Privilégiée pour le Remorquage à Vapeur sur le Nil et les Canaux d'Egypte.[23] Sa'id's liberalization measures allowed cultivators to grow what they wanted and sell it how and to whom they wished. Rural contact with the money economy was also encouraged by Sa'id's efforts to reform the system of tax collection. All these changes received a new, powerful impetus thanks to the cotton boom of the 1860s. The rise of Egyptian cotton

came thanks to the American Civil War, which disrupted the export of cotton from the American South and caused the price of cotton on international markets to skyrocket. Egypt stepped into the vacuum. As the *New York Times* reported in 1864, "Previous to our civil war in America, the sum total of this production was limited to about 500,000 cantars. In 1861, Egypt exported in all directions 600,000 cantars, without counting what she retained for her own consumption. In the year 1862 the exportation amounted to 820,000 cantars, and in 1863 it reached . . . a total of 1,287,055 cantars. By these statistics it will be seen that the exportation and consequently the production, have actually doubled since 1861."[24]

The catalytic effects of Sa'id's policies and the cotton boom on the Egyptian economy heralded a new and more pronounced role for the Greeks in Egypt. Some of the older established firms switched their general trading activities over to focusing on the purchase and export of cotton, while other Greek firms based elsewhere in the Mediterranean either opened branches in Egypt or moved their operations there altogether. Some of the Greek firms would import ginning machines, which were used to separate the cotton fibers from their seeds, the first stage of the process of moving the cotton from the hands of the cultivators to the port of Alexandria for export. N.J. Casulli was one of the existing Alexandria-based trading companies that switched to cotton, and it established a branch in the Nile Delta town of Kafr al-Zayyat in 1860. Another Alexandrian Greek house that turned its attentions to cotton was that of A. Nicolopoulo. One of the earliest newcomers was the firm of Choremi, Mellor & Company, a Greek–English partnership. The Greek partner, Ioannis or John Choremi, who was from the island of Tinos and had founded a business in London, established the company in Alexandria in 1858.

In 1860 there were two more Greek arrivals, Th. Ralli & Company and Rodocanachi & Company, both of which were branches of companies that traded as far afield as the Black Sea and England. Theodore M. Ralli emerged as a pioneer in the introduction of ginning machines in Egypt. He was a member of the largest Greek diaspora merchant families whose business interests, based in London, spread from New Orleans to India. Ralli focused his efforts on adapting to Egypt the British-made ginning machines that were used for American cotton and he was successful in 1859. He had purchased a building owned by the Khedive Sa'id in the village of Talkha on the banks of the Nile opposite the town of Mansura. The idea was to have the cotton ginned before it was shipped downriver to

Alexandria. According to the author Stratis Tsirkas, Ralli's move signaled a revolution in the Nile Delta because it brought the proliferation of ginning plants and these in turn generated a small ancillary economy of groceries and other stores throughout the Delta region.

The growing presence of Greeks there was reflected by the creation of a Greek community organization in Mansura in 1860 (making it the third oldest in Egypt) and then in the towns of Zagazig in 1870 and Kafr al-Zayyat in 1872. The Greeks arrived in Kafr al-Zayyat in the wake of the establishment of ginning plants in the town. Greeks owned six out of the eight ginning plants in Kafr al-Zayyat in 1870; the others were owned by a Greek Orthodox Syrian and an Egyptian. The community organization was called the Community of Orthodox of Kafr al-Zayyat and included Greek Orthodox Syrians; it would become exclusively Greek in 1900.[25] Next on the list of appearance of community organizations were four, all formed in 1880, in Tanta, Beheira, al-Mahalla al-Kubra, and Zifta. Their introduction to the Nile Delta was the cause of the region's dramatic transformation, with the mushrooming of big and small towns, something akin to what had happened in California and Texas. "Roads, hotels, pharmacies and *cafés-chantants* emerge suddenly and roil the marshy quiet of the life of the fellahin."[26]

The 1850s and 1860s witnessed significant arrivals of Greek merchant houses. In researching the historical background of the Alexandrian poet C.P. Cavafy, Tsirkas produced a detailed description of the mercantile activities of the poet's father, providing a fairly typical portrait of the type of Greek merchant who moved to Egypt around the middle of the nineteenth century. The poet's father Petros moved his commercial business from Constantinople to Alexandria in 1850. The Cavafy firm was already a major importer of raw materials from the Black Sea and the eastern Mediterranean in both England and France. During the Crimean Wars Petros acquired English nationality in order to protect his business. The firm's acquisition of a ginning plant in the Nile Delta, at Kafr al-Zayyat in 1860, was a sign of its growing involvement in Egypt. Petros Cavafy's wife Harikleia gave birth to their fourth son, Constantine, in 1863. By the time he reached adulthood, the family firm would not exist, but he would be destined for greater things.[27]

Among the important Greek firms established in Egypt at the time were G. Zervoudachi & Sons, bankers and cotton exporters, and C.[Constantine] M.[Michael] Salvago & Son, cotton merchants who also acquired ginning factories and branches all over Egypt. Both firms made their appearance in

1863. Constantine Salvago's family was originally from the Aegean island of Chios where the old family home is still standing. His father Michael, who was born on Chios in 1814, was based on the Aegean island of Syros and traded in textiles. He had represented Syros at the Greek national assembly that met in Athens in 1862 to decide on a new constitution for the country. He died in 1880 in Paris. Constantine, who moved the family business to Alexandria, would become one of the most influential merchants and power brokers in Egypt.

The changes in the economy brought more than the big Greek merchant houses to Egypt. In what became a distinguishing feature of the Greeks in Egypt, many of those who moved there had little or no wealth and took up all sorts of small businesses and retail trade jobs. One of the most common practices was to open a grocery store. A visitor from Greece in the late 1850s remarked with somewhat of an exaggeration that the biggest part of the retail trade in Cairo was in the hands of the Greeks.[28] These Greeks had begun arriving in significant numbers from the mid-1850s onward seeking to benefit from the freedoms foreigners enjoyed in Egypt. Political upheavals, Greek military campaigns against the Ottomans, aimed at acquiring territories Greece claimed as its own, and the corresponding lack of economic opportunities were all factors pushing many Greeks to seek more stability and better economic conditions abroad. Seeing that many of their compatriots were already established in Alexandria and Cairo, many Greeks decided to try their luck in rural areas. As one historian has noted,

here, indeed lay much of their strength: where their French and British competitors preferred the comfort of Alexandria, the Greeks, while not neglecting the seaport, moved on up the Nile, some to Cairo where they helped to make the political capital a commercial center as well, others into the farthest reaches of Upper Egypt and the Sudan, selling cloth, trinkets and hardware to the Arab cultivators and Bedouin herdsmen, lending money on exorbitant terms, and buying the products of those regions for shipment to compatriots in Alexandria and export overseas.[29]

Not to underestimate the difficult conditions the Greeks would encounter, one wonders whether the spartan lives they led in the Greek provinces made it a little easier to settle in small towns in the Nile Delta, and to go even further south down the Nile Valley. In any case, many of them were in for an unexpected reward.

The liberalization of the economy meant that cultivators often had to obtain a loan to meet their obligations. With crops being sold freely, the Alexandrian commercial houses began to send their agents to the villages, but they were at a disadvantage compared to the local merchants, many of whom were the Greeks who had already ventured beyond Alexandria and Cairo. Quite simply they became one of the only sources of capital. There was no sure way of sending money to the interior from Alexandria, and it was difficult to obtain sufficient security for any advance an agent would make to a fellah. A sophisticated institutional banking and legal network would eventually spread to the rural areas but for now, the Greek trader was in a position to make his own private arrangements with the local administration. Moreover, the Alexandrian agent was restricted in that he could provide a loan only against a future delivery of a crop, while the local Greek had money at his disposal for such purposes as weddings or the sudden visit of the tax collector. The longer the banks took to penetrate the countryside, the longer the Greeks could continue to lend at high rates of interest. Thus the Greek trader fit more naturally into the local society and profited by becoming either a lender of money to the fellahin—at a high interest rate—or a middleman between the big Alexandrian commercial houses and the fellahin.[30]

The Suez Canal

Next to the opportunities for trade and profiting from the cotton economy, the digging of the Suez Canal, beginning in 1859 and led by the Frenchman Ferdinand de Lesseps, was another factor that brought a few thousand Greeks to Egypt. The majority of them originated the islands of Kasos and Kastellorizo, the closest Aegean islands to Egypt. Ironically, Kasos joined the Greek uprising in 1821 and it was the Egyptian fleet under Ibrahim that put down the island's rebellion in a bloody fashion. For those who survived, the only means for a decent livelihood was to become sailors or fishermen; Kasos is a small rocky island with few opportunities for agricultural work. The opening of the canal offered work if not prosperity to the desperate islanders. At the canal they would use their maritime skills, especially in the dredging process, but the conditions they encountered were grim. In 1865 de Lesseps wrote that the European workers—who were mostly Armenians, Dalmatians, and Greeks, and were housed in wooden bungalows—were suffering from a variety of ailments. Both the weather and the living and working conditions were atrocious, and workers were struck by dysentery, malaria, and cholera. The numbers of laborers working on the canal at any time are difficult to establish. The Canal Company's report of 1866 puts the total number at eighteen thousand, of whom eight thousand were Europeans. Greek sources claim the Greeks numbered about five thousand—of which three thousand were said to be from Kasos. The prevalence of the Greeks often led to exaggerations of their actual numbers. A French observer claimed that the town of Port Said—established in 1859 at the northern mouth of the canal—had eight thousand inhabitants in 1867 and about two-thirds of them were Greeks. He reported a similarly high proportion of Greeks in the other two canal towns of Ismailiya and Suez. Greek sources report that in 1875, the Greeks were about 10 percent of the fourteen thousand inhabitants in the three towns.[31]

The Suez Canal opened in 1869 and that same year Greece awarded Ismail its highest honor, the Grand Cross of the Order of the Savior. Those Greeks who had gone to the canal as workers stayed on to open businesses or take maritime-related jobs. Many of them would settle in Port Said, where they formed a Greek community organization in 1865. Others would filter southward to the canal towns of Suez and Ismailiya, forming community organizations in 1888 and 1903 respectively. So great were the relative numbers of Kasiots leaving the island for the canal area, that a popular song spoke about wanting de Lesseps to stand trial for making "the desert habitable" and making Kasos deserted. The first ship to go through the canal, Kasiot sources claim, was piloted by a Kasiot.

In-between Greece and Egypt

By the mid-1870s the Greeks appeared to be feeling very much at home in Egypt. In the five decades that had elapsed since Tossizza, d'Anastasi, and Zizinia accepted Muhammad Ali's invitation to come to Egypt to do business, the numbers of Greeks had steadily increased, and setbacks such as their enemy status during the Greek War of Independence and the Crimean War, bouts of cholera, and the economic downturn that came when the end of the American Civil War brought the end to Egypt's cotton boom reduced their numbers only temporarily. Overall their numbers continued to grow. The exact figures, let alone the precise definition of who was Greek (a citizen of Greece, a Greek-speaking Greek Orthodox, or a Greek or Arab Orthodox), in nineteenth-century Egypt are very difficult to establish with any great certainty. In 1858 it was estimated that in all of Egypt there were 2,850 Greeks who were heads of families. A visitor from Greece reported that there were about seven thousand Greeks in Egypt in the late 1850s, probably a low estimate.[32] By the late 1870s that number had grown to about thirty thousand.[33] There were Greeks in almost every economic sphere in Egypt, with the exception of manual labor or agricultural work. At the top of the Greek social pyramid were the wealthy merchants whose businesses played an important role in the purchase and export of cotton and other goods. Some of them were also involved in banking and finance. Others owned ginning plants or transport companies or worked in the various ancillary jobs created by the growth of the cotton economy. In Alexandria and Cairo Greeks were doctors and lawyers. They owned hotels, restaurants, theaters, and nightclubs. Many were in the retail trade and worked for one of the Greek-owned merchant houses.[34]

Feeling at home in Egypt did not mean that the Greeks had close relations with the Egyptians or lost their connection to Greece and to other Greeks. In that sense they were similar to other Greek diaspora communities. The wealthiest Greeks established community organizations that fostered cohesion among all Greeks, and the Greek government was able to offer considerable diplomatic protection through the Consular Court and support more generally. Sometimes that support was not welcome, especially by those Greeks who regarded religion as the most salient marker of their identity and wished to cultivate ties with Greek Orthodox Syrians. But on the whole the Greeks felt close to their homeland and news from Greece dominated the newspapers published in Alexandria. Finally, less immediately visible, but just as important, was the cohesion of the merchant class, not only through kinship ties but also by favoring their compatriots in a way that impressed careful observers. Invariably, "they found their partners within their own circle of merchants and bankers especially when it was a question of preserving the Greek character of a firm." The result "was the same type of extended clan as among Jews and Calvinists."[35] This Greek clannishness, moreover, trickled down to the lower strata and it characterized most Greeks in Egypt, whatever their occupation.

A corollary to Greek cohesion and attachment to the homeland was being part of the European colonial elite and sharing in its attitudes toward the Egyptians, which is not surprising considering that the Greeks, especially their elite, functioned as a middleman minority that connected Egypt with international markets. The European elite applied one set of rules in dealings among themselves and another when dealing with the Egyptians. Most Europeans regarded them as corrupt and treacherous, or more charitably as lazy and neglectful. All of them believed they were backward and in dire need of being civilized.[36] The Greek views were somewhat different. They regarded Muhammad Ali and his successors positively, as having stood up to the Ottomans, who were the mortal enemy of the Greeks. The welcome Muhammad Ali extended to the Greeks was noted with gratitude and this respect was extended to his successors.[37] The Greeks were also aware that their homeland did not always compare favorably with Egypt. A visitor from Greece who traveled from Alexandria to Cairo by way of the recently completed railroad line noted that while Greece considered itself the leading country in the region, it could not boast of having completed an impressive project.[38] Moreover, lacking a strong government that would back them, they knew they had to ingratiate themselves with the local rulers. The wealthiest merchants saw to it that relations with the khedives and their entourage would be cordial if not close. And the Greeks knew that the attitudes and policies of Britain and France toward their own homeland were not always that different to those toward Egypt. But they certainly shared the general European view that the government was inefficient and Egypt was backward and in need of being civilized. But at least one Greek observer also believed sincerely that while all other foreign general consuls behaved in a farcically autocratic manner, the Greek was the exception to the rule.[39] While not all of them behaved like arrogant colonists, there were many incidents in which Greeks caused a public disturbance or even clashed with Egyptians. The common assertion that the Greeks in Egypt enjoyed a special relationship with the local population applies to the mid-twentieth century, not the nineteenth century. The historical record shows that "to the insult of their general success in escaping high Egyptian taxes and flaunting Egyptian justice, the immigrant European workers added the injury of drawing higher wages than local artisans for the same work," and that "European workshops tended to shun Egyptian skilled labor out of a conviction that it produced an inferior product."[40] By the same token, urban anti-European agitation in the 1860s and 1870s also involved Greeks in a planned way because they were Christians, or they provoked some kind of fracas by insulting Islam or engaged in disorderly behavior. Such incidents occurred in Alexandria, Cairo, Port Said, and Tanta. On the whole, "Egyptians in the eastern ports of Suez and Port Said seemed more aggressive toward Europeans, in contrast to Alexandria, where Italians and Greeks appear to have caused most of the trouble," with the Greek shopkeepers often clashing with Nubian guards, and Greek Orthodox believers clashing with Muslim officials.[41]

By the mid-1870s, the clock ran out on Ismail's efforts to build the country's productive capacity and he was unable to pay even the interest on Egypt's mounting debts. In 1876 the European powers—England, France, Austria, and Italy—made the first big step in controlling Egypt's finances with the appointment of a four-person commission representing each of those bondholding countries to oversee Egyptian state revenue and expenditure. The Greeks, with the exception of a few bankers, most notably Ioannis Sinadino, who was a joint owner of the Anglo-Egyptian Bank, had not been directly involved in the lending frenzy that Ismail's unwise spending had created in the 1860s. The Anglo-Egyptian Bank was one of the lucky ones because the khedive was able to bail them out before he ran out of funds completely. The rest of the Greek businessmen waited with bated breath to see how Egypt would fare under international control. But they made no plans to leave. Egypt was their home.

2

Egypt and Its Greeks under British Rule, 1882–1914

When Stephanos Zizinia passed away in 1868, he was the last remaining of the four Greek merchants close to Muhammad Ali, outlasting Casulli, d'Anastasi, and Tossizza. Zizinia was one of three wealthy Alexandrian Greeks, along with Ioannis (later Sir John) Antoniades and the physician and Egyptologist Tassos Demetrios Neroutsos, who all had a great interest in antiquarian studies.[1] The fascination of the Greeks who settled in Egypt in the nineteenth century with that country's ancient past was an early sign of the affinity many Greeks felt toward Egypt. Zizinia had amassed a huge library with about sixty thousand volumes and manuscripts that were carefully preserved by his son Menandros in his equally large home on the Place des Consuls, which was aptly named Palais Zizinia. Alas, the fire that destroyed several buildings in Alexandria in the wake of the city's bombardment by the British fleet in 1882 also consumed Zizinia's valuable collection. The unfortunate event, and the more serious loss of life and property it inflicted on the Greeks, symbolized the driving of an imperial British wedge between the Greeks and Egyptians.

The bombardment of Alexandria by the British fleet in 1882 and its occupation of Egypt that followed marked the beginning of British rule over the country and a new era for the Greeks in Egypt. Up until that point, they had gained security and prosperity by forging close ties with the Egyptian governments and maintaining a strong connection to Greece, whose diplomatic representatives in Egypt guaranteed the Greek residents would continue to enjoy the privileges afforded to them by the Capitulations. Toward the end of Ismail's rule, Anglo–French economic control of Egypt increased when Tewfik became khedive in 1879. Their increasing involvement in Egypt's affairs against the background of the country's faltering finances fueled an Egyptian militant response led by Colonel Ahmad

'Urabi that brought the Anglo–French warships to Alexandria in a classic demonstration of gunboat diplomacy that culminated in the bombardment by the British. After the British quashed the uprising led by 'Urabi and installed themselves as Egypt's de facto rulers, a third, now exclusively British, source of power cast its shadow over Egypt and the Greeks. Although Egypt did not become a British colony, or protectorate, in practice Egypt was beholden to Britain. There continued to be an Egyptian government under the khedive who was in power on paper, but it was the British administration that governed in practice. A colonial administrator, Alfred Milner, who served as under-secretary for finance in Egypt came up with the most evocative description of the new status quo when he described it as a "Veiled Protectorate."[2]

This thinly disguised form of British rule in Egypt lasted until 1914 and during this entire period the Greeks had to negotiate their status in Egypt not only with the Egyptian and Greek governments, but also with the British. The half-hearted British takeover of Egypt meant they had to observe at least part of the status quo ante and acknowledge Egypt's status as a semiautonomous Ottoman province. Most importantly for the Greeks, and the other foreign residents, the British preserved the Capitulations, even if they tried to chip away at them. Therefore the Greek community's reliance on the Greek diplomats remained, and to the extent that Egyptian political forces had some limited space to operate in, the Greeks could not ignore them either. But there was no doubt that the British mattered most to the Greeks and they soon discovered that their policies cut both ways. The erosion of foreign rights the British administrators favored somewhat curbed their privileges, but British measures to improve the cultivation and export of cotton benefited the Greek exporters. Those benefits rippled through the economy to many of the Greeks. The 1882–1914 era would see an increase in the role Greek and foreign capital played in the Egyptian economy, even though demographically the size of the Greek presence plateaued. Official figures show 37,301 Greeks in 1882, and in 1897 their number had risen only slightly to 38,208. Then there was a steep increase to 62,975 in 1907, followed by a small decline to 56,731 in 1917.

The Greeks and 1882

As 'Urabi's nationalist movement gained momentum in early 1882, a combined Anglo–French fleet arrived in Alexandria. It was an obvious show of force in support of the old status quo and Khedive Tewfik, which ultimately only managed to provoke the rebels. The Greeks in Egypt, some of whom had expressed sympathy when 'Urabi launched his movement in September 1881, changed their attitude in light of the few acts of antiforeign violence by some of the rebels. In May 1882 the Alexandrian *Omonoia* concluded that the Greeks were "experiencing the greatest of crises," and in the capital the weekly *Kairon* changed course and turned against 'Urabi.[3] The Greek government, meanwhile, sent two warships, the *Hellas* and the *Vasilefs Georgios*, to join the Franco–British fleet outside Alexandria. In an answer to a question in the Vouli, the Greek parliament, Prime Minister Charilaos Trikoupis explained that the Greek warships had been sent to Alexandria because of "the unstable situation in Egypt which could endanger the interests of Greek citizens," while the Greek diplomatic agent there had telegraphed saying the presence of Greek warships was necessary for the security of the many Greeks. His answer was met by loud acclaim from many deputies.[4] Trikoupis and many of those supporting him were openly pro-British and pro-French and saw those two powers as important allies in Greece's ongoing efforts to claim territories from the Ottoman Empire. The move obviously helped shape the attitudes of the Greeks in Egypt, many of whom were supporters of Trikoupis. Yet Trikoupis was a little uncomfortable with Greece joining this show of force, and he told the Vouli that he hoped the presence of Greek warships would not be "misunderstood" by the government and the people of Egypt.[5] Not sharing his prime minister's optimism, Alexandria's Greek consul general Cleon Rangavis decided that, under the circumstances, some of the Greek residents of the city should be given arms to defend themselves, a plan in which Ambroise Sinadino, the community organization president, also became involved. The Greek government dismissed the idea, but Rangavis turned to another plan, the creation of a European militia, which also fell through. Inevitably those mindless schemes became known and only served to strengthen Egyptian antiforeign feeling.[6]

Those sentiments came to a head on June 11 in Alexandria. According to an independent British observer, for some days prior to that event "the demeanor of the natives toward the European population of Alexandria had been growing more and more unfriendly." This included the Greeks who were regarded as part of the combined foreign powers that were putting pressure on Egypt. Among the several incidents he reported on, the eve of June 11 was one in which a Greek subject was warned by an Egyptian in a café to "take care, as the Arabs were going to kill the Christians either that day or the next."[7] What triggered the demonstrations and violence against the Europeans on June 11 is difficult to ascertain, since there are several versions. The flashpoint was on Rue des Soeurs when—according to one version—an altercation between an Egyptian who had given a ride on his donkey to a man from Malta who refused to pay his fare escalated when bystanders, including Greeks, got involved. The Maltese stabbed the Egyptian and that caused a general melee involving Egyptians, Greeks, and Maltese, who began using their firearms as snipers from the surrounding buildings. With the police slow to react, serious fighting and looting of European-owned shops and houses broke out and continued for several hours. At one point the crowd even managed to injure the British consul, who had arrived on the scene to restore order. The exact number of fatalities is difficult to establish. According to some sources 163 Egyptians, including women and children, and thirty-five Europeans lost their lives. Other counts speak of 250 Egyptians and fifty Europeans dead.[8] In any case, the event was considered as a "massacre of Europeans" and would serve as the pretext of Britain's direct involvement in Egypt's affairs a month later.

Those events in Alexandria and some smaller antiforeign incidents, some of which also included fatalities, triggered a mass flight of Europeans from Egypt and naturally reinforced their prejudice against Egyptians. Consul General Cleon Rangavis asked the government in Athens to send ships to evacuate Greek citizens as well as other foreigners opting to go to Greece. In the days that followed ships arrived at the port of Alexandria almost every day, and sailed to Piraeus or other Mediterranean ports, brimming with relieved passengers. "Alexandria, at this period," noted a British observer, "presented a curious spectacle. Beyond the business of transporting the fugitives, there was nothing else done. The shops were shut up, and the doors barred and padlocked. The banks were occupied in putting up iron shutters, and bricking up their windows . . . the streets in the European quarter presented a deserted appearance," while in Cairo "things were but a little better, the whole of the foreign populations had taken flight."[9]

The arrival of the steamship *Elpis* in Piraeus with 1,400 cramped aboard four days later was the first of a stream of arrivals. Greek Orthodox Patriarch Sofronios had to be persuaded to depart, and he left carrying the most valuable objects that belonged to the church. By the end of the month the French consul estimated that about thirty-two thousand Europeans had left Egypt. Those arriving in Greece, the authorities soon realized, were not all Greek citizens, nor did they have the means to support themselves.

Special arrangements had to be made to accommodate what were described as "refugees."[10] The wealthier Greek Alexandrians had an easier passage, among them the family of Emmanuel Benachi, one of Egypt's most important cotton exporters. His daughter, who later in life became Penelope Delta, one of Greece's leading novelists in the first half of the twentieth century, described their flight in her memoirs. The family was summering east of the city in their villa in Ramla when the June 11 riot broke out—at other times they may have been in Athens, France, or Austria in order to avoid the heat of Egypt's summer. Penelope was eight years old in 1882, but she wrote her memoirs of that era fifty years later, by which time she had acquired her considerable writing skills, and also retained a very good memory of small details. Ramla at the time was in the countryside and isolated from the center of the city. Her father learned of the events from a neighbor, who after a few days advised him to leave Egypt until things blew over. Coincidentally, on the day of the riots, the Benachis were hosting the captain and officers of the *Hellas*, one of the two Greek warships that moored just outside Alexandria. Penelope writes that her mother Virginia saved their lives by insisting they extend their visit to the midafternoon, because by the time they arrived back in Alexandria the riot—which she describes as the fellahin slaughtering Europeans—had been quelled. The next days were full of worry and unease. The men of the family took out their hunting rifles and the children were told it was because of the fear of packs of stray dogs roaming outside. A few days later they left at the crack of dawn. She was asleep when they passed through the city, but her brother Antonis claimed to have seen bloody walls and doors because they passed the spot where "the Europeans had defended themselves and from the balconies they had shot several fellahin," she explained, adding "but whoever was on the street when the murderous mobs emerged from the Arab neighborhoods was slaughtered without mercy."[11] The Benachis made it safely to the port and boarded the Greek warship for a few days and then chartered their own vessel and sailed for Greece, where they spent the summer.

Several important Greeks that had stayed helped the British in the wake of the devastating bombardment they inflicted on July 11—after the French vessels had left, registering France's disagreement with its ally's hard line. The bombardment affected the European quarter where many buildings were destroyed, either because they were struck by a missile, caught fire as a result of the shelling, or as a result of the looting that took place over the next few days. There were about 1,500 Europeans left in the city, and large numbers of them were the poorer Greeks. A few of the wealthier Greeks were still there as well. Georgios Goussios, his wife, and some employees were barricaded in the Anglo-Egyptian Bank, of which he was the manager. The widespread damages in the city included the building of the Greek consulate, which the crews of the Greek warships, after obtaining permission from the British admiral, went ashore to save from the fire that had broken out as a result of the shelling. Descriptions of the damaged inflicted on that day include information about Greek properties, for example, "a shell fell in the Rue Copt, in the stables of M. Zervoudachi, and for a quarter of an hour the neighborhood was enveloped by a cloud of dust . . . a shell fell into the house of M. Antoniadis, in the Rue Cherif Pasha." This was also when Zizinia's house and library were destroyed. Other Greek properties were completely or partially destroyed. But all this did not seem to matter because when the British landed troops to engage in battle with 'Urabi's troops, Ioannis Antoniades, the antiquarian who was director of the Commercial Bank of Alexandria and whose house had been struck by a British missile, allowed the British access to his large estate near the southern entrance to Alexandria. In doing so he enabled them to monitor 'Urabi's troops around Lake Mariut, a body of water that lies southwest of the city. This was deemed important enough for him to be knighted by Queen Victoria, who also made Constantine Zervoudachi, another leading Greek banker, a Baronet because he offered his warehouses in Alexandria to be used as a hospital by the invading British forces. As soon as the invasion was complete, order was restored and the Greeks and the Europeans started returning. The leaders of Alexandria's Greek community sent a telegram to British prime minister William Gladstone congratulating him "on the fiftieth anniversary . . . of his election as a Member of Parliament."[12]

The Greeks and the British Occupation

The response of the Greeks in Egypt to the British occupation was by no means uniform. The merchant class soon saw a significant uptick in the country's export economy and this made them mostly supportive of the new status quo. But not all of them reacted in the same way. In his study of Cavafy's historical era, Tsirkas suggested that there were two responses on the part of the Greek merchants toward the British, who became Egypt's de facto rulers beginning in 1882. The Greeks who had settled there before the 1860s, whom he described as embodying Greek diaspora banking and commercial capital and were called "first class" or first-generation Greeks, were less likely to align themselves with the British. A second "class" of Greek merchants were those who arrived in Egypt in the midst of Khedive Ismail's reforms and the cotton boom and who, Tsirkas avers, were more closely connected to British banking and financing and were much likelier to be supportive of the British, even identifying with them in many ways. Tsirkas himself conceded that this difference, being "an inter-bourgeois antithesis," should not be overstated and had not been systematically analyzed. He was after all laying out the historical background to Cavafy's life.[13] Notwithstanding the roughly-hewn nature of this analysis, it is a useful reminder that even the Greek merchant class had different approaches, and of course that it was a category in demographic flux, with old businesses sometimes closing, and new arrivals establishing new businesses. For example, one of the largest cotton and cereal export firms, Cassaveti & Company, which had branches all over Egypt, closed its operations in Egypt because Sophocles Constantinides, who had taken over after the deaths of the brothers Demetrios and Alexandros Cassaveti, decided to move to London, the company's headquarters.[14]

A recent and persuasive attempt to build on Tsirkas's view has adopted as its starting point a more pronounced emphasis on the colonial character of the British occupation—specifically the period of Lord Cromer's rule from 1882 to 1907. Enlisting recent analyses of modern empires that identify several types of resistance, this study suggests accordingly that there were three basic Greek responses to Cromer's rule: collaboration, adaptation or negotiation, and resistance.[15] These categories certainly correspond to the attitudes of the Greeks. There were several points in-between, and those attitudes also changed over time if we examine the period until 1914. Almost a year after the bombardment took place, 2,600 wealthy European inhabitants of Alexandria and other towns signed a petition asking that the occupation become permanent. Among them were many Greeks, though not Zizinia, who held on to his pro-French outlook. But over the next decades others within the Greek community would become much less supportive, and some even hostile toward the British. In particular, the British administration's hostility toward the Capitulations would obviously alienate the Greeks and other foreigners. Also, the Greeks felt they were the main target of British measures designed to regulate the retail trade, the sale of alcohol, and usurious practices in the provinces.

Cromer is the key character to understanding the nature of British rule in Egypt from 1882 through the early twentieth century. Evelyn Baring, who became the Earl of Cromer in 1901, had served as the British member of the Anglo–French commission that oversaw Egypt's finances in the late 1870s. In 1882 he was appointed British consul general in Egypt, a position from which he was able to shape government policies in the country and maintain Britain's sway over its affairs. At the end of his twenty-four-year tenure, Cromer published a weighty two-volume study entitled *Modern Egypt*, where he presented a detailed account of the country and his policies in Egypt. The journal, published by the British Royal African Society, asked Sir Henry Hamilton Johnston, who was a fellow colonial administrator as well as an explorer, botanist, and linguist, to write an extended review of Cromer's opus. Years later, Johnston would write his own account of his experiences in the colonies in a book entitled *The Backward People and Our Relations with Them*. Johnston titled his review of Cromer with the telling title "Lord Cromer's 'Modern Egypt.'" He explained, "the short title of this review almost serves a double purpose. It indicates that this article is an attempt to review the chief features of the remarkable book just published by the Earl of Cromer, but it also—accidentally—expresses the fact that Modern Egypt—since 1883—is Lord Cromer's, in the sense that it is the outcome of his work and policy." As for the book's merits, Johnston continued, stating, "I would venture, with every desire not to exaggerate, to describe it as the most important State document which has been issued for the last half century from the point of view of British Imperial policy." In the next nine pages he heaped praise on both Cromer's work in Egypt as well as the book. In conclusion, he highlights one example of Cromer's evenhandedness. Johnston asked the reader rhetorically, "what could be fairer, more in accord with actuality and opposed to fictitious traditional nonsense, than his general summing up of the character and achievements of the 40,000 Greek settlers in Egypt?"[16]

Cromer was certainly more positive about the Greeks in Egypt than he was about the Egyptians. He had praise for the wealthy Greeks but was critical of the lower-class Greeks that engaged in usury or selling alcohol. "In Alexandria," Cromer noted, "which may almost be said to be a Greek town, a great many influential and highly respectable Greeks are to be found." And he added, "Their presence in Egypt is an unmixed benefit to the country," and went on to say that "the Greeks of Egypt have, as of old, carried high the torch of civilization in their adopted country." Then came the criticism: "Still the fact remains," he stated, "that a portion of the Greek colony in Egypt consists of low-class Greeks exercising the professions of usurer, drink-seller etc." Despite his criticism of these Greeks, Cromer expressed his admiration for others, remarking "many of the small Greek traders are fully deserving of respect," and that "the Greek of this class has an extraordinary talent for retail trade. He will risk his life in the pursuit of petty gain. It is not only that a Greek usurer or *baqqal* (general dealer) is established in almost every village in Egypt; the Greek pushes his way into the most remote parts of the Soudan and Abyssinia. Wherever, in fact there is the smallest prospect in buying in a cheap and selling in a dear market, there will be the petty Greek trader to be found."

On balance, Cromer concluded, "we may therefore give the low class Greek credit for his enterprising commercial spirit." However, "his presence in Egypt is often hurtful . . . he tempts the Egyptian peasant to borrow at some exorbitant rate of interest, and then by a sharp turn of the legal screw reduces him from the position of an allodial proprietor to that of a serf," and moreover, "under Greek action and influence, the Egyptian villagers are taking to drink." Therefore, Cromer concluded, the way Gladstone said it would be a good thing if the Turks were turned out of Europe, he believed it would be an "excellent thing" if the low-class Greeks could be turned out of the Ottoman Empire and its dependencies. It was a statement with an unmistakable colonialist ring to it that illustrates the gulf between the British and the poorer Greeks.[17]

The colonial tone of Cromer's reports also entailed negative stereotyping of the Greeks. Their association with practices such as usury or the sale of alcohol, while not inaccurate, did not provide a fair picture. A recent study of the Egyptian beer industry mentions, "with the preponderance of Greeks and Italians in the distribution of alcohol, it would be easy to dismiss the burgeoning alcohol industry as a foreign imperial imposition. However, on closer inspection the picture appears to be far more nuanced. When we move our gaze from the managers of these establishments, who tended to receive the licenses, to their owners, there appears to have been a significant Egyptian contingent among the latter. For example, the British consul reported that of the 4,015 alcohol distributors in 1904, 2,257 were foreign and 1,758 were local subjects."[18]

There were of course many Greeks who engaged in illegal practices, whether it was unlicensed sale of alcohol, importation and sale of hashish, and exploitation of women sex workers. What made those practices even more egregious was the abuse of the privileges afforded to foreigners to escape prosecution. But overall, the numbers of Greeks involved in these practices was small in relation to the overall size of the Greek presence in Egypt.

For Cromer, the Capitulations were a source of evil. The privileges foreigners enjoyed, in the eyes of the British, were a relic of Egypt's Ottoman past and therefore incompatible with its new status quo, the "Veiled Protectorate." Before Cromer made his views known in print, Milner did so in a book about his experiences in Egypt that he published as soon as he returned to England in 1892. He discussed the Capitulations in a chapter entitled "International Fetters" and mentioned that in no part of the Ottoman Empire had the Capitulations "received so wide and indeed abusive extension as in Egypt."

He then listed the abuses, adding, "the impartiality of foreign judges trying their own countrymen for offences committed against Egyptians is not always unimpeachable." And he went on to single out the Greeks, saying, "this is especially the case with the judges of that foreign nationality which is most numerously represented in Egypt, the Greek." There were instances, perhaps less common than they used to be, he conceded, but still common, "in which Greek criminals—thieves, forgers even murderers—have been handed over to their consul, and have either been allowed to escape before trial or have been acquitted in the teeth of the evidence, or, if condemned in Egypt, have appealed with success to a lenient court in Athens." Worse still, those "ruffians" returned to Egypt after serving "an incredibly short sentence" and resumed their criminal activities.

Greek involvement in crime would always be invoked not only by those rightly wishing to create a more lawful environment in Egypt, but also when one wanted to cast aspersions on the foreigners and their privileges. It is notable that Russell Pasha, the British policeman whose long career in Egypt was devoted to fighting the spread of drugs, makes very few references to Greeks in his memoirs. He does, however, mention some Greeks who were working on the side of law enforcement in Egypt to catch smugglers.[19]

Milner concluded by asking rhetorically, "Can it be wondered at, under these circumstances, that the Greeks are notorious throughout the country for truculent defiance of authority, for violence and for lawlessness?"[20] Cromer's views were very similar. In a chapter entitled "European Privilege," he discussed the Capitulations in great detail and in a way that makes it obvious that he believed that they were inconsistent with the type of governance Britain was trying to put in place in Egypt. As he did with all the topics he tackled in his book, Cromer treated the Capitulations in detail, described their historical background, presented their advantages and their disadvantages, and listed what he characterized as small changes his administration had been able to introduce. Cromer then cited passages from his annual report of 1905 in which he recommended the replacement of the Capitulations, "an archaic system of government that has outlived its time which acts as a clog to all real progress," and which he described as the "main citadel of privilege."

What he wants in its place is not clear. After all, Cromer was an administrator, not a lawmaker, and the end of the chapter becomes entangled in distinctions between political and judicial internationalism. One reads through this chapter with a growing sense of the underlying irony to which the author is blind: Cromer, the principal advocate of Britain's continued presence and control over Europe, was claiming that Egypt would make big steps toward independence if it got rid of the Capitulations and the Mixed Courts, but of course, not the British, on whom "the advance of true civilization in Egypt depends."[21]

Those were the attitudes that propelled the erosion of the privileges of foreigners. Cromer tried to chip away at the Capitulatory regime. In 1884 Cromer made the approval of a £9 million international loan to Egypt, conditional upon the abolition of one of the main Capitulatory privileges that exempted foreigners from paying certain taxes. The following year he obtained a written statement from the Capitulatory Powers that enabled the Egyptian government to issue a decree in 1886 making all foreigners liable to paying property tax, which doubled the revenue for the government. A few years later, another government decree made them liable to pay a professional tax. The Greeks bore the brunt of those measures. Of the 2,210 foreigners who started to pay taxes in Cairo, about half—or 1,048—were Greek, while in Alexandria the ratio was believed to be higher. Luckily for them, following protests by both the French and Greek governments, the professional tax was rescinded in early 1892. But its abolition was also extended to Egyptians in compliance with the new principle that prevented foreigners from enjoying tax privileges over the local population. Thus the foreigners lost every fiscal advantage they had enjoyed over the Egyptians, except their exemption from paying stamp duty.[22]

Moreover, the introduction of a stricter regulatory regime for commercial business was another way in which foreigners and Greeks saw their privileges curtailed and their status equalized with that of their Egyptian competitors. In 1889 Cromer secured the approval of the Capitulatory

Powers to allow the Egyptian government to legislate on law and order in a manner that would be equally binding on local foreign residents. Police directives were issued in 1891, regulating the operation of public shops, medical clinics, pharmacies, the sale of medicine, and bookkeeping. These restrictions on the issuing of licenses for coffee shops, hotels, bars, theaters, and countryside clubs was highly damaging for the Greeks, who operated widely in these businesses. Although the police directives did not turn out to be as damaging as originally feared, their restrictions on commercial freedom and residential immunity, as well as the extension of the Mixed Tribunals' jurisdiction over certain criminal cases, persuaded Greek observers that there was a trend toward eliminating all foreign privileges. For example, Andreas Pangalos, high court judge at the Mixed Tribunals, wrote to Trikoupis, "the English occupation does not view us with a favorable eye" and that "the colony all over Egypt is going through critical times."[23]

The British and the Greek Nationality Issue in Egypt

Prior to 1882 the Greek consular officials enjoyed a broad leeway in conferring Greek nationality on individuals, and by extension the privileges and protection that came with it. This practice was frustrating to the authorities in Egypt, especially in cases of persons breaking the law and promptly claiming they were Greek.

The authorities also regarded with great suspicion the criteria the consular officials were using, namely a certificate issued by a local government office in Greece—not unusual in countries judging citizenship based on *jus soli*—but nonetheless a document that could be acquired simply through knowing the right persons and not through normal government channels. What fueled the irritation of the Egyptian authorities was that many of those Greeks were either from the Ottoman Empire or from Ottoman provinces that had become part of Greece, which meant they were Ottoman citizens and subject to Egyptian laws. The problem became acute especially after Thessaly and parts of Epirus were incorporated into Greece in 1870 and more and more ethnic Greeks arriving in Egypt from those regions claimed Greek citizenship. Both Thessaly's Mount Pelion region and Epirus's mountain region had experienced significant economic development in the late eighteenth century in terms of commerce and this triggered emigration overseas throughout the nineteenth century, with Egypt as a prime destination. All who left from those regions before 1870 were Ottoman subjects. In 1881 Egypt's minister of foreign affairs Mustafa

Fahmy Pasha requested that the Greek consular officials submit lists of persons in Egypt who were Greek nationals. Consul Rangavis refused to do so, citing the difficulties and the likelihood of wrongly excluding persons, and this triggered a dispute between Greece and Egypt over how Greek nationality in Egypt would be determined according to mutually satisfactory criteria.

As the dispute dragged on, the British authorities became increasingly involved, and as the voluminous official correspondence shows, increasingly frustrated with Greece's determination to reserve the right to determine Greek nationality. Cromer did not want to intervene on Greece's behalf, stating, in 1889, that "we should not be justified in bringing very strong pressure of this sort to bear on the Egyptian Government unless some British interest of first-rate importance were at stake." He went on to say that any British action in Egypt had to take into account the effect it would produce on "the Mahommedan population of Egypt," and added, "it must be borne in mind that the Greeks are not only disliked but despised in Egypt." It was out of the question that Britain supports the Greek views because it would cause his administration problems and "impair the moral hold now exercised by Her Majesty's Government over the Egyptian Ministers and the people of Egypt."

Referring to Greece's demand that a Greek judge be appointed permanently to the Court of Appeal of the Mixed Courts (which would adjudicate disputes over nationality), Cromer reported—uncritically—that one reason for Egypt's objections to Greek claims was "the slight degree of confidence which they profess to entertain in the Greek Judges in general," and "in M. Antoniades, the present Greek Judge on the Court of Appeal in particular." He qualified this by saying the Egyptian side was prepared to consider the appointment of a permanent Greek judge to the Court of Appeal.[24] Rennell Rodd, one of the British administrators working under Cromer and a scholar of modern and ancient Greece, was caustic in his views of the Greeks in Egypt, writing in a memorandum, "the Greek community in Egypt contains the whole strength of the money-lenders and usurers of this country; and that, though there are many wealthy and important members it contributes by far the largest proportion to the criminal class."[25]

In 1890 the Greek and Egyptian governments were close to resolving the dispute that revolved around the nationality question. Greece had agreed to almost all conditions put forward by Egypt, including its adherence to the law that imposed a professional tax on all Europeans and its support for the reforms to the Mixed Courts that Egypt proposed; it also agreed to prosecute owners of gambling houses in the Greek Consular Courts. There remained one outstanding issue: the conditions under which Greek nationals would be expelled from Egypt, with Egypt claiming the right to do so unilaterally, which was not the case with other Europeans. Cromer acknowledged that this would be difficult for the Greek side to accept, but noted the Egyptian authorities were in the right "in contending that by reason of the large number of Greeks in Egypt and the turbulent character of many individual Greeks, the Greek colony does, in fact, occupy a very special position in Egypt, and that, therefore some special measures are necessary for dealing with bad characters."[26]

Greece and Egypt eventually came to an agreement on the nationality question in 1890, although 'nationality' not only for the Greeks but also the other foreigners would always remain a very difficult concept to pin down with any great certainty in Egypt.[27] There were also lingering issues between the two sides in which the British officials continued to express their contempt of the lower-class Greeks in Egypt. The Greco-Egyptian issues over the determination of nationality required additional agreements over the types of certificates that would be acceptable to the Egyptian authorities, and the two sides needed some additional negotiations to determine the exact number of Syrian Orthodox persons who would be considered as Greek nationals. A final detail, the number of days a person would have to prove Greek nationality to the Egyptian authorities (sixty days) was agreed upon in 1906.[28] In the meantime, another difference emerged when the Greek government tried to object to Egypt's wish to regulate the sale of alcohol in the provinces, especially villages with a population fewer than three thousand. This would have entailed closing Greek-owned businesses. British administrators feared that Greece would not sign an impending commercial agreement with Egypt, seeking to get that measure reversed. Rodd, writing from Cairo to the Foreign Office, explained disapprovingly that the sale of alcohol "appears to be carried on almost entirely by Greeks, whose petty profits involve the rapid demoralization of a semi-barbarous peasantry, to whom the use of alcohol has been for centuries unknown."[29]

Greek Tobacco, Egyptian Cigarettes

The effects of a commercial treaty signed between Greece and Egypt in 1884 are illustrative of the different implications the policies of Cromer's administration could have on the Greeks in Egypt. The treaty was concluded at the urging of Edgar Vincent, the British financial advisor to Khedive Tewfik. One of its main provisions was to allow the import of tobacco leaves from Greece. Up to that point, only tobacco from the Ottoman Empire could be imported legally into Egypt, where the climate was not suitable for growing anything but low-quality tobacco leaf. Vincent's role was symbolically important because it was proof of the legitimacy of the British involvement in Egypt's commercial agreements with other countries, though it had advantages for Egypt because the import taxes were a major source of government income, all the more so because the taxes were increased substantially, from an initial 5 piasters per oke (1.28 kilograms) to 14 piasters per kilogram within a few years. Even after merchants and cigarette manufacturers in Egypt negotiated a rebate based on the value of their exports from Egypt, import custom duties on tobacco exceeded the total value of Egypt's customs receipts from other goods until 1904, and for the next decade they remained at roughly the same level.

In the meantime, the value of tobacco exports increased dramatically, especially when the Greek government persuaded Egypt to impose a total ban on tobacco cultivation in 1890. But those agreements also brought a serious drawback for Greek shopkeepers in Egypt because they included provisions allowing authorities in Egypt to control the tobacco trade and even search Greek-owned stores because they suspected that tobacco or hashish, both cultivated in Greece, were being smuggled and sold in Egypt. No doubt before those controls were implemented at least some Greek tobacco merchants would have been free to flaunt the laws. Egyptian officials appear to have overzealously implemented the new regulations. Alexandria's Greek-language *Omonoia* complained that customs officials were accusing the Greeks of being smugglers and thieves and questioned the validity of their documentation of the tobacco they were importing.[30]

Yet at the same time, the increase of Greek tobacco thanks to the Greco–Egyptian commercial treaty benefited a growing number of Greek entrepreneurs who established cigarette manufacturing plants in Egypt. Their role would be catalytic and according to an authoritative study, "the arrival of Greek tobaccomen and the change they were able to bring to commerce were the first steps toward establishing a new cigarette industry in Egypt."[31] Eventually, the Greeks would be responsible for making the 'Egyptian cigarette' famous throughout the world. Egypt's dry climate was ideal for processing the tobacco leaves into cigarettes, which was done by hand. This labor-intensive task was not a problem in Egypt where there was an ample supply of cheap labor. There was easy access to imported varieties of tobacco leaves from Greece and the Ottoman Empire which, blended in several combinations, produced the so-called 'Egyptian cigarette.' Ironically it was British troops returning home from Egypt after 1882 that helped popularize that type of cigarette in Europe. Nestor Gianaclis was the pioneer of Greek cigarette making in Egypt. Born in Gumuldjina (present-day Komotini in Greece), a town in the tobacco-producing Ottoman province of Thrace, he arrived in Cairo via Constantinople in 1869 and began manufacturing cigarettes. A story goes that after the Khedive Tewfik offered British officers Gianaclis-made cigarettes, they went looking for his 'factory' and were surprised to find a relatively small shop on Rue Mousky. But Gianaclis's business would grow thanks to the Greco–Egyptian commercial agreement, and his workforce went from about eighty in 1884 to about five hundred in 1904. In the meantime, several other Greek tobacco merchants and manufacturers moved from the Ottoman Empire to Egypt as a result of a string of measures that had established an Ottoman state monopoly. The last straw came in 1883 when the state moved from controlling the production and trade of tobacco into cigarette manufacturing, which brought the closure of about three hundred privately owned manufacturing plants. Among the Greek firms that relocated to Egypt, the most important were Dimitrino et Compagnie, Kyriazi Frères, M. Melachrino et Compagnie, and Th. Vafiadis et Compagnie. Over the next decades more Greek firms were established in Egypt and the Egyptian cigarette began acquiring an international reputation thanks to those Greek entrepreneurs.

The Export of Cotton and Its Ripple Effect
The British administration's efforts to repair Egypt's finances and increase government income included a mixture of free-trade policies and improvements in the country's infrastructure, especially measures to enhance land irrigation, all of which were designed to increase the production and export of cotton. The relative success of those policies had enormous benefits for the wealthy Greek cotton merchants and other foreigners, who quickly consolidated their interests by creating the Alexandria General Produce Association in 1883. It was a body that regulated the marketing of cotton, cottonseed, cereals, and other produce. Out of the twenty-four founding members, fifteen were Greeks. Its first president was Theodore Ralli, and the vice president was Emmanuel Benachi.[32] The association purchased cotton and other goods, graded products, and delegated to itself the au-

thority to settle all disputes, not only between its own members but also between its members and outsiders. Its critics, including Egyptian cultivators, resented its control over the market and complained that it was "a state within a state."[33] It is a reminder that any benefits accruing to Egypt from the creation of wealth in the cotton sector passed first through the filter of the foreign elites. Thousands of other Greeks stood to gain from the prosperity of the Greek cotton elite, either because they were engaged in ancillary jobs, benefited from the wealth that trickled through the rest of the economy, or were able to take advantage of the improvements in community schools, hospitals, and other services funded by the wealthy. The several hospitals the Greeks established in Egypt, aside from the care they offered their patients, Greek and non-Greek, also had the sophisticated types of laboratories that enabled pioneering medical experiments and new methods to be practiced and adopted.[34]

The Greeks were prominent in the cotton exporting business. From 1882 until the First World War four large firms exported about 40 percent of the Egyptian cotton crop each year, and one of them, Choremi, Benachi & Company, was Greek-owned. It evolved out of one of the oldest and biggest exporters, Choremi, Mellor & Company, established in 1858, with Joseph Mellor being the partner based in Liverpool and Ioannis Choremi based in Alexandria, though he also owned houses in Liverpool. When both men decided to retire they divided the company. Ioannis moved to Athens and left his son-in-law, Emmanuel Benachi, in charge, with his brother Lucas Benachi, Ioannis Choremi's brother Demosthenes, and Thomas Davies, a cotton broker based in Liverpool, as the main shareholders.[35] After 1882, Benachi made a critical decision to establish branches throughout Egypt, and he did so with the help of the Bank of Alexandria's directors and fellow Greeks, Vasilios Georgalas and Constantine Sinadino. The firm also acquired cotton-ginning plants in the Nile Delta and embarked on a widespread import business of goods from many other countries. Choremi, Benachi & Company was the biggest cotton exporter in 1911–12. The other big Greek exporters were Pilavachi & Company (which exported the fourth-highest quantity in 1913–14), Andritsakis, Barsoum & Company, N.G. Casulli, and Rodocanachi. Several other Greek exporting firms would be established during the First World War era and become significant players in the cotton exporting business beginning in the 1920s.

The cotton exporters after 1882 did not limit themselves to exporting cotton or acquiring ginning plants. They directly or indirectly encouraged the continuous experimentations to find new types of high-quality cotton because all types were vulnerable to insects, the boll weevil, a beetle that feeds on the cotton plant, the bollworm, or various fungal diseases. Even a successful type of cotton such as the Ashmuni could not be expected to maintain its high yield or quality for much over two decades. To produce a type of resistant cultivar was a challenge that attracted mostly Greeks, many of whom owned cotton-growing land or were associated with one of the exporting firm's own properties where they conducted their experiments. Their efforts would bring them in conflict with British authorities who favored the status quo, and in any case their work had mixed results with some notable successes. One of the earliest came when Ioannis Cartalis discovered the Bamiah in 1873. It was considered superior to the Ashmuni, which was the most commonly planted in the 1880s, and gained popularity but before long experienced degeneration and disappeared, along with the Gallini that had been discovered by another Greek, Anastasios Milcovitch. The Mit-Afifi or Afifi type developed by Pericles Canavas, a Greek farmer and merchant, was considered superior to the Ashmuni, but growers were reluctant to take a chance with a new cotton cultivar for obvious financial reasons. Canavas got some help from fellow Greeks, "two important firms, Messrs Voltos Bros and Cartalis Bros who introduced the [Canavas] cotton to their . . . districts and clients."[36]

Failures of new types could exact a toll on their inventors. Zafiris Parachimonas, after working as the purchasing manager of the Cassavetis cotton merchant company in Upper Egypt, acquired his own property and tried his hand at developing a new variety of cotton. In 1890 he came up with one cultivar he named Zafiri which initially looked promising. He spent time and money advertising it to cultivators, but ultimately its staple was weak, demand plummeted, and Parachimonas "sustained financial loss and depression in health." Luckily, he tried again and in 1892 he produced the Abbassi, named after Khedive Abbas II, which did moderately well. Success fell to his son, Nicholas Parachimonas, who was born in Greece and studied agriculture in Montpellier in France before following in his father's footsteps in Egypt. Parachimonas went on to become one of the most distinguished and successful agronomists in Egypt, and worked hard to publicize the need for a wider acceptance of new cultivars by those involved in the cotton industry.[37]

But the Lancashire cotton manufacturers were hostile to the introduction of new cultivars of cotton because it involved costly adjustment to the machinery and was usually sold at a higher price than the type it was replacing. Moreover, their influence on British administrators in Egypt meant another obstacle in the promotion of new types of cotton, because the administrators were in a position to block its cultivation. Even the very successful Sakel, developed by Greek agriculturalist Ioannis "John" Sakellaridis and introduced in 1912, quickly becoming the most dominant type of cotton in the decades that followed, needed the help of Choremi, Benachi & Company. It has been argued that this brought "an inherent economic alliance between Egyptian landlords, Greek cotton-exporters in Alexandria and village-based Greek entrepreneurs and usurers. This alliance was, of course, based on mutual interests, but as it developed in opposition to the interests . . . of the Lancashire textile groups, it placed some members of the Greek community of Egypt on the side of the Egyptians in the developing contradictions between Egyptian landlords and British economic interests."[38]

The construction industry was a major beneficiary of the profits the cotton boom created. Many of the wealthy Greeks built houses and, proof of the ensuing construction boom, many Greeks arriving after 1882 were architects and civil engineers who became building contractors. Penelope Delta writes that in 1883, barely a year after the city's bombardment, "all the most distinguished Greeks of Alexandria bought plots of land on the Rue Rosette just outside the city limits . . . and all that area was named the Quartier Grec . . . it was the most beautiful neighborhood of Alexandria." And after that house was completed, her father built another one in Ramla, for use in the summer months.[39] A few years later, Penelope's little sister Argine would marry Mikés Salvago, the cotton exporter and one of the richest men in Egypt during the first half of the twentieth century. Their house in the Quartier Grec was a classical-style villa (now the Russian Cultural Center) and gardens occupied an entire block. By that time, the extended Benachi family had several homes in that neighborhood. The house of Penelope's brother Antonis was described by an admiring American visitor as "unique as a museum—jewelry, arms, medals, porcelain, embroideries, textiles, almost every sort of art in its finest examples."[40] Greek contractors undertook the building of many houses and several public works such as government buildings and major irrigation projects on the Nile. One of the best examples was the Société Anonyme des Immeubles d'Egypte that Georgios Zouros established in 1884. He had begun working as a contractor in Egypt in the 1850s along with his brothers-in-law Pandelis Trehakis from the island of Chios and Themistocles Sarris from the island of Syros. The company was awarded major projects by Khedive Ismail, including a wing of the Ras al-Tin Palace in Alexandria and the task of participating in bringing down one of the 'Cleopatra's needles' obelisks that were shipped to London and New York. In the 1880s the company began building houses around Alexandria's Place des Consuls and several central streets. After his retirement his nephews Antonis and Demetrios Trehakis took over the firm. They continued to undertake major projects including the enlargement of the port of Alexandria and the building of the Khedival Library in Cairo. One of the most successsful Greek contractors was Nikolaos Nicolaou, who from the 1890s onward built a total of 250 villas and houses east of the expanding city between the suburbs of Ibrahimiya and San Stefano. According to the 1897 census, out of 282 foreign contractors, 101, or slightly more than one in three, were Greeks. This was obviously a lucrative business because the 1917 census recorded 1,563 foreign contractors, among whom 352 were Greeks.[41]

The wider ripple effect—in terms of Greek entrepreneurial activity that the prosperity of cotton brought after 1882—is captured in a list of "the most important" Greek-owned firms established between 1882 and 1900 in Egypt and Sudan. Out of a total of eleven, four were involved in the cotton sector, two were real estate agents, and five were engaged in the import and export of a wide variety of goods.[42] Almost all the Greek firms survived the economic downturn in 1907; the Zervoudachi banking firm was the only big Greek casualty. Meanwhile more and more Greek entrepreneurial initiatives were taking root in Egypt. Ioannis Lagoudakis had established a plant that manufactured cigarette papers, and he had sent his brother-in-law, G.E. Anastasiades, to France to study papermaking. Lagoudakis's business was so successful, he had clients in the United States, including the Philadelphia-based Stefano Brothers cigarette company. He visited there in 1900 and saw that machines were replacing manual cigarette rolling, so upon his return to Alexandria he decided to switch to paper-making and established the first successful combined color printing and paper mill in Egypt.[43]

Greek Community Life

The community organization in Alexandria experienced a tremendous expansion in its activities after 1882, benefiting immensely from the prosperity the cotton boom brought to the wealthiest Greeks. The number of Greeks in Egypt increased by 40 percent to sixty-four thousand from 1897 to 1907. About 40 percent of them would settle in Alexandria and the remainder were equally divided between Cairo and the provinces. The new arrivals were not wealthy merchants and would soon be making use of the services provided by community organizations. Clearly the wealthy benefactors believed in the value of continuing to maintain the cohesion of the city's Greek population, its Greek identity, wellbeing, and public image and standing. A big part of the organization's growth in Alexandria was due to the inspirational leadership and generosity of Georgios Averoff, who served as president from 1885 when he replaced Theodore Ralli. Like the community organization's first president Tossizza, Averoff was born in Metsovo, a village on the commercial routes of the western Balkans, in 1815 and moved to Cairo aged twenty-two to join his brother Anastasios, who owned a small trading business.

Averoff was of Vlach origin; the Vlachs were a Balkan nomadic ethnic group who, like most of those in the southern Balkans, were 'Hellenized' and considered themselves Greek, even though the mountainous regions that were their home had not yet been incorporated into Greece. From what little exists in terms of information about his personality it seems he was—like most Greeks from mountain regions—plain-spoken and some-what gruff in a no-nonsense way, and like many Metsovo Greeks, deeply patriotic and conservative in terms of morals.[44] A young teacher who arrived from Metsovo described their encounter as down-to-earth. Aver-off, who was playing with his *komboloi* (worry beads), offered him coffee and inquired whether the newcomer could speak in the Vlach language. At a subsequent meeting Averoff reprimanded him and called him an "anar-chist" because he had heard the teacher was in favor of using the vernacular over the purist, archaic form of Greek.

Averoff was clearly not conservative in his investments, and willing to take risks. In what is one of the most spectacular rags-to-riches stories of the Greek diaspora, he became the richest Greek in Egypt thanks to his astute commercial activities and acquisition of land. He also became one of the community's and Greece's greatest benefactors. Averoff was most cer-tainly an example of the older, first-generation Greek merchants who did not have ties to British capital and were not beholden to the British. Tsirkas believes he was elected president of the community organization despite the opposition of the 'anglophile' elite that included Benachi, Sinadino, and Zervoudachi. In any case, Averoff took over at a crucial moment because the community organization had a deficit of 500,000 gold francs, of which he contributed half while others, including Patriarch Sofronios and leading community members such as Antoniades and Zervoudachi, also contributed to help the community pay its debts. That they were 'anglophiles' suggests that intra-elite tensions had subsided or that Averoff marshaled broad support. From that moment onward the community organization began expanding its initiatives.

Averoff funded the creation of a Greek-language high school that was named after him and recognized by the Greek government, which meant its graduates were eligible to take entrance exams at the University of Athens. Three years later, in 1894, Averoff funded a building to house the girls' preparatory school, a move that helped improve the school's overall performance considerably. In 1899, when he was honored by the erection of a statue, he announced he was donating a sum of money that would go to create a Greek 'industrial' (vocational) school. Averoff had already made several significant contributions to Greece. He was one of the main donors of what became the Athens Polytechnic, one of the country's most respected higher education institutions. He funded the construction of a prison for adolescents and the refurbishment of the Panathenaic Stadium, where the first modern Olympic Games took place in 1896.

Averoff's tenure as president of the community organization, which lasted until his death in 1899, was emblematic of the way the Greeks positioned themselves in relation to their homeland, the Greek consulate, and the British administration. He was passionately concerned with Greece's progress domestically and in terms of its foreign policy. By agreeing to serve as president of the community organization, he ensured that the position would continue to be held by a prominent Alexandrian Greek, not the Greek consul, preserving the community organization's autonomy. In 1887, the Greek government officially recognized a new charter the community organization adopted—naming the Greek consul as its "honorary president." Averoff was not openly identified with the British, and had expressed his admiration for France publicly on one occasion, but nonetheless earned the respect of the British, even receiving a personal message from Queen Victoria, a rare honor for a foreigner.

Averoff's death in 1899 was the end of an era. He was the last of the older pre-1860s generation, and from then on the leadership of the Alexandria community passed into the hands of the younger 'anglophile' generation of merchants. He was replaced by Constantine "Costi" Salvago, the Chiot merchant who put up 25 percent of the capital for the creation of the National Bank of Egypt in 1898, which served as the country's government bank and the bank of issue for Egypt's currency. A few years earlier, Salvago partnered with Benachi and Zervoudachi and outbid Averoff and Ioannis Pezmazoglou, a Greek banker who had become director of the Anglo-Egyptian Bank in 1882, in a competition for the ownership of the Egypt branch of the Bank of Athens. Constantine's decision to contribute LE500 annually to the community was the first item of a long list of projects he had in mind, but he was only able to fund an eye clinic at the Greek hospital before he died in 1901, aged fifty-six.

Emmanuel Benachi was elected to replace him, and he would lead the community organization during one of the most creative periods in its history. The organization's finances which had required Averoff's rescue were now on a very sound footing, "such was the confidence of the Greeks in the organization and so great their interest in its affairs, that it was rare that a wealthy Greek drawing up his will would not bequeath it a substantial sum of money."[45] The community's standing with the British administration was also in good shape. Both Salvago and Benachi were known anglophiles, and Cromer's respect for Benachi was also well known and mentioned proudly by his daughter Penelope Delta in her memoirs.

Both under Benachi, who was president until 1911, and under his successor Mikés Salvago (Constantine's son), the community organization's main priority was the improvement of the schools and their infrastructure, a sign that the community leaders saw a future in Egypt for the younger generation. The better educated the Greeks were, the more they could contribute to the community's cohesion, its prosperity, and of course its standing in Egypt. The community organization purchased a large plot of land, 52,800 square meters in the Chatby neighborhood of Alexandria. It was there that a 'commercial school' was built thanks to a LE16,500 contribution from the Salvago family. Named after Constantine Salvago, this was a vocational school with four departments—mechanical, woodwork, ironwork, and electrical—which opened its doors in 1908.

On the Chatby plot, Emmanuel and Virginia Benachi contributed LE20,000 for the establishment of an orphanage for girls and an institution that provided meals for the orphanage, pupils of the community schools from poor families, and the poor of Alexandria. A donation of LE15,000 from George Zervoudachi for a building to house the upper school classes of the Tossizza and Averoff schools completed the network of Greek buildings at Chatby. The schools remained the community organization's main focus when the younger Salvago became president. The curriculum of the

Salvago school was enhanced and reoriented away from technical skills and toward topics that would provide the knowledge required in business and commerce. The Greek community organizations in Cairo and elsewhere also focused on the need to establish a viable educational infrastructure. With the help of generous donations from a few of its members, the organization in Cairo acquired a girls' school and a boys' high school, as well as a new church and a hospital soon after its reorganization in 1904. Around the same time Greek (preparatory) schools were either improved or established in each of the towns of the Nile Delta, the Canal Zone, and in Upper Egypt, where there was a significant Greek presence.

Ties with Greece and Egypt

At the turn of the century, Greece began to pursue its territorial claims on the Ottoman Empire all the more vigorously, and this cause found an enthusiastic audience among the Greeks in Egypt. The banker and entrepreneur Georgios Goussios led a small group of volunteers who went over to Greece to fight in the short-lived Greco–Turkish War of 1897. Anglophilia was no obstacle to supporting Greece's cause. Penelope Delta, Emmanuel Benachi's daughter, at times found the two sides of her childhood puzzling. In her memoir she described an incident aboard the ship that was taking them to Piraeus in 1882, which divided the English and the Greek children into two feuding sides. "And yet," she remarked, "everything that was English in our house was held in high esteem: English furniture, English silver, plates, glass, English linen, English soap (Windsor soap, later Pears soap, were the only ones, except the Cretan one for the clothes, that ever entered the house). English polish for the furniture, powders for the silver, threads, needles, buttons were all English, and we were raised to respect every English product." She goes on to say, "at the same time however, our upbringing remained Greek and each time our Greekness clashed with something foreign, our patriotic heights went to being chauvinistic."[46]

While they prepared for a long stay in Egypt, the Greeks also maintained close ties with their Greek homeland, that is, their place of origin but also the Greek state. Averoff's commitment to his birthplace Metsovo and to the domestic and foreign policies of the Greek government was typical in that sense. His last major contribution came in his will, where he bequeathed a sum of money for the Greek Navy to build an armored cruiser that was named after him and would play a pivotal role in Greece's maritime dominance over the Ottoman fleet during the Balkan Wars of 1912–13.

Obviously all others made more modest contributions either through their own initiative or by responding to appeals by Greece, as for example during the run-up to the interim Olympic Games that took place in Athens in 1906. In order to finance that event, the Greek Olympic Committee appealed to the Greeks abroad for funds and the Greeks in Egypt responded generously. In 1909 came a big turning point in Greek politics with the rise of Eleftherios Venizelos, a politician from Crete who would become one of the country's greatest statesmen. Venizelos's pro-European, promodernization agenda appealed to many Greeks in Egypt, especially the merchant class. Emmanuel Benachi was so enamored with Venizelos's vision that he went to Athens and ran on the Venizelist ticket in the Greek elections of 1910 and was elected deputy, subsequently becoming a government minister. In 1914 he was elected mayor of Athens. In the meantime, when Greece entered the Balkan Wars against the Ottoman Empire, which resulted in substantial territorial gains, hundreds of Greeks from Egypt went to fight for their homeland.

Close ties with Greece did not preclude some rare but significant signs of solidarity with the early beginnings of Egyptian nationalism. In 1893, under the penname "Philaleth," Menandros Zizinia published a pamphlet titled *L'Angleterre et Abbas II*, in which he described Cromer as a "true dictator" and called upon Britain to "end the military occupation of Egypt." Intelligence reports from Khedive Abbas Hilmi II's personal network of informants also show that a developed sense of solidarity with the Egyptian nationalists was shared across wide sections of Egypt's Greek community in the 1890s. In 1896 Zizinia allowed the nationalist leader Mustafa Kamil to speak on the subject of Egyptian independence, a speech which Kamil repeated to an all-European audience at the same venue. In the late 1890s and early 1900s, journalists and writers such as Nicolas Haikalis, Ioannis Gikas, and Petros Magnis published articles in the Greek-language newspapers of Alexandria expressing sympathy with the fledgling Egyptian nationalist movement and criticizing Cromer's policies.[47]

The readers of the *Omonoia*, one of the several Greek-language publications in Egypt, opened their paper on the morning of January 19, 1914 with a sense of déjà vu. Its banner headline, usually reserved for world events, featured instead a protest against excessive regulations that were strangling the Greek retail trade.[48] The *Omonoia* and its sister paper, the *Tachydromos*, had been openly critical of the measures the British administration had introduced in the 1880s. By the early 1900s both newspapers had become much friendlier toward the British, but as the front page on that day indicated, the attitude of the Greek press could not be taken for granted. Indeed, nor could the attitude of the Greeks, or more accurately the various groups that were part of the broader Greek entity in Egypt. Rather, those attitudes were always in flux because the Greeks in Egypt were in-between their Greek homeland, their Egyptian home, and British rule in Egypt. They were constantly repositioning themselves in order to defend their interests and gain a sense of security. The post-1882 era had presented several challenges, not only political but also economic and cultural. Overall the Greek response had been effective, and the community grew in status and influence in the decades that followed. It had managed to become more rooted in Egypt, closer to the Greek homeland, and found a modus vivendi with the British administration. Within a few months, in 1914, a new political landscape and new challenges would arise.

3
The Erosion of Privilege, 1914–52

B ritain abruptly dropped the veil over its rule in Egypt when the Ottoman Empire sided with the Central Powers following the outbreak of the First World War. Although Egypt's dependency on the Ottoman Porte had remained a little more than a legal technicality, it needed to be ended so Egypt could be fully deployed on the side of the Anglo–French alliance. This was both good and bad news for the Greeks in Egypt. Their interests, and for most, their sympathies, lay with the Allies on the side of the conflict that generated the Great War. So the announcement of the protectorate met with a warm welcome on their part. But the elimination of the Ottoman framework raised the question of what would happen to the Capitulations and the status of Egypt's foreign residents. Indeed, the British authorities posed the question, but before any answer could be given the war ended and Egypt emerged transformed. A popular indigenous nationalist movement posed its own questions to the British administration: When would it leave and let Egypt rule itself? For the next three decades, the future of the Greeks and other foreigners would be envisioned through the lens of Egypt's ongoing struggle for independence from Britain.

The Wartime Protectorate
It took three years for Britain to decide to do something about the Capitulations after it declared Egypt a protectorate. The war years were hardly the time to risk antagonizing the Capitulatory Powers, especially those fighting on Britain's side. In 1917 Britain formed a mixed commission of Egyptian and foreign experts to examine the reforms that the anticipated end of the Capitulations would require. In charge was Sir William Brunyate, a British official who had served in the British administration in Egypt. One year and

134 sessions later, the Commission concluded its work and proposed the replacement of the Capitulations and the 'Kitchener' Constitution of 1912 with a new legislature with an upper house composed by British officials, representatives of the foreign communities, and Egyptians. Unsurprisingly, the Egyptians would be in a minority in that body. The Commission also called for a radical restructuring of the judicial system with the unification of the Mixed, Native, and Consular Courts and what Brunyate described as "the Anglicization of the law and legal institutions in Egypt."[1] The strong negative reaction from the Mixed Courts coupled with Egyptian opposition to the implications of the Anglicization doomed the Commission's recommendations.

The Commission's proposals and Britain's refusal to allow a delegation of Egyptian nationalist leaders to travel to London in November 1918 to negotiate an end to the protectorate triggered widespread demonstrations in Egypt. Sa'd Zaghlul, an experienced politician who had originally collaborated with the British but then turned against them, emerged as the country's nationalist leader. A mission of inquiry under Milner, who had served in the British administration under Cromer, recommended that Egypt be given a modified form of independence but the British government rejected this proposal, only to witness continued nationalist demonstrations and unrest in Egypt. Among one of Milner's proposals was the abolition of the Capitulations—evidently, this was becoming a permanent feature in all British blueprints of Egypt's future. Crucially, Britain decided that the Capitulations were part and parcel of Egypt's foreign affairs which, the thinking was, would remain under British control in return for the relaxation of its management of Egypt's domestic affairs. Thus, while the Foreign Office pondered the degree of internal freedom it would grant Egypt—because Milner's view that the protectorate be abolished was regarded as too large a concession—the wheels began to turn in planning the end of the Capitulations.[2]

The Greek government turned out to be very accommodating to British approaches, which is not surprising because it was relying on the Great Powers for diplomatic backing in its ongoing conflict with the Ottoman Empire. It had been British Prime Minister David Lloyd George who of all the Great Power statesmen had been the most supportive of Greece's territorial demands. The primary one was for Greece to be part of the parceling-out of strategically important areas of the Ottoman Empire, pending a decision of its long-term future. Greece gained the right to provisional control of the city of Smyrna (present-day Izmir) and its hinterland. In May 1920, when the British ambassador in Athens, Earl Granville, was instructed to open negotiations with the Greek government, Greek troops, who had landed in Smyrna a year earlier, were engaged in battles with Turkish nationalist forces.

Lord Curzon, the British acting foreign secretary, sent Granville a briefing document which stipulated that Greece should agree in principle to the future abolition of the whole system of Capitulations and allow Britain a free hand in implementing this process. Curzon, in anticipation of Greek concerns, indicated that Granville could drop a suitable hint that the Greeks should feel confident "there will always be some Greek judges on the Bench," adding however, "no pledges or undertakings" could be given because other foreign powers might claim similar assurances. Granville was also told that the British authorities in Egypt would proceed with the appointment to the new Mixed Courts of existing judges unless Greece entered into the proposed agreement with Britain. More specifically, the message read, "Cambas, the Greek judge in the Mixed Courts of Appeal, is a first-rate man, and occupies a great position at Alexandria; we should therefore be glad to proceed to his definite appointment as soon as possible, an additional reason why the Greeks should sign the agreement without delay."

When the Greek government informed the Vouli of the negotiations, some deputies expressed concern that an independent Egypt might take away the privileges of foreigners, but those fears were allayed when the British side agreed to state publicly that Greek citizens would be treated on an equal footing with British citizens in Egypt. In September 1920, the Greek parliament ratified the treaty signed by the two countries. Greece had not made much trouble for Britain over the Capitulations, unlike France, Italy, and the United States, countries that had expressed strong concerns about the proposed ending of the Capitulations.[3]

The Anglo–Greek agreement over the principles that would guide the end of the Capitulations represented a significant turning point in the relations between Greece and the Greeks in Egypt. The Greek government was choosing quite consciously to place the need to preserve British support for its foreign policy goals over the short-term interests of the Greek communities in Egypt. The prime minister at the time, Eleftherios Venizelos, had visited Egypt five years earlier, after King Constantine I, with whom he had disagreed over Greece's stance in the First World War, had forced him to resign as prime minister. The Anglophile Venizelos had recommended that Greece join the Anglo–French alliance, while the Germanophile king, who was also head of state, wanted Greece to remain neutral, a position that was to the advantage of the Central Powers.

Venizelos traveled to Egypt in April 1915 ostensibly as a private citizen. Twenty-five thousand cheering Greeks lined the streets of Alexandria waving Greek flags and gave him a rousing welcome. He traveled in an open car along the three-mile route from the port to the Greek Club in the city center, where the aged president of the Greek community, Mikés Sinadino, was too overcome with emotion to make his speech. Similar scenes took place in all the towns Venizelos visited on his rail journey to Cairo and then along the Suez Canal. At Kafr al-Zayyat, where his train made a brief stop, the sirens of the Greek-owned cotton-ginning mills added to the general pandemonium with loud and prolonged blasts.[4]

Thanks to Britain and France's intervention, Venizelos was reinstated as prime minister and Greece promptly entered the First World War on their side. Throughout the war, and from the time of his visit, the Greeks of Egypt offered Venizelos and Greece's war effort significant material and political support. Even before Venizelos returned to the post of prime minister, a congress of all-Greek community organizations held in Alexandria in 1916 pledged their support to Venizelos in manpower and money, which continued during and after the end of the Great War.[5] Such was the support for Venizelos among the majority of Greeks in Egypt—who were also those supporting the royalist side—that there was little criticism of the attitude of Athens toward the situation in Egypt.

Beginning in 1919, demonstrations supporting the nationalist agenda swept through Egypt, and continued through 1922. While clearly anti-British, the movement did not express strong views about the future of the Capitulations. Yet this was a challenge to the status quo and the events themselves also affected foreigners, forcing them to reflect on their status and their future in Egypt. In the case of the Greeks, when a few lost their lives and others were injured during four days of violent demonstrations in Alexandria in May 1921, this caused greater alarm among the community than the initial uprising in March–April 1919, which had spread throughout Egypt. The beginning of the three-year unrest in Egypt was peaceful, and a nationalist demonstration in Alexandria in March broke out in applause as it passed outside the Greek consulate. But in the space of a few days there was extensive destruction and looting of more than forty Greek-owned shops in Cairo and in small towns in the Nile Delta and Upper Egypt. Ten Greeks lost their lives, four of them in Cairo. The violence was directed against foreigners because of past disputes, either randomly or in a targeted manner, not exclusively against Greeks. Armenians also suffered, especially in Cairo. The Greek consul general in Alexandria, Antonios Sachtouris, cabled Athens, explaining that the Greeks incurred losses and damages not because they had opposed the movement but because it had taken on a character of religious fanaticism and because the local population was well aware of the devotion of the Greeks to England.

The Greek-language press was at pains to prove that none of the violence had been explicitly "anti-Greek" and described the looters as hooligans, wholly unrepresentative of the average Egyptian, adding that those killed in Cairo had been mistaken for Armenians who had opened fire on the demonstrators. The press prominently reported several incidents in which Egyptians protected Greeks from angry demonstrators. The Wafd leadership was also anxious to portray the harm inflicted on the foreigners as incidental. To this end, extraordinary scenes took place outside the Greek consulate in Cairo in March 1919, at the height of the troubles. While a crowd of concerned Greeks had gathered outside, a nationalist delegation arrived, including an army major, 'alim (a religious teacher), judge, lawyer, and doctor, followed by a large crowd of Egyptians. The delegation expressed its sincere regret that Greeks had accidentally fallen victim to the disorders and made a moving speech stressing its fraternal feelings toward the Greeks.

Consul Sachtouris recalled later that he was overcome by emotion, especially when they spoke about the wish of an entire people for freedom, and noted ruefully that the Greek revolution against the Ottomans a century earlier had also been slandered. Sachtouris, speaking publicly, agreed that the Greek victims had lost their lives by accident, and expressed his solidarity with the nationalist movement. He drew parallels between the Greek revolution and the Egyptian movement, adding hyperbolically that if the Greek blood spilt would irrigate the tree of Egyptian freedom, then it was worth it. The delegation, according to Sachtouris, described the Greeks as agents of civilization and progress throughout Egypt.[6]

The incident Sachtouris had witnessed improved his perception of the Egyptian nationalist movement, but among the community there was a range of reactions, from supportive to suspicious, and there were growing questions about the role of the British. Among white-collar professionals, many of whom held leadership positions in Greek organizations in Alexandria, there was a growing sense that the British were no longer prepared to intervene with the type of gunboat diplomacy they had exercised in 1882. If the British were unwilling to take a stronger line other than sending the Milner mission—which some Greeks regarded as a sign of weakness or indifference—perhaps the solution was to work toward a better understanding with the nationalists.

The growing feeling that the British either could not or would not protect the foreigners crystallized following the events of May 1921, when demonstrations in Alexandria escalated into riots that lasted for two days in the poorer quarters of the city. By the time British forces restored order, forty-three Egyptians, twelve Greeks, two Italians, and another European were dead. The numbers injured were also high: 129 Egyptians, forty-six Greeks, twenty-one Italians, and a few other Europeans. The Greek Chamber of Commerce reported that one hundred shops, ninety of them Greek-owned, were burned or looted and that Greek shopkeepers suffered losses amounting to LE100,000. The normally staid front page of the Greek-language *Tachydromos* carried a banner headline that exclaimed "Anarchy and Fear in Alexandria—Many Victims Massacred." The stories that emerged of particular incidents ranged from young fathers being killed to Egyptians stepping forward and protecting Greeks from angry mobs. The *Tachydromos* regarded the events as proof that there was no protection by the British and what was at stake was whether the Greeks would be able to continue living in Egypt. But the Alexandria community organization chose to keep faith in the British.

President Mikés Salvago wrote to Lord Allenby, the British high commissioner, to thank him for the intervention of his forces, which he described as the only safeguard for the lives and property of foreign subjects, and expressed the hope it would continue in the future. Salvago was one of the few foreigners who still trusted the British and his message may have been more of a public relations gesture than a sincere sentiment. One Greek consular official, Nikolaos Lelis, would report to Athens that he had to pressure a British office to quell rioting that threatened Greek lives and property. The officer acceded to Lelis's request, even though apparently his orders were not to intervene. This is an indication of a much less-involved British role in 1921 compared to 1919, when the demonstrations were portrayed as being antiforeign, possibly to undermine Egyptian efforts to gain concessions at the Paris Peace Conference.[7]

The Post-protectorate Era

In 1922 Britain decided to satisfy some of the Egyptian demands for independence and abolished the protectorate it had established eight years earlier. But Britain circumscribed the independence it was granting by continuing its control over the security of communications of the British Empire in Egypt; the defense of Egypt against foreign aggression; the administration of Sudan, and the protection of foreign interests and minorities in Egypt. Clearly the retention of British management of matters foreigners faced meant the issue had become a potential Anglo–Egyptian bargaining point, because in practice Britain had shown diminishing interest in preserving foreign privileges. A Foreign Office internal communication in 1935 stated explicitly that beginning in 1922, Britain had treated the Capitulations as a bargaining chip when negotiating with the Egyptians. Thus after 1922, while some Greeks had hoped to arrive at an arrangement with the Egyptian nationalists, they would still have to deal with the British in determining their future in Egypt.

The issue of foreign privileges in Egypt was never a priority for Zaghlul's nationalist movement but it became important for his opponents, politicians such Ahmed Ziwar Pasha, who led parties that were not inclined to confront the British. Ahmed Ziwar Pasha came to power in 1924, after the British forced Zaghlul out of office in retaliation for the murder of Sir Lee Stack Pasha, the governor general of Sudan and commander-in-chief of the Egyptian army who was shot by militant Egyptian students while traveling in his car in Cairo. The Greek reactions to the ousting of Zaghlul, who had condemned the assassination, showed their sympathies toward the nationalists. The Greek consul general in Alexandria visited his British counterpart to offer his condolences and explain that the large presence and geographical dispersion of Greeks in Egypt meant they could not risk antagonizing the Egyptians by publicly supporting the British. Greeks living in the provinces went further and sent telegrams to Allenby stating they were living in harmony with the local Egyptians and criticizing the British measures against the nationalists. An embarrassed Greek embassy tried to portray the event as the result of Egyptian pressure on the Greeks, but the *Tachydromos* noted drily that the British remembered the foreigners only when their own interests were threatened.

Many Greeks, including leading members of the community in Alexandria, maintained close contact with the nationalists. In 1924 two Greeks, journalist Nikos Caravias and architect Nikolaos Nicolaou, were elected to the Municipal Council of Alexandria as Wafd-supported candidates. Greeks ran for council positions again in 1926 with the Wafd's support. Zaghlul's death in 1927 was bad news for the Greeks and the other foreigners in Egypt, because he had focused the nationalist movement's efforts on exacting concessions from the British and putting the issue of foreign privileges on the back burner. His absence increased Britain's chances of persuading nationalist and moderate politicians that in signing the planned Anglo–Egyptian Treaty, the Capitulatory regime had to be drastically modified.

The moderates, who took power in 1924, did not dare challenge British influence but instead raised the issue of foreign privileges as a way of currying favor with the electorate. A year later the Egyptian government formulated a decree against drug trafficking and submitted it to the Mixed Courts so as to make its provisions and penalties applicable to the Mixed Courts. When the courts balked at passing the decree in its entirety, the government drafted a proposal for the modification of the Mixed Courts to enable it to deal effectively with unlawful activities of foreign shop owners. From January 1927 onward, the progovernment Egyptian press launched a vigorous campaign in favor of curtailing the Capitulations and limiting the power of the Mixed Courts.[8]

The prospect of abolishing, or at least restricting, foreign privileges in Egypt became less certain with the appointment of Lord Lloyd as British high commissioner in 1925, but that lasted only until his dismissal four years later by the new Labour Party government. Allenby's successor was a conservative and an old-school colonialist who reported to London in 1927 that he believed that the immunity from taxation foreigners enjoyed should be preserved. He pointed out that although foreigners were not taxed directly, they were subject to taxes on land and houses, judicial fees, fees on the registration of property and mortgages, and other dues. He believed that rather than abolish the Capitulations, new taxes could be imposed with the consent of the Capitulatory Powers. With regard to the laws of inviolability of domicile and freedom from arrest, Lloyd noted that those privileges had eroded with time and there were instances where Egyptian police could arrest foreigners. Finally, he added, even the Egyptians did not support the abolition of the Mixed Courts if it meant giving novel and exceptional powers to the British authorities.

Lloyd's beliefs were a throwback to the past. He wished for even stronger British rule in Egypt but also thought the Capitulations should be preserved and modified. His argument was that the brains, character, and culture that had helped Egypt achieve progress were almost exclusively foreign. Meanwhile, Egypt's ambassador in London had approached the Foreign Office with the suggestion that Britain should support the principle of taxing foreigners, something Lloyd dismissed, thereby incurring London's displeasure. When the Labour Party won the elections of 1929, the differences between the high commissioner and the Foreign Office brought his dismissal and replacement by Percy Lorraine, who had served in Athens.[9] Egypt's *al-Ahram* newspaper commented that among the issues he faced was an outcry from foreigners living in Egypt because of the possibility that the forthcoming treaty would end the immunities many of them enjoyed under the Capitulations system. The newspaper added that those who hate equality are unjust, cannot advocate peace, and are unable to conform to the spirit of the age. It need not have worried. Lord Lloyd, it turned out, had embodied the last hurrah of the Capitulations.[10]

The foreigners felt abandoned after Lloyd's departure because Britain was back to the position that their privileges should be curtailed and the Egyptian side was applying pressure toward that goal. An ominous sign was that King Fu'ad had been speaking out against the Capitulations and the Mixed Courts for the first time since he became head of state in 1917, that he was doing so to distract from the unpopular prime minister he had appointed did not make much difference. The Foreign Office would be alarmed with Egyptian calls for the abolition of the Capitulations and the Mixed Courts without something to replace both. Change was on its way, but it would happen on Britain's terms. By the end of the 1920s, with negotiations underway for an Anglo–Egyptian Treaty designed to further limit Britain's presence in Egypt, plans were also made for the abolition of the Capitulations, the transfer of the jurisdiction of the Consular Courts to the Mixed Courts, and the application of Egyptian legislation to the foreigners.

A Community on Its Own

Even though both Egypt and Britain were questioning the privileges of all the foreign communities, the communities themselves were unable to cooperate among themselves and present a united front. Even in multiethnic Alexandria, the celebrated cosmopolitan culture and the significant foreign economic interrelationships failed to produce a common political strategy. The British businessmen were the most vociferous opponents of the plan to limit the advantages foreigners enjoyed and as an insular community not an ally the Greeks could enlist. The French community were evidently set on negotiating on their own, hoping they could bargain on the basis of the 1904 Anglo–French Agreement that stipulated that in the event Great Britain introduced into Egypt reforms involving changes in the system of Capitulations, France would entertain such proposals with the understanding that Great Britain would agree to similar suggestions in Morocco.[11] There was no question that the two largest foreign communities, the Greeks and Italians, would cooperate. Both communities were closely associated with the governments of their homeland and relations were strained due to Italy's occupation of the Greek-inhabited Dodecanese Islands in the Aegean. As Italy's designs on the eastern Mediterranean grew in the 1930s, more Italians in Egypt identified with the policies of their homeland. A British diplomat reported to London that out of the twenty-seven thousand Italian subjects in Egypt, almost all supported Italian dictator Benito Mussolini, with the exception of about ten thousand Italian Jews. About one thousand Italians had joined blackshirt profascist organizations.

The only meaningful cooperation among the foreigners in Egypt came at the level of their diplomatic representatives. Beginning in 1927, consultations between the Greek ambassador Athanasios Politis, and his French and Italian counterparts, who had different personalities, would prove fruitless because neither the British nor the Egyptian governments were prepared to listen. British views of the three reveal the considerable differences in personality. They liked Politis because he was "a pleasant, cultured individual of strong British sympathies." H. Gaillard, the French ambassador in Egypt since 1921, was the dean of the diplomatic corps in Cairo who moved easily among government circles thanks to his knowledge of Arabic that he had acquired during a previous appointment in Morocco. The British considered him a self-satisfied petit bourgeois in mentality and appearance, because he was "short and stout," but they acknowledged that despite his objectives of preserving France's cultural and intellectual dominance in Egypt in addition to its commercial interests, he made himself amenable to the British residency. Italy's ambassador, Marchese de Paterno, was a great admirer of Mussolini to whom, according to Lloyd, he bore a great resemblance. The British unforgivingly noted he was the only diplomat to wear all his medals at social functions and left his "dull wife" behind, appearing in the company of a lady of doubtful reputation. Notwithstanding the differences in personality and the divisions among the respective communities they represented, the three diplomats arrived at the conclusion that if Britain went ahead and unilaterally surrendered its Capitulatory privileges, their countries could do very little. Any pressure they might exert risked a confrontation with Britain, thus the best way to try and preserve foreign privileges would be to come to an understanding with the Egyptian government with a view to extending the judicial scope of the Mixed Courts. The British and the Egyptian governments did not respond to the messages they received from the ambassadors, a sure sign that foreign communities would find it difficult to influence policy.[12]

Politis then turned to legal experts within the Greek community in Alexandria while he alerted Athens to the unfolding impasse. He first consulted with Georgios Roussos, an attorney at the Mixed Courts who had served as Greek ambassador to Washington and for three brief stints as Minister of Foreign Affairs of Greece thanks to his close ties to Venizelos; Nikolaos Vatimbellas, who was also an attorney at the Mixed Courts; Stavros Vlachos, a judge at the Court of First Instance; and Constantine Vryakos, a judge at the Court of Appeal. Their meetings, held in late 1927, were focused on low-key tactics such as the need to preserve the majority of Greeks and Europeans in the legislative assembly of the courts and, oddly enough, the need to preserve the number of judges from Scandinavian countries because they tended to be more sympathetic toward the Greeks appearing before them, compared to most French and Italian judges.

In response to Politis's messages, the Greek government called a meeting to discuss those issues. Held in Athens in 1929, it was presided over by Prime Minister Venizelos with Andreas Michalakopoulos, the minister of foreign affairs, also attending. Venizelos had already stated publicly that he agreed with the abolition of the Capitulations and the meeting quickly affirmed its support for Politis's low-key approach. Following the arrival in Greece of about 1.3 million ethnic refugees from the Ottoman Empire a few years earlier, no Greek government had the time or resources to offer any practical help to the Greeks in Egypt. This knowledge had shaped Politis's moves, of which the government approved, though it decided to offer symbolic support by arranging Michalakopoulos's visit to Egypt in February 1930. Its purpose was to foster close relations with the Egyptian government, raise the community's morale, and possibly mitigate the effects of the impending end of the Capitulations. After his meeting with King Fu'ad and government officials in Cairo, and a visit to the Pyramids, Michalakopoulos went to Alexandria for a series of visits to Greek schools, official dinners, and a meeting with leading members of the community and legal experts with whom Politis had interacted. The gathering hammered out the Greek strategy, basically affirming the delicate approach already in operation. The whole issue boiled down to the future of the Mixed Courts. The number of foreigners in those courts was not proportional to the size or wealth of each community, thus the imminent reorganization could well work against a country that was not fully involved in the discussions and in close contact with the Egyptians.[13]

Michalakopoulos's visit to King Fu'ad was not a mere formality. Many Greek leaders in Egypt regarded the monarch as likely to see that their interests were protected. Casting around for ways to ingratiate themselves with the Egyptians, several Greeks commissioned a statue of Muhammad Ali that would be erected in his hometown of Kavala in northern Greece. Michalakopoulos invited Fu'ad for a visit to unveil the statue. This caused great excitement in the Greek press in Alexandria and Cairo, and speculation about the advantages this would offer the Greeks ran rampant, but unfortunately the king's failing health and continued political instability in Cairo meant the visit never took place. What did take place to honor the king was a fawning Greek-language biography written for the occasion of the visit by Radamanthis Radopoulos, the secretary of the Greek Community of Alexandria. Radopoulos portrayed Fu'ad as an enlightened, open-minded, and progressive monarch, drawing close parallels between him and his modernizing forebear, Muhammad Ali. As soon as the book appeared, Politis, the acting Greek ambassador at the time, arranged for Radopoulos to visit the palace and receive Fu'ad's commendations personally. It was a well-publicized event in which the Greek-language press extolled the virtues of the monarch.[14]

Intellectual Outreach

It was no coincidence that at the same time Politis was conducting negotiations over the future of the Capitulations and the Mixed Courts, he was also writing what became the standard history of the Greeks in Egypt. His two-volume *History of Hellenism in Egypt* appeared in Greek and French in 1928–30 and was a well-researched and systematic treatment of the Greek presence in Egypt.[15] The underlying themes were that the Greeks functioned as the pioneers of Western civilization and contributed to Egypt's modernization. Politis, who was as much a man of letters as he was a diplomat, shared the growing awareness of a number of Greek intellectuals that a prerequisite for forging a political alliance with Egyptians was to assert the rights they believed the Greeks had earned through their role in the making of modern Egypt. Politis decided that he could use the access he had to diplomatic records in order to contribute in that direction. Historically, Politis explained, the Greeks had settled in Egypt in antiquity and had maintained a continuous presence there. Thus the Greeks and Egyptians had a longstanding interrelationship, which he claimed ought to distinguish the Greeks from other foreigners. The two-volume work functioned not only as the standard account of the history of the Greeks in Egypt, and remained so for decades, but also as a statement of Greek claims on Egypt.

The book was well received, with one exception. One of the bishops of the patriarchate of Alexandria, Christophoros, whose district was situated around Zagazig in the Nile Delta, took issue with many things in the first volume of Politis's book, and published a critique of almost twenty-five printed pages. Christophoros claimed his purpose was to offer some advice to the author, who he knew was preparing the second volume. Among other things he believed that the author had overlooked the role of the church and had also not recognized that the Greeks in Egypt, compared to earlier times, were experiencing a general decline in the post-First World War era. He faulted the community organizations for trying to marginalize the patriarchate.[16] It is true that Politis's narrative attributed the success of the Greeks to their entrepreneurial spirit and their (secular) communal organization. A decade later, Christophoros would become patriarch and try to strengthen the relative importance of the patriarchate. The tension between the secular and religious leadership of the Greeks in Egypt would continue into the second half of the twentieth century.

Another voice that believed in an assertive Greek statement in Egypt was Evgenios Michaelides, who was born in Jerusalem, studied at the prestigious Greek Orthodox Seminary of the Holy Cross, went to Lebanon to study Arabic, and settled in Alexandria, where he was a teacher at the Greek schools on his way to becoming one of the leading Greek–Egyptian intellectuals. Michaelides, thanks to his knowledge of Arabic, quickly became aware of how little leading Egyptians were aware of the positive role the Greeks had played in their country. He urged his fellow Greek–Egyptian thinkers to do something about it, and published a study on the past and future of the Greeks in Egypt in 1927, elaborating the need for their history to be known and suggesting that their future could be ensured by maintaining their close ties with Egypt and continuing their positive contributions.[17] The argument that the Greeks were present in Egypt since that ancient era that Michaelides emphasized dovetailed nicely with the concept of 'phara-onism' (al-fir'uniya) that pointed to an Egyptian identity that went back to ancient Egypt, which some nationalist thinkers were elaborating in the 1920s. Also reinforcing this historical point was a second claim, namely that the Greeks in Egypt had functioned as agents of progress and civilization.

One of the earliest public enunciations of the theory of Greco–Egyptian ties that went back to the ancient era had come from Georgios Arvanitakis, a journalist and publisher who arrived in Egypt in 1899 at the age of twenty-seven. He had grown up in Jerusalem, where his father had taught at the Greek Orthodox seminary of the Holy Cross and where he later taught mathematics. Arvanitakis was somewhat of a polymath and beyond mathematics he also acquired some knowledge of philology, his-tory, and archaeology, as well as geography. In 1902 he became a member of the Khedival Geography Society and later authored one of the earliest geography books on Egypt, which was published in Greek and used in the community schools. In 1925, Arvanitakis delivered a paper in French at the eleventh International Geographical Congress held in Cairo on the contri-butions of the Greeks to the civilization of modern Egypt. He opened with some historical background, pointing to the Arab conquest of Egypt as an event that almost ended the continuous presence of Greeks in the coun-try, and which is preserved thanks to the presence of the Greek Orthodox Church in Alexandria, until it begins to grow again under Muhammad Ali. From then on, according to Arvanitakis, the Greeks coexisted with their Egyptian hosts in a mutually reinforcing dialectic, and contributed in many ways to the country's Europeanization and progress.[18]

These studies by Arvanitakis, Michaelides, and Politis were the open-ing salvoes in what became a steady outpouring of articles, pamphlets, and books on the topic of the future of Greeks in Egypt. Michaelides's output was prodigious. It included studies of fellow intellectuals who investigated the past, present, and future of Egypt and the Greek presence. Many others would follow suit and join the conversation. The content of those studies would shift away from the themes of ancient presence and contribution of the Greeks to exploring the practical ways Greeks could integrate into Egyptian society.

The End of the Capitulations

It is unlikely that any kind of strategy by Greece would have deflected Egypt from its determination to abolish the Capitulations and curtail the powers of the Mixed Courts. In 1937 the inevitable happened. By that time the political landscape in Athens had changed dramatically. In 1936 General Ioannis Metaxas engineered a coup and established a right-wing dictatorship. His regime took its name from the date Metaxas seized power, August 4. Venizelos had died earlier that year, and so had several other of the country's political leaders. The last elections had produced a stalemate and the head of state, King Georgios II, supported the coup, so there was little resistance to Metaxas's action. Twenty years earlier, Metaxas had opposed Venizelos's vision of a Greater Greece, so he was an unlikely candidate to altering Greek policy toward Egyptian affairs. Predictably, Metaxas stuck to the stand-off policies of his predecessors. In 1927 the Egyptian government had handed the Capitulatory Powers a circular note that included six points of reform. The underlying philosophy was to increase Egyptian presence on the various bodies of the court. Protection of foreigners had to be compatible with Egypt's sovereignty.

In its negotiations with Egypt in 1928 over a new treaty between the two countries, Britain committed to using its influence to modify the Capitulations and by extension the Mixed Courts in a draft form of the treaty, which was signed in 1936. The main points of the treaty were the termination of the British military occupation of Egypt, allowing only a continued presence around the Suez Canal for twenty years, the right of Britain to reoccupy Egypt in case of an emergency, and continued British control of Sudan. But there was also an article stating that Britain recognized that the Capitulatory regime "was no longer in accordance with the spirit of the times" and that the Egyptian government and the king desired its abolition without delay. An addendum to the treaty set out in detail the method that would be followed to end the Capitulations and affirmed that Britain would actively collaborate with Egypt and use its influence with the other Capitulatory Powers. Thus the end of the Capitulations became a foregone conclusion.[19] The Metaxas regime in Athens simply went along with the process.

The one Greek institution in Egypt that the impending abolition of the Capitulations did not affect was the Greek Orthodox Patriarchate of Alexandria. As the abolition of the Capitulations became more likely, there was a steady stream of articles and studies the patriarchate issued that drew a clear distinction between the nature of the Capitulations and the status of Greek Orthodoxy in Egypt. After their formal abolition, the church's position became even more explicit. It argued that the Capitulations, which were an agreement between two states—that is, secular, not religious, authorities—had decreased the powers the old millet system had granted confessional communities. Specifically, the Consular Courts that emerged as a consequence of the Capitulations were supposed to hear disputes of a commercial nature and criminal cases. But over time, the Consular Courts had encroached the sphere of personal status that covered marriage, divorce, adoption, guardianship, and inheritance, which the Church claimed to be under its jurisdiction. Over the years, the spokesmen of the patriarchate asserted, the jurisdictional scope of its Patriarchal Courts had grown smaller. This had happened simply because Greece and the other states involved had refused to recognize many decisions issued by the Patriarchal Courts. This example illustrated the differences between the old or "historic" privileges that had been granted to the Greek Orthodox and the rights that the Capitulations had awarded to Greek citizens.

In the wake of the abolition of the Consular Courts, the church argued that the right thing to do was to allow all cases of personal status contested between Greek Orthodox litigants to revert to the Patriarchal Courts.[20] The Egyptian constitution of 1923 had not affected personal status laws, allowing the religious courts to decide matters of personal status. But the rising tide of nationalism generated moves to reform the system of religious law by unifying it and having mixed family courts presided over by Muslim and non-Muslim judges.[21] Despite the efforts of the Egyptian government, opposition by the religious establishments and the advent of the Second World War helped postpone any resolution of the status of the religious courts in Egypt, and they remained in place until the mid-1950s. In the immediate post-Capitulations era the patriarchate was emboldened by the shrinking of Greek secular jurisdiction in Egypt. First under Patriarch Nikolaos V, who took office in 1936 after the death of Patriarch Meletios, and then under Christophoros II, who became patriarch after Nikolaos's death in 1939, the patriarchate became all the more assertive in its relations with community organizations, challenging them over a wide range of issues, from school curricula to real estate ownership throughout his tenure, which lasted until 1966.

The formal abolition of the Capitulations came at a conference held in the Swiss city of Montreux in April 1937. Egypt issued an invitation to the Capitulatory Powers along with a draft agreement to be discussed by those attending. The Greek delegation was led by Nikolaos Politis, a senior Greek diplomat, who was the uncle of Athanasios Politis, and the

Alexandrian lawyer Georgios Roussos, the Alexandrian judge Constantine Vryakos, and another diplomat, Constantinos Sakellaropoulos. Roussos traveled from Alexandria on the same vessel as the leader of the Egyptian delegation, Prime Minister Mustafa al-Nahhas Pasha and his colleagues. In a private letter to his fellow Alexandrian lawyer Nikolaos Vatimbellas, Roussos said he spoke with the Egyptians on the ship, but avoided answering the questions about what Greece's attitude would be, saying he had no contact with Athens. But he assured them Greece would be favorable to Egypt's demands. Al-Nahhas assured him, repeatedly, that the Greeks were the most likeable of all the foreigners and were wanted in Egypt. But the Greeks should not make any demands officially at the conference because it would be difficult for Egypt to distribute favors all around. Vatimbellas wrote back saying that he thought the Egyptians were making promises to everyone, but he was certain they would not keep their word, and there was no reason they should, having already secured Britain's support.

Nonetheless the Greek delegation gambled on ingratiating themselves with Egypt. France suggested the commonly accepted transition period should be eighteen years rather than twelve, which Egypt had put forward with Britain's backing. Italy agreed with Egypt. Greece much preferred an eighteen-year transition period but it agreed to the twelve years in order not to displease Egypt. After some intense negotiations between al-Nahhas and François de Tessan, an experienced French politician (who would subsequently join the wartime resistance, was arrested, and died in Buchenwald), Egypt got its way, and the transition period was fixed at twelve years. There was greater and concerted opposition by the European delegations over the exact implications of the end of the Consular Courts, which was inherent in the abolition of the Capitulations. The second article of the proposed treaty stipulated that foreigners would be subject to Egyptian legislation in criminal, civil, commercial, administrative, fiscal, and other matters "subject to the application of principles of international law." Politis, the head of the Greek delegation, doubted that the reference to international law would provide sufficient protection to foreigners, and took steps to make a separate agreement with Egypt specifically designed to protect Greeks from discrimination in the employment of foreigners, though he also noted there was nothing to prevent Egypt from unilaterally abrogating that agreement.[22]

With the core of its demands satisfied, Egypt could afford to make small concessions on issues such as the composition of the Mixed Courts and the status of foreign organizations, which were of vital interest to the

Greek side. Politis stated that while the Greek organizations, understandably, would now be subject to Egyptian law, they should also be officially recognized as Greek institutions. With Britain, France, and Italy also interested in such an arrangement for their own ethnic institutions in Egypt, Greece was not alone in pressing Egypt on this point. Thanks to an intervention by the British delegation, Egypt eventually agreed. The parties also agreed that no relevant clause would be included in the text of the treaty. Letters would be exchanged between al-Nahhas and the heads of the British, French, Greek, and Italian delegations which represented countries with ethnic organizations in Egypt, affirming that their foreign status would be recognized.

The Greek parliament ratified the Montreux Treaty in September 1937, stating, as did the other signatories, that it was retaining the Consular Courts in Egypt to deal with matters of personal status and other cases in which Greek law was applicable. In Egypt, the Greeks were following the developments in Montreux with an increasing sense of anxiety with few seeing a silver lining. Their public support for the Capitulations notwithstanding, they had held out hope that the Greek delegation could extract some concessions from the Egyptian government that would mitigate the effects of the impending change. The news that Egypt was prepared to affirm its good intentions toward the foreign communities by concluding treaties of establishment (governing the status of the foreigners) and friendship with the various powers offered little relief. Mikés Salvago, the president of the community organization in Alexandria, wrote to Metaxas expressing his fears. Unless Egypt provided concrete guarantees, he noted, the abolition of the Capitulations would lead to the end of the Greek presence in Egypt and cause many Greeks to move to Greece.

There were a few optimistic voices. Andreas Delmouzos, the Greek ambassador in Cairo, thought the newly established equality before the law of both foreigners and Egyptians could ensure the security and long-term presence of foreigners in Egypt. It was a view at least one Greek lawyer in Alexandria had expressed prior to the conference. But more importantly, the day after saw no particular plan being formulated by Greek diplomats, community leaders, or Greek ethnic organizations.[23]

The end of the Capitulations however would not discourage Greek entrepreneurship and while not discounting the significance of that development, it is important not to exaggerate its immediate effects. A study of Greek and Jewish entrepreneurship in interwar Egypt has found that

"Montreux, in fact, did not cause major changes in the participation of Egyptian Jews and Egyptian Greeks in establishing new companies. The participation of Egyptian Jews increased in the 1930s by 9 per cent over the previous decade, reaching 24 per cent, while Egyptian Greek participation decreased slightly by 1 per cent, to 16 per cent . . . Egyptian Jewish–Egyptian Greek partnership increased significantly by 8 per cent, reaching 25 per cent. Exclusively Egyptian companies increased by 4 per cent to 7 per cent of the total number of companies." The Greeks were sufficiently well established and integrated into the Egyptian economy that they were prepared to adapt to new circumstances.[24]

The 1940s

The dust from the Montreux conference barely had time to settle when the outbreak of the Second World War brought the reoccupation of Egypt by Britain and therefore the process of Egyptian independence was suspended. Arguably the reintroduction of British control galvanized nationalist feeling, which emerged even stronger. And all the while, the countdown to the abolition of the Mixed Courts, scheduled for 1949, continued. The wartime period also brought the arrival of the Greek exiled government and units of its military forces that escaped before the Axis Powers occupied Greece. Greece had joined the Allied side when it was attacked by Italy in 1940 and it had managed to repulse the Italian army and hold its ground until early 1941. But the Greek armies, even with the help of British forces, were no match for the superior German forces that launched an offensive across Greece's northern border in the spring. The British, along with some Greek military units, warships, the king of Greece, and the government, retreated until they reached the island of Crete, the southernmost point of Greece. They contemplated making a stand there but yielded to the ferocity of the German airborne attack. The next stage of the retreat was to make the 650-kilometer trip across the sea south to Alexandria.

Safely in British-controlled Egypt, the Greeks—with British approval and support—established a government in exile and the headquarters of Greek army and navy units that managed to reach Egypt. During the war the king and the prime minister would spend time in London, where the other Allied exiled governments were established, but a Greek government delegation remained in Cairo. Egypt became the destination of politicians and others who succeeded in escaping Greece.

The problem with the creation of a Greek émigré population in Egypt during the war was that it experienced a series of upheavals, divisions, and conflicts that absorbed their energies and interrupted their ongoing efforts to confront the steady erosion of their privileges. The Greek distancing from the British that had taken place during the run-up to the abolition of the Capitulations was quickly forgotten. To some extent those changes were understandable if we consider that in the summer 1942 the Allied forces had stopped the advance of General Erwin Rommel's army at al-Alamein, just over one hundred kilometers along the coast west of Alexandria. Egypt was in danger of falling to the Germans and much more was at stake than the foreign privileges. By the same token, the post-al-Alamein relief and euphoria was centered on Britain's role and no one seemed worried about the future.

A public talk about the past, present, and future of the Greek community organization in al-Ibrahimiya district of Alexandria by Cleomenis Nicolaou, its popular and respected president, was mostly a celebration of the four-decade work of the organization. Speaking in February 1942, Nicolaou expressed his pride in the progress the organization had achieved in serving the needs of the twenty thousand Greeks who inhabited the district. He praised the generosity of local benefactors who had funded the establishment of the Church of St. Nicholas, the Pratsikas and Kokkinarios community schools that had one thousand students in 1940, and funded the assistance to poorer Greeks. He went on to speak about the need for changes in the school curriculum, more vocational training, and a greater focus on health and hygiene study and practice, which would guarantee "our national future." Nicolaou did not mention the need to learn Arabic or make any allusion to forging closer bonds with Egyptians. He called on the community's "young women and ladies" to redouble their philanthropic efforts. He concluded by saying that the community organization was looking ahead to a future driven by its faith in the Greek spirit.[25]

The community organization in Alexandria lurched into action in September 1944 when it became obvious that the war—at least in Greece—was about to end and the postwar era and the abolition of the Mixed Courts were around the corner. The word αναπροσαρμογή (readjustment) became the term Greeks used to summarize what they needed to do to preserve their position in Egypt. President Salvago, in a letter to the Greek ambassador, raised the issue of the "treaty of establishment" discussed at Montreux, a bilateral agreement between Greece and Egypt that would, hopefully, ensure the protection and well-being of the Greeks living in Egypt. Salvago suggested an agreement to replace the Capitulations with a more direct form of security provided by Greece. But it took two years for the Greek leadership to produce a draft document.

Polys Modinos, a distinguished lawyer of the Mixed Courts in Alexandria, was asked to produce a draft that was discussed by a committee that included diplomats, jurists, and presidents of several ethnic organizations. What they produced was a legal document that envisioned equal rights for native Egyptians and foreigners (a felicitous way of demanding that there would be no discrimination against foreigners) and spoke of reciprocity in the way Greek interests would be treated in Egypt and Egyptian interests treated in Greece. The only problem was that there were no Egyptian 'interests' in Greece so in order to make the concept more realistic, the committee considered whether the Greeks in Egypt could finance the building of a mosque in Athens or provide grants to enable Egyptian students to study at Greek universities. The next steps proved even more challenging because the British reserved the right to play the role of consultant in all the bilateral agreements that Egypt would enter into with former Capitulatory Powers. But with anti-British sentiment on the rise in Egypt, the Greeks prudently decided to keep their exchanges with the British diplomats secret.[26]

Throughout this process, the Greek community had the full backing of the Greek government, only because the end of the war had brought an economic downturn in Egypt, causing some Greeks to return to Athens in search of work. At the time, Greece was experiencing considerable political turbulence because of escalating clashes between the right-wing promonarchist government and the communist-led left-wing opposition that soon led to a civil war that broke out in 1947. With Britain unable to continue supporting the government side, the United States intervened. The Truman doctrine that the US president announced in March 1947 would ensure enough military backing for the government side to enable it to win the war in 1949.

The possibility that unemployed or marginalized Greeks from Egypt settling in Greece might support the Left in the ongoing conflict was one of the reasons why the Greek government wished to discourage any movement from Egypt to Greece. Another fear was that the initial trickle of arrivals would grow, triggering memories of the huge influx of Greek refugees from Turkey in the 1920s, which caused considerable social tensions and severely tested the government's ability to cater to their needs.

It was not only the Right versus Left conflict that was escalating into a civil war in the north of the country that the government had to deal with. There was widespread domestic unemployment because the Axis occupiers had destroyed Greece's economic infrastructure. There were food shortages and the widespread destruction of homes, including entire villages, had left thousands without homes. The devaluation of the British pound in September 1949 affected the value of the Egyptian pound, and the Greek press warned that even the Greeks from Egypt who had gone to Greece with money to spend faced difficulties. The Ministry of Foreign Affairs was already instructing Greek diplomats in Egypt to find alternative destinations for Greeks in Egypt wishing to emigrate.[27]

The efforts to achieve an acceptable agreement on the future status of the Greeks in Egypt to help them 'readjust' to the new circumstances came up against a wave of rising nationalist sentiment in Egypt. In September 1945 Egypt demanded a modification of the Anglo–Egyptian Treaty that would terminate the British military presence and allow Egypt to annex Sudan. There were also nationalist sentiments directed against foreigners, sparked by the end of the domestic economic boom the war years had brought to Egypt. As early as 1944 the Greek embassy told Athens that it was likely that the labor market crisis that was beginning would result in foreigners becoming scapegoats as the Egyptian government scrambled to deal with difficulties including its unpopularity.

Indeed, the government promulgated a law in 1947 that increased the quota of Egyptian citizens that joint-stock companies were required to include in their administration and workforce. Several Greek observers noted that the Egyptians were conflating foreign occupation with not only the British but also foreign residents. In the summer of 1946, the anti-British demonstrations in Alexandria and Cairo that turned violent resulted in the destruction and looting of Greek-owned shops. The numbers of those affected were not great, but the symbolism of targeting Greek establishments was worrying.

The United Nations partition plan for Palestine, which recommended the creation of an Arab and a Jewish state, brought a new round of nationalist protests in Egypt in November 1947. Egypt's delegates at the assembly were vociferous in their condemnation of the plan. With the interests of the Greeks in Egypt in mind, Greece was the only European country to vote against the resolution. Six months later, the Greek side submitted its draft of the treaty of establishment to the Egyptian government, a document that tried to make the case that the Greeks had a special place and deserved special treatment. As Modinos put it, a foreigner who has lived all their life in Egypt whose ancestors also lived in Egypt is not a foreigner, and could therefore be regarded as Egyptian. The contradiction in Modinos's logic was that the Greeks who should be considered "Egyptian" were requesting that the old privileges be phased out over a longer period than that envisioned by Egypt. There was no immediate response.[28]

In May 1949, an Egyptian commission declared that the government's obligation not to discriminate against foreigners was limited to the so-called transitional period. In other words it did not apply after the impending end of the Mixed Courts. The Greek leadership desperately sought help from Athens, but none was forthcoming. Then in August, two-and-a-half months before the Mixed Courts would close their doors, the Egyptian government sent a counterproposal to the Greek committee.[29] There was optimism on the Greek side until the last minute, and without having seen the text the *Tachydromos* relayed the assurances of Egyptian officials that foreigners had nothing to worry about. This, the newspaper believed, confirmed the welcoming climate toward foreigners.[30] But when the committee read the text it was extremely disappointed to discover that the message contained the standard text sent to all other foreign communities.

It was a sign of things to come when Greco–Egyptian negotiations began in mid-September. Two weeks later the discussions concluded with no final agreement, and on October 15, 1949 the Mixed Courts marked their end with a ceremony that took place at Cairo's Opera House. A few days earlier, the last formal adjournment in Cairo included speeches heralding a new era for Egypt.[31] In Alexandria, the *Tachydromos*, despite the widespread concerns of the Greeks, reiterated its confidence that the Egyptian justice system and its courts would rise to the occasion. The Reuters news agency noted laconically that "all foreigners in Egypt now become subject to the purely Egyptian national courts."[32] It did not explain that negotiations were still pending to finalize the status of foreigners in Egypt. As things turned out, it was correct to ignore that point.

The nationalist Wafd party won the 1950 elections and put an abrupt end to negotiations, announcing it would issue a law regulating the status of resident foreigners. The law, it became clear, would adhere to international practices and make a distinction between nationals and non-nationals. It was the end of an era and the beginning of a new one. But not many Greeks in Egypt saw it that way. In 1951 the consul general in Alexandria informed Athens that the morale of the Greek community had reached its lowest point.[33]

4

The Greeks, Economic Change, and Egyptianization, 1914–52

Egypt's quest for independence in the post-First World War era entailed not only political demands for the end of British rule, but also strategies for the country's economic wellbeing. Egyptians began envisioning their economic independence against the backdrop of significant changes the economy experienced in the 1920s and 1930s. Economic nationalism grew out of the country's experiences during the First World War years, the interruption of foreign trade, and shortages of food and basic goods, all of which exposed the flaws and weaknesses of the economy's overwhelming emphasis on the cultivation and export of cotton. During the war, investors, exercising caution, formed only six joint-stock companies, four of them with Greek or Jewish participation, a sign of their willingness to adapt to the prevailing conditions.[1]

The cotton sector of the economy also began facing serious difficulties. Successive agricultural crises in the 1920s, a worldwide downturn in international demand for cotton, and the Great Depression of 1929 brought a sharp deterioration of trade, forcing the cotton-focused economy to diversify.[2] All this produced a sustained effort to promote industry and manufacturing. In 1930 Egypt gained tariff autonomy and the government imposed customs duties that protected whatever domestic industry already existed. Until then, the lack of protections and government indifference toward industry—for example, necessary raw materials were taxed as 'luxuries'—had placed obstacles in the way of the nascent industrial sector. There was also a widespread sentiment that the changes that needed to be introduced could be implemented effectively only if Egyptians took charge of their agriculture, finances, and industry. That produced incremental legislative steps to force private, foreign-owned companies to 'Egyptianize' by employing a greater proportion of Egyptians or including more Egyptians on their boards of directors.

These new developments in the Egyptian economy affected the Greeks differently depending on their social class and profession. The businessmen, cotton merchants, and exporters and bankers, falling profits notwithstanding, remained active and retained their position as the community's elite. Significantly they were on the boards of directors of joint-stock companies with other foreigners and began investing in the fledgling manufacturing sector, as were Greek entrepreneurs, who were becoming part of the emergent domestic bourgeoisie. These businessmen displayed the adaptability that Greeks practiced throughout their time in Egypt, so much so that it is difficult to think of some of them as 'exporters' or 'bankers' because of the breadth of their investments in all sectors of the economy. For example Mikés Salvago, the cotton magnate and banker, was also on the board of companies that ranged from textiles to rail and river transport. Greeks went into business with other Greeks, foreigners, and Egyptians, thus their economic roles were as complex as their identities.[3]

The few Greeks involved in manufacturing, primarily in the food and beverage sector, did well, especially after Egypt acquired tariff autonomy. New Greek entrepreneurs, focused on the manufacturing sector, began to emerge during this period. Soon their names featured among the leaders of the Greek community organizations. These Greek manufacturing enterprises also began to include Egyptians on their boards.

Another indication that the Greek business elite's status remained strong between 1914 and 1952 was that aside from 'Egyptianization' this period also witnessed an 'indigenization' of company boards and shareholding in Egypt. The years between 1914 and 1933 saw the formation of 153 companies. In fifty-one of them, the majority of capital came from overseas, but 102 were subscribed locally. The proportion of shares held in Egypt rose from a third to half of the total. This trend was maintained after 1933, and according to one estimate, foreign capital in Egypt in 1948 constituted only 15.5 percent of the country's national wealth. Meanwhile, Egyptians and foreign residents in Egypt were playing an increasingly important role in the direction of joint-stock companies. According to an in-depth study of Egyptianization, in 1946 out of a total of 342 joint-stock companies, overseas foreigners dominated only forty-three, albeit the most heavily capitalized. The remaining 299 companies had significant indigenous participation of resident foreigners, including Greeks as well as Egyptians. There were eighteen firms in which the board was predominantly constituted of Syrians, twenty-two Greek companies, and thirty-eight Jewish firms; these firms were almost exclusively in the hands of foreign residents in Egypt. Another sixty firms were run by Egyptians and of the remaining companies, the largest number were directed by mixed boards of Egyptians and foreign residents. Moreover, the transformation that had taken place between 1920 and 1950 was striking. In 1920 most boards of business firms were predominantly made up of one ethnic group. Firms depended on large European branch banks and were managed by board members based overseas. By 1950, such firms were no longer so prominent and those that existed were much more 'Egyptian,' meaning they were directed by foreigner residents of Egypt. Even more prevalent were companies run by a mixed board of Egyptians and foreign residents.[4]

The other Greek social strata, however, found it much more difficult to adapt to the new socioeconomic climate. Egyptianization for them did not simply mean the obligation to include Egyptians on the boards of their companies. For white-collar professionals, shopkeepers, and employees the interwar period brought increasing competition with Egyptians, who were becoming better educated and gaining access to funding that enabled them to go into business or seek employment thanks to new quotas mandating the hiring of Egyptians. A sure sign of the steady transformation of the Egyptian economy and society was the gradual disappearance of the Greek grocer-middlemen in the provinces, as well as efforts by Greek employees and workers to mobilize to defend their living standards. The Second World War brought a mini-economic boom and some relief from the effects of Egyptianization, but in the postwar era the difficulties began to mount.

The Slow Decline of the Cotton Economy

On the eve of the Great Depression of 1929 the Greek exporting houses accounted for over 25 percent of Egypt's cotton export. It was a sign that despite the slowing down of the country's export sector after the First World War, Greek exporters were still in a robust position and most certainly still the wealthiest group among the Greeks. But overall the picture was changing. The value of Egypt's cotton exports reached just over LE77 million in 1920, but that was an inflated figure that probably had to do with demand that had shored up during the First World War. It fell by over half the next year, and for the rest of the 1920s it varied between LE38 and LE56 million. The 1920s brought several difficulties for cultivators in terms of preserving the quality of the soil and the level of the cotton yield per feddan; there was a growing need for fertilizers, improved drainage, and better-quality seeds.

The end of the protectorate in 1922 brought greater involvement and control of the production and commerce of cotton by the Egyptian government, something foreigners viewed as a mixed blessing. There was friction between the foreign-dominated Alexandria General Produce Association and government officials after Egyptian landowners formed their own organization and protested what they saw as the association's engineering of artificially low prices. In 1930, the government replaced the association with a Commission of the Cotton Exchange, which included cotton growers it appointed—the reason given was that through greater supervision, the state could better serve the interests of cotton growers.

By then the effects of the Wall Street crash and the drop in international demand for cotton were becoming obvious. The value of Egypt's cotton exports in 1930 was just under LE24 million, almost half the previous year's, and it dropped to just under LE18 million in 1932, the lowest of the entire period between the two world wars. For the rest of the 1930s it improved gradually but never surpassed the LE30 million barrier. Throughout the interwar period the two great Greek-owned firms, Choremi, Benachi Cotton Company and C.M. Salvago Company, remained the biggest exporters, followed by Rodocanachi & Company, Andritsakis, Barsoum & Company, N.G. Casulli, Joakimoglou & Company, and G.D. Sarris House. In the 1930s, the presence of other foreigners and most importantly Egyptians on their board of directors was a common feature of the big Greek-owned exporting firms. The names of the board members of the Choremi Benachi Cotton Company were Lucas Ant. Benachi, Alexander L. Benachi, George J. Choremi, Thomas E.H. Davies, John E. Lloyd, John H. Lloyd, Auguste Th. Sinadino, Themistocles A. Sinadino, Skender Soliman, and Ahmed Ziwar Pasha.[5]

Landownership by foreigners, including Greeks, also experienced changes after the First World War. During the 1920s and 1930s there was a contraction in the acreage owned by Greeks. This was a trend that had begun before the First World War, when Egyptians were buying up land with the help of better credit facilities and making improvements to its quality. Thus foreigners could no longer profit by improving land they purchased and then reselling it. The trend was accelerated after the war, and by the mid-1920s the two biggest Greek-owned firms, the Société Anonyme du Béhéra and the Union Foncière d'Egypte, had sold about half the land they owned in 1907. The only landowning company established by Greeks in the interwar period was the Kafr al-Zayat Company S.A.E. in 1937, and the Zerbinis brothers who were involved in its founding were not cotton exporters but manufacturers. Overall, Greek-owned land, which was 687,764 feddans, representing 12 percent of the total owned by foreigners, decreased to 428,726 feddans by 1937, or 7.4 percent of the total owned by foreigners. The contraction in Greek landowning was much more pronounced than in the cotton exporting business.[6]

The biggest changes during this period came with the sharp decrease in the numbers of small Greek merchants in the provinces, who for decades had played the role of middleman or moneylender, "facilitating the work of the fellah" as one Greek diplomatic report noted. By the late 1920s their numbers had diminished, either because some banks had extended their credit facilities to the remote provinces or because Egyptian merchants were no longer prepared to accept the high rates of interest involved in borrowing from Greeks. There were also instances of violence with Greek *nazirs* (superintendents) of rural estates, not necessarily because of anti-foreign sentiment but yet another development that made the provinces less attractive. According to the Greek embassy in Cairo there were fourteen murders of Greeks in the provinces between July 1931 and February 1934, and most of the perpetrators had gone unpunished. This added to the steady Greek exodus from rural Egypt. Initially it was the smaller Greek merchants who were unable to compete with the growing number of Egyptians who were benefiting from the greater availability of credit. But gradually even the wealthier Greek merchants in Upper Egypt and towns of the Nile Delta began moving to Alexandria and Cairo.[7]

Greek and Turkish Tobacco versus Virginia Leaf

The absence of government measures to protect cigarette exports, the continued taxation of imported tobacco, the manufacture of Egyptian-blend cigarettes in a number of European countries, and the launching of a blend of Virginia and Turkish tobacco cigarettes in the United States put increasing pressure on cigarette manufacturing firms based in Egypt. Nestor Gianaclis Limited established plants in Frankfurt, Geneva, and Boston, and Kyriazi Frères transferred almost all its production to Amsterdam and Hamburg. Miltiades Melachrino, the owner of *M. Melachrino & Company*, moved production to New York and closed down the business in Egypt, and when he returned he became involved in the cotton trade. Two other Greek-owned firms, Cigarettes Coutarelli and Papatheologos Frères, turned to the Egyptian market, which up until then was the preserve of

Armenian-owned firms. Needless to say, the Greek government, focused exclusively on tobacco exports to Egypt, was of little practical help to the Greek-owned cigarette firms in Egypt.

Difficulties for cigarette manufacturing in the 1920s included a series of strikes by workers opposed to the introduction of cigarette-making machines. Mechanization was a one-way street in the aftermath of the First World War and cost cigarette rollers their jobs. At the Coutarelli firm their number dropped from 172 in January 1920 to fifty by June 1921, at the Papatheologos firm over the same period their numbers went from 175 to eighty-four. And faced with strikes—one of the earliest took place at Coutarelli in 1917—the owners met to coordinate their strategy and agreed to threaten an industry-wide lockout. In the 1930s the consumption of cigarettes and other luxury goods such as coffee declined because of the effects of the Great Depression on Egyptian consumers. Cigarette manufacturers launched aggressive promotional campaigns and the Société Anonyme des Tabacs et Cigarettes Papatheologos ended up giving away expensive cameras, but nothing stopped the downward trend of cigarette consumption.[8]

But the single event that caused the demise of the Egyptian cigarette was the arrival of the Eastern Tobacco Company, which belonged to British American Tobacco, a multinational company. Eastern's arrival in Egypt meant much more than a change of ownership, it represented the introduction of Virginia leaf tobacco at the expense of the Greek and Turkish tobacco that, blended together, made the internationally famous Egyptian cigarette. Eastern had already acquired one cigarette company in Egypt, Maspero Frères. In the 1920s it gained control of several Armenian-owned cigarette companies that focused on the domestic market and in 1935 took over the Greek-owned Société Anonyme des Tabacs et Cigarettes Papatheologos. The owners, the brothers Stergios and Alecos, had expanded after the First World War and installed machines with the help of the Bank of Athens, but nonetheless saw profits drop in the mid-1920s.

Eastern Tobacco began by marketing a blend of Virginian, Greek, and Turkish tobacco cigarettes in the 1930s without much success. But with the arrival of large numbers of British troops in Egypt in the 1940s the tide finally turned in favor of the Virginia leaf cigarette. In 1938 only 13 percent of tobacco imports were Virginia leaf but in 1946 they had risen to 46 percent. The Egyptian cigarette in terms of mass consumption had had its day, and so had the Greek presence in the country's cigarette industry, with the exception of Cigarettes Coutarelli, which managed to adapt and survive.

The owners of Cigarettes Coutarelli focused on the Egyptian market and by 1928 had installed a total of twelve machines at its plant in Alexandria, where it employed about two thousand people. Cigarettes Coutarelli were last in line in Eastern's takeover bid. Three brothers, Constantinos, Dimitrios, and Alciviades Coutarelli, had moved to Egypt from the Mount Pelion region in Greece and established the firm in 1890. Constantinos, the driving force behind the enterprise, died in 1925, but his sons Achileas and Angelos stepped in to keep the business going. There was not much difference between the asking and selling price but no deal was concluded in the end and Cigarettes Coutarelli remained in business with control of 30 percent of the market. Eastern controlled the rest.

In 1945, according to one source, the company had five thousand employees. Other survivors were the smaller Greek firms that focused on the export of mostly handmade cigarettes, which had become a luxury consumer good, or producing cheaper cigarettes for the domestic market. Nestor Gianaclis had already diversified his investments and gone into wine manufacturing. His cigarette firm focused on the domestic market after the First World War. The company remained in the family after his death in 1932 but it was soon purchased by the Greek tobacco company Papastratos. In 1948 the company employed 558 workers, but that number fell as the company's output declined and demand for machine-made cigarettes rose.[9] The definitive end of the Greek role in cigarette manufacturing came with the nationalization of the economy in 1961. The Coutarelli firm was renamed the Nasser Cigarette Company.

Greeks in Manufacturing and Industry

The interwar period was the era in which industrialization began in Egypt. But there was a vibrant manufacturing sector before the First World War in some areas in which Greeks had a significant presence. It involved mostly food and beverage manufacturing, which saw further development in the 1920s and 1930s. Initially, this sector faced difficulties due to the government's fiscal policies. A tax on sugar, aimed at alcoholic spirits and imposed in 1919, had an adverse effect on the profits and employment capabilities of Greek-owned distilleries, including Bolanachi and Klonaridis, which were established in the late nineteenth century, and one established by Andreas Zottos in 1918. A tax on cocoa was bad news for Greek confectionery manufacturers including The Royal Chocolate Works of Egypt.

The soft drinks industry, of which four of the five big firms were

Greek-owned—Spathis, Valsmamides (Ariston), Koutsoukos (Blue Cross Mineral Waters), and Dimitriou (Sinalco)—used domestic sugar and benefited from post-1930 protectionist measures. The importation of machinery in the interwar period enabled the development of domestic flour milling. There were several flourmills owned by Greeks, including the Dilaveris Brothers. Their Alexandria-based plant, established in 1914, was soon producing twenty-five tons of flour a day. Andreas Halkousis and Nicholas Atherinos established another big flour mill in Alexandria in 1929, producing twenty tons a day, as did the flourmill owned by the Vasilopoulos Brothers and Tsakalis, established in 1930. In 1933 Kimon and Constantinos Atherinos established a plant that produced a hundred tons a day.[10] Other smaller Greek ventures in the food sector included the establishment of poultry farms by Ganoselis and Capaitzis.

The construction industry, in which several Greeks had become involved during the nineteenth century, was another sector that attracted newer entrepreneurs. Nicholas Syrigos had the largest cement factory in Alexandria at the end of the First World War. Other Greeks owned wood-processing and marble-cutting plants. An enterprise immune to the difficulties plaguing the industrial sector before 1930 was an iron foundry established by the Zacharis brothers in 1904. The growing volume of machinery imported into Egypt at that time created the need for repair shops and ironworks. With their business picking up, the brothers soon introduced automated machinery and were able to fulfill major orders such as collapsible metal pavilions for the British Army, the conversion of sailing ships into steam-powered vessels, and the construction of beer fermentation vats. In the 1920s and especially after the 1930s the firm took on a series of major projects, including warehouses for the port in Alexandria, warehouses for the Cotton Exchange, and hangars for the British Air Force base at Abuqir. The Lagoudakis paper manufacturing firm also did well after 1930. It was handed down to relatives and was in operation after the revolution of 1952.[11]

The most ambitious project in terms of beverage manufacture was the introduction of vineyards for the purpose of producing wine in Egypt by Nestor Gianaclis, the cigarette manufacturer. Viniculture had existed in Egypt in ancient times but had eventually disappeared. Gianaclis studied a number of classical Greek texts, which commented favorably on wine produced around Lake Mariut, south of Alexandria. He confirmed the authenticity of his sources and put his capital and his imagination to work.

He purchased three thousand hectares (7,413 acres) of desert land about seventy kilometers southeast of Alexandria and brought the first vines from Greece in 1903 along with Greek experts to supervise the creation of the vineyards. The first good wine was produced thirty years later, in 1933, just before Gianaclis's death. The occasion of the production of wine in modern Egypt was marked by a visit to the Gianaclis estate by the Egyptian prime minister, Isma'il Sidqi Pasha, escorted by several cabinet ministers and a flurry of publicity. The project was a major success in land reclamation and viniculture, but the Greek commentators also proudly pointed out that Gianaclis had revived a Hellenic–Ptolemaic practice that had remained dormant for twenty centuries.

An early manufacturing project was in the form of the Société d'Egrenage et Dépôt de Graines, which produced oil and soap from cottonseeds, while it was also involved in cotton ginning. The founders were a Greek national, Georgios Goussios, and two brothers, G.I. and G.M. Sursock, who belonged to the Lebanese family that became the bankers of Khedive Ismail. If there was an element of risk to the project, Goussios was no stranger to adventure. He had fought in Garibaldi's army in Italy in 1866, returned to Egypt, and then went to Greece to head a group of Greek irregulars who were fighting the Ottomans. Upon his return to Egypt he ended up as director-general of the Anglo-Egyptian Bank. He had remained barricaded in the bank during the bombing of Alexandria in 1882 in order to protect it from looters. Goussios and the Sursocks were joined on the board of directors by two Jewish bankers, A. Bimenstein and Jacques Goar, and a Greek financier. The list of subsequent board members, up to 1955, reads like a list of Egypt's leading British, French, Greek, Jewish, and Lebanese financiers—the first Egyptian was Ahmed Ziwar Pasha, a lawyer and former prime minister, who was chairman of the board from 1934–44.

But the company's twentieth-century history is usually associated with the Zerbinis family, which was originally from Genoa but settled on the island of Mytiline in the fourteenth century. Ioannis Zerbinis moved to Egypt in 1871 at the age of seventeen to enter into the employment of a relative. Later, he began trading in cotton in Kafr al-Zayyat, where he met Goussios and joined him in the fighting in Thessaly. The two men continued their association upon returning to Egypt, and Zerbinis became managing director of the Kafr al-Zayat Cotton Company in 1899. He held the post for thirty years until his death and was succeeded by his elder son Dimitri, who was born in Alexandria in 1903. Ioannis's thirty-year reign as managing director was a period of constant expansion for the company, which set up a second factory in Alexandria and rebuilt and enlarged facilities at Kafr al-Zayyat after they were destroyed by fire. Both factories ginned and pressed cotton. A soap-manufacturing plant was installed in 1902 to supplement the cottonseed refinery, which expanded in 1924, enabling the production of sixteen tons of good-quality edible oil per day. The company's profits grew substantially, from LE6,667 in 1899–1900 when Ioannis took over to LE39,170 in his last year, 1929–30. In 1936 the company expanded into land development in the Kafr al-Zayyat region.[12]

Theocharis Kotsikas, who used the Latinized spelling of his name "Cozzika," pursued another early manufacturing project, an alcohol distillery. He moved to Alexandria from his hometown of Karistos in Greece, well aware that his uncle Ioannis had amassed a fortune through trade in Sudan and along the Red Sea. Theocharis also went into trade and managed to become the main supplier to Lord Kitchener's expeditionary force to Sudan between 1896 and 1898. One of the commodities he was dealing with was alcohol and he decided that rather than continue to import it he would invest in the manufacture of alcohol in Egypt. Helped by his brother Polychronis, he established a distillery in Turah, south of Cairo, which produced alcohol from molasses, a by-product of Egypt's sugar cane processing industry. The alcohol was used for lighting and the production of fertilizes, perfume, and spirits. By the early 1900s the plant was producing 1.5 million kilograms of 95–96 percent-proof alcohol, contributing to a steep drop in imported alcohol from abroad; on the eve of the First World War the plant's output had reached 6.5 million kilograms annually. The plant began producing carbonic acid for the production of soft drinks in 1936.

Theocharis died in 1932 and his nephew Theodore P. Cozzika, who was born in Cairo in 1899, took over the business. Theodore, like his uncle Theocharis and his father Polychronis (who died unexpectedly in 1922), was active in the affairs of the Greek community organization in Cairo and made substantial philanthropic contributions to the community, his ancestral hometown Karistos, and the Greek state, which recognized his services by awarding him several medals. But unlike the older generation, Theodore managed to combine business with pleasure, and was associated with retired American film actress Pearl White. After her death he married Despina, a granddaughter of Emmanuel Benachi. He owned several Rolls-Royces and a stud farm in France, from where he sold a horse to Winston Churchill. Theodore also served as aide-de-camp to Prince Andrew of

Greece when the Greek royal family spent time in Egypt during the Second World War. Another remarkable fact about Theodore is that he built a small mosque on the grounds of the plant for use by the workforce. He sold the Cozzika business in 1949 to an Egyptian businessman.[13] Theodore Cozzika's flamboyant lifestyle was the exception to the rule. Most Greek businessmen, although well-off, lived more ordinary lives while contributing to the growth of Egypt's manufacturing sector.

The Greeks and Egypt's Post-1930 Industrialization

The introduction of protective tariffs and other measures that benefited industrial projects ushered in a new era of industrialization focused primarily on the substitution of imports of consumer non-durables, especially cotton textiles. It also brought investment from abroad. Even the Egyptian state-funded Misr Group, whose goal was to develop an indigenous industrial sector, went into joint ventures with British and other foreign firms. The Association des Industries en Egypte, another group that promoted industrialization and represented foreign residents in Egypt, had been calling for easy entry of foreign capital and technicians into Egypt. The post-1930 era brought the emergence of a new generation of Greek industrialists, even though the Greek Chamber of Commerce in Alexandria offered only limited support to promote industrialization, and remained focused on facilitating trade and cotton exports. There were rumors that a Greek bank would be formed in Egypt for the purpose of assisting small Greek industries, but these were denied by a representative of the National Bank of Greece branch in Egypt. But new Greek industrialists did emerge.

Symeon Pialopoulos and Constantinos Delios were fairly typical examples of the new Greek industrialist. Pialopoulos moved to Egypt from Istanbul in the early 1930s. Even though the country's textile industry was dominated by two big firms, the Filature Nationale d'Egypte and the Société Misr pour la Filature et le Tissage, he felt he could capture part of the market by producing materials woven from high-quality cotton, wool, and vegetable fibers. In doing so he would be following the pattern of other Greek entrepreneurs specializing in quality goods. After operating his plant in a rented space he moved to his own premises, where he installed the latest machinery imported from Britain with financing from the Ottoman Bank. Pialopoulos employed British technicians for woolen materials and French experts for dyeing. His chief engineer was Egyptian, as was his workforce, and the office staff were Greeks.

Soon Pialopoulos managed to build a second, more advanced factory just south of Alexandria, which was in 1952 the pride of Greeks in Egypt and of Egypt's industrial sector because it contained the most modern technology and machinery, according to an account of a Greek industrial entrepreneur in Egypt. The factory was designed by a French architect and built by a Greek contractor, Miltiades Kokkinos, whose business began as a small company in the 1920s but grew steadily. Between 1937 and 1948 it had erected over one thousand buildings in Alexandria and Cairo.[14]

In 1946 the company was renamed Selected Textile Industries S.A.E., with a share capital of LE700,000. It was one of the most important Greek-owned businesses in post-1930 Egypt. Unlike Pialopoulos, Delios had been in Egypt for several years before he decided to invest in the manufacturing sector, having brought out a Greek-language commercial publication in the 1920s. In the late 1930s he established a knitted clothing manufacturing plant in Alexandria and later expanded into the manufacture of cotton undergarments that were sold in all of Egypt's leading department stores.[15]

Other, smaller textile businesses were started by several Greeks including Christos Loukakis's Société des Soies el Ghazala in Cairo in 1946, the Roussopoulos, Perakis & Company rope manufacturing in Benha, Dimitrios Philipides's Cleopatra Oriental Carpets in Alexandria, with twenty-one looms and a workforce of about ninety persons, and the undergarment firm of Constantinos Theotokas.[16] Of the many small ventures into manufacturing in the 1930s, those that grew significantly were Yangos Chrysovergis's Egyptian Coconut Oil Company, Nicholas Yamodis's rice mills, Antonios Ververis's ironworks, Michael Galanis's metal fixtures manufacturing plant in Cairo that employed 360 persons, the cement and porcelain factories of Dionysios Kannelatos in Alexandria and Theodoros Efstratiou in Cairo, the Sarpakis Brothers' gold mining operations in the Red Sea area, which led to a road being built from Qena on the Nile to the Red Sea port of Safaga, and Constantinos Nanopoulos's Rotaprint Papermill, which he acquired from a Jewish businessman in the late 1940s.

Meanwhile, Greek merchants invested in industrial firms in the 1930s and sat on their boards. Mikés Salvago and his son Constantine sat separately on the boards of such diverse companies founded from 1929 onward as the National Petroleum Company (1929), Egyptian Copper Works (1936), S.A.E. Cabra (1934), and the Société Egyptienne des Pétroles (1932). What information there is on investments and shareholdings reveals that Alexandros Alexandroff and Theodore and Xenophon Casdagli put up 7 percent of the capital of Beida Dyers, a company jointly sponsored by Bradford Dyers and Banque Misr; Alexandre and Jean Choremi, Byron Dellaporta, and Jean Pilavachi put up 14.5 percent of the capital of the Egyptian Independent Oil Company (1938); Constantine Lagoudakis and Mikés Mavros held shares in the Société Fiancière pour le Commerce et l'Industrie (SEFINA) S.A.E. (1938); Alexandros Rallis held shares in the S.E. pour l'Exploitation des Mines et Carrières (1938); Armand Mustaki held shares in the National Contractors Company of Egypt (1938) and later joined the board of the Matexa textile company; Theodore Cozzika was on the board of the Société Nationale du Papier (1934).

Symeon Pialopoulos, a Greek who invested in the textile industry, remembers that he and the other Greeks who were becoming involved in manufacturing ventures in the 1930s had little help from Greek banks or the Greek Chamber of Commerce. This was probably due to institutional inertia rather than a result of the predominance of the cotton exporters over Greek economic life in Egypt. After all, they themselves soon began to participate in industry-oriented investment. Unencumbered by the weight of institutional responsibilities, both well-established and newly emerging Greek businessmen were responding to new opportunities opening up in Egypt. To be sure, the Greeks had benefited from the colonialist structures the British had installed and maintained in Egypt, and had played their role in the country's uneven development and integration into the global economy. But that had been their meal ticket rather than part of an ideological agenda. Likewise, the new circumstances in the interwar period created by Egypt's economic nationalist movement attracted their interest to the extent that it held out the prospect of continued prosperity.

Egyptianization Measures

Egypt's post-1922 'Egyptianization' policies to enhance the presence of Egyptians in the economy through legislative measures mandated an increase of Egyptians on the boards of private companies, a greater proportion of Egyptian employees in those companies, and measures that would increase the number of self-employed Egyptians and in white-collar professions. The Greeks had particular reason to be alarmed. Even as late as the 1940s, about 33 percent of them worked in clerical jobs, about 26 percent were in white collar professions widely defined to include doctors, teachers, drivers, nurses, and waiters, 13 percent were technicians of various kinds, about the same proportion were classified as handicraft laborers, about 8 percent were shopkeepers, and the remaining 7 percent were merchants, industrialists, and businessmen. And there was a domino effect to be considered.

If a Greek-owned business succumbed to Egyptian competitors and closed, that usually meant the loss of jobs for the business's Greek employees. The general secretary of the Greek Grocers Association in Alexandria made precisely that point in 1937. Lastly, the Greeks were especially affected by interwar Egyptianization measures because their numbers had grown. The total number, according to Egypt's *Annuaire Statistique* of 1927 had grown over the previous decade, reaching just over seventy-six thousand in terms of Greek citizenship and just under one hundred thousand in terms of Greek ethnicity irrespective of citizenship status. Indeed, both those numbers would show a roughly 20 percent drop by the time the 1937 statistics were published, the effect of Egyptianization measures of the 1930s that had barely gone into effect.[17]

The first Egyptianization measure came in July 1923 when a ministerial decree ruled that a new joint-stock company had to have at least one director with Egyptian nationality. Then in 1927 another law stipulated that boards should have at least two Egyptian directors and one-quarter of the employees should be Egyptian. The Greek Chamber of Commerce along with the other European country chambers of commerce in Egypt lodged protests. They need not have bothered because the government never got round to ensuring that new companies would comply. But in the 1930s, the increased number of graduates of secondary and higher education, the consequence of long-overdue educational reforms implemented in the post-protectorate era, produced demographic and political pressure on the foreign-dominated private sector. In response to protests and unrest the government considered doubling the quota of Egyptian employees to 50 percent and having a minimum of 90 percent of workers be Egyptian. Those measures were first implemented in 1940. Apparently the government wished to see the restrictions on employment practices apply not only to foreign nationals but also to naturalized foreigners, and even the Copts, whom it considered overrepresented in the private sector, benefiting from the preference of foreign employers for them rather than Muslim Egyptians.[18]

In the case of the Greeks, the workers and shop employees were the category most immediately affected by these measures, because Egyptian workers accepted lower wages and proved to be just as capable, as the Greek ambassador informed Athens. But Greek office workers were also affected.

Thanks to the education they had received at the community organization schools that included French and English, hundreds of Greeks worked as clerks in foreign-owned firms in Egypt. Because of the Egyptianization measures many were losing their jobs or were unable to find employment. This triggered a debate among community leaders and educationalists about the need to change the curricular orientation of the schools with a view to offering more technical skills, but any change was of course going to come too late for those who had assumed they would find employment.

In some cases even Greeks in the liberal professions faced problems. For example, those without a medical degree from an Egyptian university had to pass an exam in order to be allowed to practice medicine in Egypt. The difficulties this entailed led the Greek government to recommend aspiring doctors to stay in Egypt to study and not return to Greece.[19] Yet it was unlikely that Athens could offer any concrete help to mitigate the Egyptianization of the economy, given its inability to pressure Cairo diplomatically, as the case of the Capitulations had demonstrated. Its advice that Greeks petition to acquire Egyptian nationality was not practical because the Egyptian government had already shown it conferred nationality on very few foreign applicants. Attempts at creating organizations to foster cooperation between Greeks and Egyptians, such as forming a friendship association or the proposal to create a Greco–Egyptian bank to finance joint Greek and Egyptian economic ventures went nowhere. The bank had been envisioned by Marios Lascaris, the director of the Bank of Athens in Alexandria, who had also served as president of the Greek Chamber of Commerce of Alexandria. Lascaris's family were ethnic Greeks of the Ottoman Empire who had lost their fortune when the Greeks were expelled in 1922, leaving him particularly sensitive to the potential dangers that the rise of Egyptian nationalism could pose for the Greeks. But the vision of a joint Greek and Egyptian bank proved to be too bold a move for the rest of the Greek banking community in Egypt.

A group of small businessmen in Alexandria formed ELPOA, the Greek Popular Progressive League of Alexandria in 1930. It functioned as an umbrella group for fourteen Greek trade associations and unions it had formed and a pressure group working toward securing better funding for Greek businessmen from both foreign and Greek banks in Alexandria. Its initial membership of 250 grew to over 1,250 and in 1931, its president, Georgios Zacharis, the iron foundry owner, claimed it was the most powerful Greek organization in Egypt, a calculated swipe at the community organizations which businessmen like him felt were ignoring their problems. ELPOA was raising apparently controversial issues, such as the need for the Greeks to take Egyptian citizenship and a radical change in the curricula of Greek schools. Such was the energy generated at the group's first meeting that the Greek ambassador worried ELPOA would undermine the predominance of the community organizations. He even prevented ELPOA from calling a national meeting of Greek businessmen and offered assurances that the Greek diplomatic representatives were working toward finding the best solution for the future of the Greeks in Egypt. That patently false claim appeared to reassure the ELPOA members and the organization held back from implementing its program.[20]

The only area where a more practical response appeared possible was in education, steps of course that would benefit the younger generation. With the encouragement of a strong and progressively minded teachers' union, educationalists recommended the teaching of Arabic and more technical and vocational subjects that would prepare students for the changing socioeconomic environment in Egypt. The teaching profession was one of the few areas where liberal and radical ideas were welcomed, and also where women could pursue a successful career. Angeliki Panayotatou, who had studied medicine in Athens, was placed in charge of the medical services of several Greek schools as well as philanthropic institutions, while pursuing research into cholera and other diseases in Egypt.

Judging by the reformist spirit sweeping through a major conference on Greek education in Egypt held in 1931, one might have expected a series of changes in the years that followed. But the system was slow to react, and by the end of the decade little had changed except that the numbers of Greek children going to American, Egyptian, English, French, and Italian schools had grown overall.

The Averoff High School of Alexandria was at the forefront of plans for reforming the educational system of the Greeks in Egypt. Beginning in the late 1920s several administrative changes were introduced to permit better monitoring of the teaching as well as the curriculum. The school was well aware that it could not rely on advice or help from Athens, because the Greek government had never shown serious interest in its educational efforts, even though it regularly sent inspectors to Alexandria. In 1932 a teacher at the school drew up a proposal for the creation of a section that would teach students technical skills, echoing similar demands that were being published in the ethnic press. In 1940 there were suggestions that the two last grades be divided into two different tracks, "practical" and "classical"; in other words, one would focus on mathematics and science and the other on the humanities. The plan was eventually implemented in 1946 and concerned the three last grades of high school. The process, already laboriously slow, was delayed even more because the plan required the approval of the Greek government.

A proposal that students attending the Averoff Girls' High School—which was established in 1938 and focused on the so-called "classical studies"—could attend the boys' "practical" section was approved but it came up against Egyptian laws that prohibited mixed classes. By the late 1940s the school was trying to align its final examinations with the requirements of Farouk University in Alexandria. Overall, the school tried to move from its original concept as a Greek school that happened to be in Egypt toward becoming a Greek-language school serving the interests of young Greeks who were born in Egypt and planned to stay there. But many believed that the transformation, especially in terms of adapting its curriculum to the changing reality of Egypt, had been more rhetorical than effective.[21]

The war brought a brief respite from direct Egyptianization measures, with the exception of the introduction of a law making Arabic obligatory in all business dealings and the end of the war brought legislation that shop signs be written in Arabic. More importantly, the issue of creating more positions for Egyptians on company boards and in the workforce resumed in earnest. The war years had brought increased employment thanks to the needs to provide supplies as well as food and drink for the thousands of Allied troops stationed in Egypt. There were roughly one hundred thousand British and Dominion troops stationed in and around Cairo; in 1941 the British Army was spending an average of four and a half million pounds sterling a month. Prices were going up, but that was benefiting middlemen and retailers, many of whom were foreigners.

British officers arriving in Egypt were struck by the contrast between the privations experienced in wartime Britain and the leisure and luxury of life in Cairo. While rationing had become the norm in England, "the corner shops and Greek groceries of Cairo were packed with butter, sugar, eggs and paraffin . . . oranges and dates were piled into round baskets in the greengrocers," while "the resourceful Greeks who ran the black market . . . did their best to keep the city well-stocked with goods of all sorts." It was a challenging task but "the little Greek boats and their indomitable crews ran cargoes as far as Tunis and Algiers, from where they brought back Italian cheese and spaghetti, medical supplies, stockings and condoms."[22]

By the same token, the end of the war and the departure of British troops brought an abrupt drop in the consumption of goods and services and widespread unemployment. An official estimation that foreign employees earned on average twice as much as Egyptian employees in the private sector, coming on top of data that showed a growth in population and higher rates of unemployment, fueled the process of limiting foreign privileges. The Greeks, especially those involved in the food and beverage industry and the service sector, felt the effects of the departure of foreign troops most acutely. And the seven thousand or so Greeks of Egypt who had been drafted by the Greek forces, upon being demobilized, found that their old jobs either did not exist any more or had been taken by Egyptians or other foreigners. Greeks who had sided with the Left during the uprisings in the Greek military units in 1943 and 1944 found out that the old ties of solidarity among Greeks did not exist any more when they asked for more assistance from politically conservative businessmen.

Some respite would come for the Greeks in the late 1940s with the departure of other foreigners. When Italy entered the war in June 1940 on the side of the Axis Powers, the British authorities in Egypt arrested 5,800 Italians who were members of the fascist party and sent the rest of the Italian men to civilian internment camps. Only Italian Jews and known antifascists were not interned. Meanwhile, the British forces commandeered a number of buildings owned by Italians.[23] By the end of the war in 1945, the wartime experiences of most Italians and the loss of jobs meant that many started leaving Egypt.

Armenians, 1,700 of them, responded to the invitation issued to the Armenian diaspora to move to the Soviet Socialist Republic of Armenia and boarded a vessel in Alexandria, optimistically looking forward to a new future. The Palestinian question at the United Nations and the war of 1948 triggered a stream of Jewish emigration to Israel. Paradoxically, while the departure of foreigners opened employment opportunities for some Greeks, it also deprived many others of their most regular clientele.[24]

With the war finally over, the Ministry of Commerce and Industry produced a draft of the long discussed 'companies law' that aimed to strengthen the presence of Egyptians in the private sector as well as increase government control. The draft law called for high quotas of Egyptian employees, more equitable salaries, a greater reliance on Egyptian-owned capital, and a greater presence of Egyptians on the boards of directors. The law was intended to apply to both joint-stock and privately owned companies and to have immediate and retrospective effect on existing companies. As Egypt's ambassador to Greece Mahmud Sabet Pasha explained in an interview with the *Tachydromos* correspondent in Athens, all his country was doing was ensuring that qualified Egyptians did not remain unemployed, and foreigners, especially law-abiding Greeks, had nothing to worry about. But such reassurances from official lips rang hollow to most foreigners in Egypt.

The foreign-dominated Federation of Egyptian Industries launched the earliest protests and began working on an alternative set of proposals, an acknowledgment that something had to be done to redress the imbalance between foreigners and Egyptians. In 1946 the government countered with a new draft that took into consideration some of the criticisms and focused the measures only on joint-stock companies. After a great deal of debate and various amendments, the parliament passed the law in February 1947, and it went for consideration to the Senate. One British source claimed that sixty thousand foreigners including Greeks would lose their jobs. The Greek Chamber of Commerce in Alexandria hosted a meeting with the British, French, and Swiss chambers of commerce and all agreed the law was prejudicial. But rather than launch a common protest, the representatives of the other chambers told the Greeks that they preferred to work through their respective embassies. Given the perennial inability or unwillingness of Greece to apply pressure, the Greek Chamber of Commerce felt helpless and unable to offer any credible alternative to the Company Law. Indeed, the Greek embassy did next to nothing while both the British and French diplomatic authorities delivered their objections to the Egyptian government.

The Greek press in Egypt, as it had when dealing with the impending end of the Capitulations, tried to put on a brave face. Days before the Senate was to consider the law, the *Tachydromos* reported on a public meeting held at the Greek Chamber of Commerce in Alexandria to discuss the situation of the cotton economy in the country, with Greek and Egyptian businessmen present. The Egyptians had offered a justification of the Company Law, claiming it was designed to ensure that Egyptians with the right qualifications would find employment. This had been well received at the meeting. The newspaper added its own commentary, noting that the Greeks agreed with the law as long as it would be implemented fairly and their attitude would surely guarantee the close cooperation between

Greeks and Egyptians in the months ahead. Privately, the Greeks were not so optimistic.

The chamber, along with the Greek community organization in Alexandria, therefore went ahead and submitted a memorandum to the government and the Senate. They requested a five-year grace period and a revision of the 1929 Egyptian nationality law so that Greeks born in Egypt could become eligible for Egyptian nationality. The 1929 nationality law reflected Egypt's wish to assert its sovereign right to regulate the status of Egyptians and foreigners. Its provisions were unfavorable to European residents because, rather than taking into account the time spent living in the country, it granted Egyptian nationality to applicants who were considered assimilated "or those deemed to be easily assimilable because of their ethnic or religious origins."[25]

Invoking the sentiment many Greeks had that Egypt was their home, the memorandum noted that most Greeks had lived in Egypt for generations, their fortunes were completely tied to Egypt's, and they knew Egypt better than Greece.[26]

In early July 1947, after making minor amendments, the Senate passed the law. It required that at least 40 percent of the board members of companies be Egyptian, 51 percent of the stock of new companies be held by Egyptian nationals, 75 percent of the white-collar employees be Egyptian and receive 65 percent of the salaries, and 90 percent of the workers be Egyptian and receive 80 percent of the wages. It also sought to separate the public and private sectors by barring government officials or recent government officials from sitting on the boards of joint-stock companies. Finally, the law sought to dissolve interlocking directorships in order to ensure that companies received the time and energy from their board members they deserved. It stipulated that no person could serve on the boards of more than ten companies or be the managing director of three. Foreign businessmen continued their opposition, claiming that the three-year transition period was too short, but most firms responded positively and began including Egyptians on their boards and hiring Egyptian employees and workers.[27]

The foreign communities also shifted their attention to testing the legislation's definition of 'Egyptian.' No one doubted that this was another milestone in the steady reduction of privileges for foreigners resident in Egypt and for the first time codified the restrictions placed on them. Like all previous steps taken toward the Egyptianization of the economy, it was

challenged by some foreign and Egyptian businessmen, the phased imple-
mentation process was complicated, and the measures were not applied
consistently. Overall it would have its intended effect. In the period immediately after the measures became law, its challengers tested its integrity
by probing apparent loopholes. One was the somewhat vague distinction
between employees and workers, which allowed businessmen to fudge the
numbers and ethnicity of their workforce. The other was its use of the term
'Egyptians' that allowed questions on the exact definition of the term, for
example, whether it signified officially naturalized Egyptians, those with
Egyptian passports, or those born in Egypt.

Ultimately the government made it clear that the law considered
Egyptians all those born in Egypt with an Egyptian name as well as those
who had obtained a nationality certificate prior to November 4, 1947. The
Greeks who had obtained such certificates more recently had done so on
the basis of the Egyptian nationality law of 1929 that made all those born
in the old Ottoman Empire, known as *mutamassirun*, eligible. It also conferred eligibility on those born in Egypt to apply when they reached the
age of majority, as well as those who could prove they had been continu-
ously resident in Egypt for ten years. To have taken advantage of the 1929
law meant renouncing the privileges accorded by the Capitulations until
1937 and the Mixed Courts until 1949. Needless to say, there was a scramble to beat the November 4 deadline. One report claimed that six thousand
Greeks had applied in November. But throughout the year there had been
a steady stream of applications. In January 1947, a front-page article in the
Tachydromos reported that many Greeks had acquired Egyptian nationality
and many others wished to do so soon.

The consideration of who was eligible for Egyptian nationality
exposed yet again the hopelessly complicated status of so many foreign
residents in Egypt. Ottoman documentation was often lacking. Those
with no official Greek or other nationality but were tried in native courts
and served in the Egyptian military were another category on the margins
of the law. The government's instinct was to treat such cases in a strict
manner, bearing in mind that the general idea was to benefit the native
Egyptian population. Ultimately, the government introduced a new and
more restrictive nationality law in 1950, which decreed that longtime
residents had the right to apply for nationality—they were no longer
automatically eligible. It also delayed the inclusion of naturalized citizens
in the Egyptian quota of the workforce.[28]

5

Greek Cultural and Social Life

Greek Independence Day, March 25, was celebrated in an especially grand manner in Alexandria in 1930 because the events also commemorated the centenary of Greece's independence. The centenary of the uprising against the Ottomans had not been formally observed in Athens or elsewhere in 1921 because of the ongoing military campaign in Asia Minor. Thus the Greek government decided that it should be honored in 1930, which was a hundred years since the Great Powers recognized Greece as a sovereign independent state. The festivities in Alexandria began with a service at the Greek Orthodox Cathedral officiated by Patriarch Meletios Metaxakis. There were also prayers offered in memory of the Greeks from Egypt who had died fighting for Greece between 1912 and 1922. In the afternoon twenty-five thousand Greeks packed the Municipal Stadium to watch a parade of 2,500 schoolchildren, athletes, boy scouts, and girl guides, followed by Greek dances and track and field games. The main speaker, Paleologos Georgiou, the director of the Greek schools, spoke about how freedom was at the core of Greek ideals.[1]

The Greek centenary celebrations that took place all over Egypt were a reminder of the strong ties the Greeks of Egypt maintained with their homeland, which were part of sense of being culturally Greek. When one thinks of the presence of modern Greek culture in Egypt, it is difficult not to consider the importance of the poet Constantine Cavafy—C.P. Cavafy, as he liked to be known. Even though the Greekness of the Greeks of Egypt was produced and maintained by the geographical closeness of Greece, their status in Egyptian society, and their ethnic associations and the schools, the fact that among them lived one of the greatest modern Greek poets is enough 'proof' that Alexandria was a 'Greek' city. Cavafy was born there in 1863, the son of businessman Petros Cavafy, and spent a few years in England and then Constantinople before his family returned to Alexandria in 1885. By that time his father's business had been dissolved and he had died, leaving relatively little to his children. After returning to Alexandria, Constantine traveled very little from the city, where he worked at the irrigation department in the Ministry of Public Works, a job that left him time to write poetry. His residence in the city and the fact that several of his well-known poems were set in Alexandria, albeit in its era of Hellenistic greatness, served to cement his identity as a Greek and an Alexandrian poet. His presence alone in Alexandria would make the city a center of Greek letters and underscore the close cultural ties between the Greeks of Egypt and their homeland. Cavafy's Greekness was set on a much broader canvas. E.M. Forster, the British poet who met him in Egypt during the First World War, wrote that Cavafy "was a loyal Greek" however "Greece for him was not territorial" but was instead the broader influence of its civilization. Cavafy "could be caustic about the claims of the tight lipped little peninsula overseas."[2]

Unlike the great poet, most Greeks living in Egypt maintained close ties with Greece, which they considered their homeland, even those who were born in Egypt.

The geographical proximity of Greece and Egypt—Crete, Greece's southernmost island is only 650 kilometers from Alexandria, closer than Aswan in Upper Egypt—was matched by the close ties the Greeks in Egypt maintained with their homeland. In the interwar years, the demographic size of the Greek presence in Egypt and its relative affluence, coupled with the ease of travel between Greece and Egypt, contributed to a sense that Alexandria, Cairo, and the canal towns were part of a Greek world spread out throughout the eastern Mediterranean. That world shrunk dramatically after the expulsion of Greeks from the Ottoman Empire but it lived on in Egypt. Greece itself, roiled by the enormous task of accommodating 1.2 million incoming refugees and no longer interested in projecting itself throughout the eastern Mediterranean, could not focus on the needs of the Greeks of Egypt. Yet the Greeks of Egypt remained as strongly attached as ever to Greece. In the words of the director of the Xenakion schools in Cairo, the Greeks in Egypt followed developments in Greece very closely in the interwar period. Thanks to Greek-language education and "the preservation of Greek traditions they avoided assimilation and becoming absorbed by their surroundings."[3]

1. Nestor Gianaclis Ltd cigarette tin containing twenty cigarettes, ca. 1920s. In response to market conditions in Egypt in-between the two world wars, Gianaclis began focusing on the export market. Author's personal collection.

2. Advertisement for Spathis' Cola. Nikolaos Spathis opened the first carbonated water factory in Egypt in 1884. The Mineral Waters and Wines and Spirits Company was registered in Cairo and Alexandria. Photograph courtesy of ELIA/MIET Photographic Archive.

3. The Benachi and Choremi families at the Benachis' house in Alexandria, ca. 1889. Standing, left to right: Ioannis C. Choremi, Emmanuel Benachi, Demosthenes C. Choremi, unidentified servant, Constantine J. Choremi. Sitting, left to right: the four children of Demosthenes Choremi (Aristeides, Constantine, Karteria, Alexandros); Penelope, daughter of Emmanuel and Virginia Benachi (the future Penelope Delta); Virgina Benachi, née Choremi; Alexandra, Penelope's sister; sitting cross-legged is Tom Davies, a business partner of Emmanuel Benachi and Alexandra Benachi's fiancé; Argine, the youngest Benachi sister; cross-legged on the right is Alexander, son of Emmanuel and Virginia Benachi. Copyright 2018 by the Benaki Museum, Athens.

ΜΕ ΤΗΝ ΕΥΚΑΙΡΙΑ ΤΗΣ ΠΑΡΟΥΣΙΑΣ
ΤΟΥ ΕΛΕΥΘΕΡΙΟΥ ΒΕΝΙΖΕΛΟΥ,
ΣΥΓΚΕΝΤΡΩΣΙΣ ΣΤΟ ΣΠΙΤΙ
ΤΟΥ ΣΤΕΦ. ΚΑΙ ΤΗΣ ΠΗΝΕΛΟΠΗΣ ΔΕΛΤΑ

4. Eleftherios Venizelos visits the house of Stephanos and Penelope
Delta in Alexandria, 1915. Sixth and seventh from the left are Mikés
Sinadino, president of the Greek community organization of Alexandria,
and Antonios Sachtouris, Greece's general consul in Alexandria. On
the floor, second from left, is Mikés Salvago, the future president of
the Greek community organization of Alexandria. Venizelos is third
from right in the seated row. Penelope Delta (née Benachi) is to his left.
The photograph is signed by Venizelos. Copyright 2018 by the Benaki
Museum, Athens.

5. Choremi Benachi Cotton Company advertisement. Copyright Elie Politi, Annuaire des Sociétés Égyptiennes par Actions (Alexandria: Procaccia, 1938).

6. C.M. Salvago & Company advertisement. Copyright Elie Politi, Annuaire des Sociétés Égyptiennes par Actions (Alexandria: Procaccia, 1938).

7. March 25 celebration (Greek Independence Day), sometime in the 1930s, at the Greek Orthodox Church of Constantine and Helen in Bulaq, Cairo. Near the church steps in white uniforms are the students of the Achilopoulio Women's School; in the foreground are the Cairo Philharmonic and the Greek Boy Scouts bands. Photograph courtesy of ELIA/MIET Photographic Archive.

8. Visit of Christophoros II, Greek Orthodox patriarch of Alexandria, to the Greek community in the Nile Delta town of Mit Ghamr, 1950s. Photograph courtesy of ELIA/MIET Photographic Archive.

9. A lottery ticket issued by the Greek community organization in Ibrahimiya in April 1951 to support fundraising for its philanthropic activities. Photograph courtesy of ELIA/MIET Photographic Archive.

10. Salvago family photo at home in Alexandria, Easter 1945. From left to right: the fifth person is Angeliki "Kiki," wife of Costantinos Salvago; next is Julia Salvago, daughter of Mikés and Argine Salvago, and the future Mrs. Melas; Argine Salvago, née Benachi, wife of Mikés Salvago; Irene, daughter of Constantinos and Kiki Salvago; and Thamar and Manolis Loukas Benachi. Copyright 2018 by the Benaki Museum, Athens.

11. The Automobile Electrical Repair shop of Manolis Coutroubakis at 1 Doubreh (now Soliman al-Halaby) Street in the Tawfiqiya neighborhood of Cairo, taken a few years after the shop opened in 1926. Coutroubakis is seated, wearing a dark colored shirt. Standing behind him are the Egyptian employees. Coutroubakis arrived in Egypt from Crete with his mother in 1905 when he was five years old, and he  attended the Abet School for Boys in Cairo. Over the decades his shop acquired an excellent reputation, his customers including members of the families of Nasser and Muhammad Naguib, as well as businesses such as Groppi's pastry shop, the Hassan Allam construction company, and the EgyptAir airline company. Coutroubakis handed over his shop to his employees when he left Egypt for Greece in 1973. Photograph courtesy of Maria Adamantidis Coutroubaki Personal Archive, Athens.

12. Nasser and Archbishop Makarios, the leader of the Cypriot anticolonial struggle, in Alexandria, 1958. Photograph courtesy of ELIA/ MIET Photographic Archive.

The preservation and promotion of ties with Greece and a sense of Greekness continued, quite remarkably, against a background of serious obstacles in an Egypt experiencing a cascade of socioeconomic changes. There was an economic downturn in the wake of the First World War, and another after the Wall Street Crash of 1929, and especially in the 1930s, Egyptianization measures were on the rise. Greek presence in the provinces was growing smaller and smaller—though demographically, the total number of Greeks in Egypt still hovered around one hundred thousand on the eve of the Second World War. The economic difficulties put pressure on the Greek ethnic associations, contributions diminished, and welfare needs took away funds that might have been used for schools or cultural activities. Despite all this, the interwar period witnessed a continued involvement in Greek party politics. Community organizations continued their work of instilling and preserving Greek identity through the schools and cultural initiatives, such as the commemoration of national Greek holidays. Ethnic associations continued their activities and new ones emerged. The ethnic press, notwithstanding a few losses, continued to flourish: Cairo had five Greek daily newspapers on the eve of the Second World War. Literary circles continued meeting, debating, and published a number of journals in the 1920s and 1930s. There was a stream of artists, singers, theater companies, athletes, and sports teams that arrived from Greece to exhibit, to perform, and play. Journalists recorded their amazement at what they considered the huge size of the Greek communities in Egypt's major cities, the many Greek shops and businesses they saw everywhere, and of course, the wealth of the upper classes, for the benefit of their readers in Greece. The playwright Alekos Lidorikis, who toured Egypt in 1938 and published his impressions in an Athens daily, remarked that "Alexandria is not a Greek colony; it is a second, small Greece that stretches from the city center all the way to Ramla and Ibrahimiya."[4]

Political Ties with the Homeland

On the eve of the First World War, when Greece became involved in the Balkan Wars, a total of thirteen thousand Greeks went from Egypt to fight in the Greek army. The volunteers came from across the Greek social strata; among them were Emmanuel Benachi's two sons, Antonis and Alexandros. Theocharis Cozzika, the owner of the alcohol distillery, was far too old to enlist, but he and his brother Polychronis made a significant financial donation to the Greek state and funded repairs that the battleship *Averoff* required. Thaleia Flora-Caravia, the wife of Nikos Caravias, the editor of the Alexandrian daily newspaper *Efimeris*, went to the front as a correspondent, even though she was a painter rather than a journalist. She produced a series of sketches depicting daily life at the front that are currently being exhibited in several museums in Greece.

The community organization in Alexandria contributed toward sending over a Red Cross field hospital with twelve doctors and a staff of ten nurses, two pharmacists, supplies, and three hundred boxes of medical instruments. Many Greek employers continued to pay the volunteers' wages, and a committee was arranged for assistance to be offered to their families. Greece emerged victorious from the Balkan Wars with territorial acquisitions that included Macedonia, Epirus, and several islands in the northern Aegean, including Chios, Lesvos, and Lemnos, and further south, the island of Crete. But very soon the country suddenly became politically polarized. When the First World War broke out in 1914, King Constantine favored neutrality, which would have benefited the Central Powers, while Prime Minister Venizelos believed Greece should fight on the side of the Anglo–French Entente. The clash between the two men was the beginning of Greece's so-called national schism that mortally divided the country's politics between supporters of Venizelos and supporters of the monarchy for the next three decades. The conflict divided the Greeks of Egypt, with the majority supporting Venizelos. It was an attitude that came naturally because of Venizelos's alignment with Britain and France, two powers with great political and cultural influence in Egypt. There could be no doubt that Britain was acting against those who were not aligning with the Entente. It deposed Khedive Abbas II in December 1914 because they believed he was sympathetic to the Central Powers, and replaced the "Veiled Protectorate" with a formal one. Nonetheless, there were supporters of the king of Greece in Egypt, a sign that the polarization and its intensity had carried over to Egypt, remaining after the First World War and the Greco–Turkish war that ended in 1922.

The Venizelist and promonarchist divisions in Egypt remained even when it was obvious that neither side in Athens was courting support from its diaspora communities as they had done in the past. The end of the Greco–Turkish War had extinguished the Great Idea, the plan to create a Greater Greece incorporating Ottoman territories considered historically Greek within Greece's borders, and given the inundation of refugees whose resettlement became possible thanks to American aid, both Venizelist and monarchist governments had much less reason to call on the support of diaspora Greeks. They were also not in a position to offer any effective diplomatic or material support. In the case of Egypt, all the Greek Ministry of Foreign Affairs did was to advise the Greeks to find a way to deal with the nationalists and to make token representations to the British and Egyptian authorities. There were several meetings held in Athens and Venizelos's Vice President and Minister of Foreign Affairs Andreas Michalakopoulos visited Egypt in 1930 but was unable to obtain any favors for the Greeks at a time when the abolition of the Capitulations was drawing closer and closer. The Greek consular authorities in Egypt were also ineffective despite their efforts made in consultation with the community's leaders. And yet, the umbilical cord to the homeland was much too strong for the Greeks to contemplate cutting it. Homeland politics continued to loom large in their lives and on the front pages of their daily newspapers, and Greek consuls in Egypt were present at every important community event.

It was the turn of the monarchists to make their presence felt among the Greeks in Egypt between 1936 and 1940. In the early part of 1936 Venizelos and other major Greek political figures died, while the rise of the communist party added to the tensions with which the ongoing rift between Venizelists and monarchists had imbued Greek politics. Using the communist threat as a pretext, Ioannis Metaxas, a staunch anti-Venizelist former general whom the king appointed prime minister in 1936, established a dictatorship, with the king giving his tacit support. The regime took the name of the date Metaxas seized power, August 4. The regime's supporters in Egypt were a minority but they had the support of the Greek ambassador and consular authorities. They established a branch of the regime's youth organization, known by its Greek acronym EON, but its numbers remained low. The outbreak of the Second World War would bring a new phase in the close relationship of the Greek of Egypt with the homeland's politics.

Community Organizations

The mainstay of the connection with Greece, and more generally the preservation of Greek identity, continued to be the community organizations, the church, and the schools, along with a constellation of ethnic associations and clubs. The growing numbers of Greeks placed greater demands on the services the community organizations provided, which meant the establishment of a growing number of associations, clubs, and societies. As long as there remained a wealthy class of Greeks in Egypt, the community organizations were in a position to maintain their function. Mikés Salvago told the Greek Ministry for Foreign Affairs in 1924 that they were a substitute for the Greek state for the benefit of the Greeks of Egypt. A few years earlier, the president of the Greek Consular Court in Alexandria, speaking to the newly arrived Greek ambassador, explained the multiple functions of the community organizations—which were inspired by "the Hellenic idea." These included the moral and material development of the Greeks of Egypt, the "cultivation of the Hellenic spirit and the idea of the motherland." The schools, operating on the basis of the curricula in Greece, promoted Greek culture and language. The hospitals cared for Greeks, kept them healthy, and enabled Greeks to engage in medical and scientific research.[5] Clearly the underlying concept for the community organizations and the other ethnic associations was that the Greeks of Egypt were a Greek diaspora community that should maintain ties to the homeland.

Thirdly, because these ethnic institutions relied exclusively on donations by the wealthy—the Greek state did not contribute a penny—the philanthropic contributions signaled a hierarchical structure in the community writ large, with the wealthy on top and owed deference and respect from the rest of the Greek community. This enabled the wealthy to assume a hegemonic role through which they exercised a degree of control while maintaining their status through benevolence rather than force. No doubt their personal motivations for giving may have also been based on their Greek Orthodox faith, which values philanthropy, or deeper, psychological motivations.[6] But because of the ethnic nature of this form of philanthropy, it was frequently described as a form of patriotism and a benchmark against which patriotism could be measured. A Greek judge wrote in 1920 that the major benefactors "are the most ardently Greek of our citizens" and they "undoubtedly deserve our admiration and gratitude for their unselfishness, their generosity and their dedication in administering communal affairs and in providing multiple protection to the deprived popular classes."[7]

All this gradually began to change in the early 1920s when the total number of Greeks in Alexandria had increased and more persons in need made claims on the resources of the community organizations. This was due to the adverse effects of the First World War on many Greeks with low-paying jobs and the arrival of ethnic Greeks who had fled Turkey. The community organization in Alexandria introduced a 12.5 percent across-the-board salary reduction of all employees except those in the Greek hospital. Two years later, the organization created a department of "information and statistics" whose purpose was to identify wealthy Greeks in the city who were potential contributors.

That year, 1923, the community organization sought permission from Greece's Ministry of Foreign Affairs to transfer from Athens to Alexandria its deposits of gold drachmas. Greek laws forbade currency exports and the organization cited the need "to pursue its national objectives without hindrance." With the homeland struggling to deal with a huge influx of refugee ethnic Greeks from Turkey this was not a good time to ask for favors. Even in the best of times Athens expected to take rather than give to the diaspora, and therefore it rejected the request. At the same time the organization's executive committee noticed a decline in the number and size of the bequests it had received. This, it discovered, was because the Greek government had raised inheritance tax and death duties, which also applied to Greek citizens living abroad. This meant that potential donors withheld contributions to the community organization, prompting Salvago to write to the Greek Ministry of Foreign Affairs, which eventually relented and awarded the organization a quarter of the inheritance taxes it collected in Egypt.

In 1930, the government reduced the inheritance tax but by then, as Salvago explained in another communication to the ministry, it was too late to make up for the lost income from donations because more Greeks were leaving the provinces and moving to Alexandria, while at the same time the community organization was reeling from the effects of Egypt's economic crisis. Salvago ended by saying the Greeks of Alexandria had reached the end of their tether as many had used up all their savings and were out of a job. Had he been asked, he could have backed up all he was saying with plenty of facts. The non-paying patients treated at the Greek hospital in Alexandria had increased from 876 in 1920 to 1,864 in 1933. At the Greek schools, the percentage of students on free or reduced fees had jumped from 68 percent during the 1921–22 school year to 97 percent in the 1933–34 school year. In 1934–35 the operational budget of community organization institutions showed an LE10,000 deficit.[8]

There was only one significant donation the community organization received in the interwar period: LE60,000 from Theocharis Cozzika followed by another LE50,000 contribution from his wife Angeliki, intended for the establishment of a new Greek hospital. It was the largest single donation since the time the Salvago family had contributed over LE100,000 in 1901. The cornerstone was laid in 1932 and there followed several years of debates within the community organization over whether it could undertake the administrative costs and responsibility of running such a large institution. Ultimately in 1938 the old hospital was closed and the new one was inaugurated. It was a grand, imposing building that contained the latest in medical and scientific equipment, with 350 beds for patients. While its layout followed the appropriate needs for a medical facility, "details such as the stylized classical entrance and the neo-Byzantine arcade surrounding the main courtyard" conferred "a Greek identity to the building."[9]

Inevitably the difficulties the community organization of Alexandria experienced led to challenges to its "undemocratic" structure. This had become a favorite theme of the *Tachydromos*, especially when the organization issued one of its frequent appeals for funds. "It is not enough for Mr. Salvago to launch an appeal and for the Patriarch to second it," thundered an editorial in 1927. "What he must do first is to pull down the wall that divides the organization from the community," the paper suggested, adding "there should be a system whereby every Greek, from the simple breadwinner upward can contribute his penny and be allowed to express his opinion on communal affairs and exercise control over the organization's finances."

In response to this and other voices, the Alexandria community organization launched a membership drive and within a year its members increased tenfold, but the income from dues only quadrupled because the actual amount paid varied according to income. Over the next few years the membership numbers fell because many felt they could not keep up the annual payments even at reduced rates. It vindicated the supporters of the status quo who saw the community organizations as bodies that combined notions of aristocracy and democracy. Everyone, they said, benefited from the range of services, but only a few paid and therefore had the right to govern.[10]

Greek Schools

The community organization-run schools, the few run by the patriarchate, and the private Greek schools remained the most important instrument that reproduced Greek identity and ties with the Greek homeland. Ironically perhaps, the slowness with which the educational system responded to the urgent calls for reform and anticipation of the Egyptianization of the economy in the interwar period ensured that the curriculum would remain effective in promoting Greekness. Rooted in the old perspective of regarding the Greeks of Egypt an extension of Greece, the community organizations judged the performance of their school according to the standards and curriculum of the schools in Greece. This meant an emphasis on subjects such as Greek language, literature, history, and religious education. An inspector sent to Egypt by the Greek Ministry of Education in 1939 reported that he was very impressed by the standard of teaching, the students, and the facilities of the Greek community organizations schools, and that the schools functioned the same way as schools in Greece. Moreover, the Greek schools in Egypt compared favorably to schools in Greece and other diaspora communities, in many ways going beyond the curriculum, for example, in the existence of student-run councils and the quality of student-run magazines the high schools published. In terms of the numbers of those magazines that appeared between 1915 and 1936, in Greece or abroad, Alexandria came fourth overall with seventeen, Mansura eighth with eight magazines, and Cairo tenth with four. Mansura's high ranking was due to the quality of the teachers and the outstanding facilities the schools there acquired in 1926, which gave them an excellent reputation and made its boarding school well-known in Greece and other Greek diaspora communities. Reflecting the ties to Greek culture the schools cultivated, the most important and longest-running magazine at the Mansura schools was named the *Glaux*, the ancient Greek name for owl, a symbol of wisdom. Although the magazine was primarily populated by articles in Greek, it included articles in Arabic, French, and English.[11]

Greek education became a battleground that pitted conservatives against reform-minded teachers in the interwar period. Their debate, initially at least and especially through the 1920s, was centered around whether the schools should switch from the more archaic and formal *katharevousa* form of the Greek language over to the more vernacular form known as *demotike*. The reformers focused on language but also sought to introduce more modern teaching methods as well. This was a debate polarizing the educational and intellectual world in Greece and reflected among the Greeks of Egypt. Even the name of the organization advocating reform in Alexandria, founded in 1919 and which spread to the rest of Egypt, Εκπαιδευτικός Όμιλος Αιγύπτου (Educational Society of Egypt), was the same as the one founded in Athens in 1910, the Εκπαιδευτικός Όμιλος (Educational Society). Greek intellectuals in Egypt became involved in the conflict over the most appropriate form of Greek at the same time as the subject was boiling over in Greece prior to the First World War.

In the educational sphere in Egypt, the first big step toward language reform in the schools came in 1918 thanks to Athanasios Marselos, a thirty-year-old teacher at the community school at Kafr al-Zayyat who had been born near Smyrna and attended Smyrna's prestigious Evangeliki School before going on to study at the equally respected Maraslio School in Athens. After school administrators objected to Marselos's advocacy of the *demotike* and the parallel de-emphasizing of ancient Greek, which was considered sacrosanct by the educational establishment, he resigned and opened a private school in Kafr al-Zayyat. Despite the support it received from the supporters of the *demotike* in Alexandria, it lasted only three years, after which it succumbed to a lack of funds. But the school galvanized the reform movement in education, which began to gain ground steadily throughout the Greek schools in Egypt.[12]

The overall statistics on schools point to growing numbers throughout the interwar period. Figures comparing the school years of 1912–13 with 1927–28 show that the total number of Greek schools grew from forty-six to fifty-seven and the number of students from 8,177 to 11,949. The only region where the numbers dipped was that of Upper Egypt, something that was expected because of migration to Cairo and Alexandria. But by the late 1920s the numbers were impressive. In 1927–28 there were twelve schools with 2,592 students in Cairo, fourteen schools with 6,600 students in Alexandria, six schools in Port Said and Tanta, five in Zagazig, four in Mansura, and three in Tanta and Minya. The primary and secondary school teachers were all from mainland Greece, Cyprus, or the Ottoman Empire but beginning in 1930 more of the teachers were Egyptian-born Greeks.[13] A study of the Greek schools in Mansura offers a good picture of the situation of Greek education in interwar Egypt. With 1,500 Greeks living in the town and many within commuting distance, Mansura's Greek schools flourished during that period, not only in terms of the numbers of students, but also of teachers and the quality of the curriculum. This success was achieved by a purposeful adaptation to the changing circumstances, including the introduction of Arabic-language classes, thanks to the community organization treating the schools as its primary responsibility at the expense of any other activities.[14]

Cultural and Intellectual Life

Cavafy singlehandedly made Alexandria a recognized center of Greek letters during the first half of the twentieth century. By the mid-1920s literary circles in Greece were vigorously debating whether Cavafy was the equal to Kostis Palamas, who was considered by many at the time as Greece's national poet. In 1926 the Greek government awarded Cavafy a medal in honor of his contributions to Greek letters. Notwithstanding the recognition he gained toward the end of his life, Cavafy led a somewhat marginal existence. As one of his biographers puts it, "though he continued to take part in the social life of the established Greek community and though he remained keenly aware of having been born a rich man's son, his poverty and perhaps more important, his homosexuality inevitably made him to some degree an outsider." Thus his early and middle-aged life in Alexandria "was clearly restricted . . . partly *mondain*, partly secret, limited in literary and intellectual associations."[15]

Those Greek literary circles that Cavafy was part of were important enough to gain recognition and respect from the intellectual establishment in Athens. Their activities ranged from activism on issues of education to the publication of magazines and the promotion of Greek letters. Two of the many Greek-language literary magazines published in Alexandria made the city an important center of Greek literary production in the second decade of the twentieth century. *Nea Zoe* (*New Life*) appeared in 1904, published by a group of young men who also established a literary society by the same name. They soon embraced the growing trend in Greece, support for the *demotike* form of Greek. Very soon *Nea Zoe* was publishing pieces sent by major Greek poets and writers. But the refusal to publish one poem on moral grounds prompted some members of the group to leave and begin publishing another literary journal, *Grammata (Letters)*, beginning in 1911. It soon established itself as another prestigious venue for the publication of Greek prose and poetry. After running into trouble with the censors over a piece that mentioned incest, *Grammata* ceased publication for a few years and reappeared in 1920 for a short while, with an even greater emphasis on philosophical and sociological articles that reflected the ongoing anxieties and concerns about western civilization in the post-First World War era.

Cavafy, not wishing to alienate either group, was in contact with the editorial boards of both journals. Another important Greek intellectual who was part of those literary and intellectual circles was the Marxist sociologist Georgios Skleros. Following his studies in Germany, Skleros settled in Helwan near Cairo prior to the First World War because he suffered from tuberculosis and believed the dry climate was beneficial to his health. He spent the last years of his life in Egypt, where he completed two of his three major studies and gave several public lectures. He died there in 1919. Skleros is considered the intellectual 'father' of Greek Marxist and sociological thought.

Nea Zoe and *Grammata*, both of which ceased publication in 1921, were the most prestigious literary magazines, but they were only the tip of the iceberg. The 1920s and 1930s witnessed two more respected publications, *Alexandrine Techne (Alexandrian Art)*, which ran from 1926 to 1931, and *Panegyptia (Panegyptian)*. One of the editors of *Alexandrine Techne* was Rika Singopoulou, who along with her husband Alekos was very close to Cavafy. She wrote that the journal aimed to promote modern Greek literary production of Alexandrian Greeks. Between 1920 and 1940 there were eight Greek printing houses in Alexandria, three in Cairo, two in Port Said, and one in Kafr al-Zayyat, Mit Ghamr, and Zagazig. One in Alexandria belonged to the Greek Orthodox patriarchate, which published several journals. Between 1914 and 1952 over forty journals and about a thousand Greek-language books were published in Egypt. The journals ranged from literary and religious to economic and sports-oriented.

Most Greeks in Egypt may not have been interested in developments in the literary world, but many of them read one or more of the many Greek-language newspapers and magazines published in Egypt. Their coverage of Greek events, from politics to high or lowbrow culture and sports, connected their readers with the homeland, and coverage of community events helped strengthen Greek ethnic identity. Of course the fact that with few exceptions they were in Greek indicates the depth of that identity. The Alexandrian *Tachydromos* and the Cairene *Phos (Light)*, both of which had begun publication in the late nineteenth century, remained the largest circulation Greek newspapers. In 1910 the *Ephimeris (Newspaper)* appeared in Alexandria and became the liberal *Tachydromos*'s conservative rival. And in 1916 the *Kleio (Cleo)* appeared in Cairo as the competitor to the conservative *Phos*. What is striking is the number of newspapers that appeared after the First World War. Several that came out in the 1920s were short-lived, but in 1932 the publication of the *Anatole (East)* in Alexandria was another direct challenge to the *Tachydromos*. The new paper was also liberal but gave extensive coverage to the concerns of the community about its future. The liberal-leaning *Kyrix (Herald)* appeared in Cairo in 1936 and lasted until 1947, while the *Emera (Day)* appeared in Alexandria in 1942. There were also many short-lived satirical newspapers that were evidently popular in the interwar period.

Cavafy died in 1933 on his seventieth birthday, April 29. Especially after English translations of his poems began appearing after the Second World War, his reputation and interest in his work have grown. The Greek cultural environment that bred him has receded into relative obscurity though it is recognized in studies of the history of Greek letters. The richness of that environment was remarkable given growing concerns about Egyptianization, thus serving as a reminder that for many Greeks Egypt was their home, and Greece their homeland, and they saw no contradiction in embracing both at the same time.

Greece Comes to Egypt

The establishment of a Greek microcosm in Egypt during the Second World War brought an interregnum in the ongoing process of determining the status of the Greeks because of the prevailing wartime conditions and the wholehearted involvement of many Greek residents in Greek political conflicts between 1940 and 1944. The Greeks in Egypt were no strangers to the passions of Greek politics, but the wartime era presented entirely new challenges. Metaxas's death in early 1941 had helped discredit his dictatorial legacy, which suffered at a time when Greece was fighting against much worse forms of dictatorship. Meanwhile, within occupied Greece, the small communist party, well-versed in clandestine activity because of the persecution it had suffered during the interwar period, was able to take the lead in organizing a resistance movement against the Axis occupiers.

The communists were careful to present a patriotic antifascist front and call for a democratic postwar Greece, but their ideological track record and their attachment to the Soviet Union meant their appeal among Greeks was far from universal. Soon republican and right-wing organizations, along with collaborationists, emerged. Occupied Greece witnessed both acts of sabotage against the Axis and internecine political conflict. All this, as had been the case with the Venizelist royalist clash in the interwar period, was reproduced among the ranks of the Greeks in Egypt as well as those in exile. The British saw the creation of this microcosm as an opportunity to gauge public opinion in occupied Greece. The BBC requested information from the British embassy in Cairo about the discussions the Greeks there were holding in order to determine the content of its broadcasts to occupied Greece.

Initially, the Greeks of Egypt put aside their partisan differences and supported the homeland when it entered the Second World War in October of 1940 by repelling an Italian attack launched over the Greco–Albanian border. They continued to offer material support for Greece's defense, which ended in May 1941 when the king, the government, Greek forces, and British units that had also been fighting the Axis invaders were evacuated to Egypt. One of the British officers who arrived in Egypt and Greece and who would have a continued involvement in Greek wartime affairs, and then write books about Greece, noticed that "the devotion of Egyptian Greeks to their little country across the water has always been intense . . . it is an insatiable nostalgia. When the Germans occupied Greece, the Greeks of the outer world suffered mental agonies as great as the physical agonies of their cousins at home."[16] Indeed, community leaders established a National Committee of Greeks of Alexandria after Italy's attack on Greece, with the goal of invigorating the morale of the community and offering help. The committee expanded its scope and was renamed the National Committee of Greeks in Egypt and in just over six months raised LE150,000. The lawyer Georgios Roussos, a known Venizelist, was president, and the presidents of the community organizations of Alexandria and Cairo were on the board of directors.[17]

The arrival of the king, the exiled government, and the military and naval units to Egypt, and the subsequent ideological battles they fought over what would be Greece's postwar political future dragged the Greeks of Egypt away from patriotism and into a vortex of political partisanship. The king of Greece, Georgios II, and the government arrived in Egypt to a mixed welcome by the Greeks. The very fact they had fled Greece under Axis occupation was a blow to the morale and pride of the Greeks of Egypt.[18] But the ambivalence in the reception was because many regarded the government as a continuation of the Metaxas dictatorship, even though the dictator had chosen to fight rather than capitulate to fascist Italy. He had died before Greece's defenses began to crumble because Nazi Germany sent troops to do the job the Italians had been unable to carry out. By the time of the evacuation to Egypt the prime minister of Greece was Emmanuel Tsouderos, a moderate Venizelist.

Over the next year the government shed the pro-Metaxas ministers and the dictatorship's legal framework, but it continued to face instability because the emergence of a communist-led resistance movement during the Axis occupation threw into doubt the chances that a postwar Greece would welcome back the king. Foreign Office officials were aware that by establishing itself in Egypt the government had to assert itself early on. One of them noted in an internal memo that "I think the King and

M. Tsouderos are fully alive to the danger that the large Greek colony in the Middle East . . . may get out of hand unless under strong government control."[19] The British authorities in Egypt were exercising censorship on the Egyptian and ethnic press. It was a necessary wartime measure, but it also made them familiar with the particular and strong political affiliation of the Greek newspapers, which had a total daily circulation of about twenty-five thousand. In Alexandria the *Tachydromos*, which had the highest circulation, was Venizelist. The *Anatole (East)* and the *Imerisia Nea (Daily News)* were right-wing and the *Ephimeris* was center-left. In Cairo the *Phos*, the second largest in circulation, was right-wing and the *Kyrix* was left-wing.

As soon as they arrived in Egypt the king and government did their best to increase their popularity by attending meetings of the various committees and organizations working for the Greek cause. There was a committee of the Greek Red Cross and several newly established relief organizations, such as the Soldier's Parcel, Soldier's Vest, Cairo Committee for the Greek Soldier, and Sailor's House in Alexandria. The community organization in Alexandria placed its modern hospital, the Kotsikion, at the disposal of the Greek Armed Forces, and the organization in Cairo allowed the army to set up its headquarters on the top floor of its Xenakion School.[20] There were many social occasions as well, including visits to the Greek-owned family houses in the Quartier Grec in Alexandria and the Cairo suburb of Heliopolis. Publicly, all the Greeks patriotically demonstrated respect and support for the king and the prime minister. But just below the surface many had started questioning whether Greek politics had moved on from the Metaxas dictatorship and whether the king was prepared to go along with the new antifascist democratic climate that the struggle against the Axis had created. And when the king and the government left Egypt to travel to London via South Africa, their absence allowed the political debates to come out in the open.

The presence of Admiral Sakellariou, who was an admirer of the late dictator Metaxas and remained in charge in Cairo as vice president of the government, contributed to the suspicion many Greeks in Egypt harbored toward the government. He confirmed those views when he allowed the Metaxas regime's youth organization EON to continue functioning in Egypt, though it changed its name and officially at least came under the protection of the Greek Orthodox Patriarchate of Alexandria. It ceased operations in 1942 only after the British authorities asked the patriarch to withdraw his support and he promptly complied.[21]

Patriarch Christophoros II's involvement in the Metaxas youth organization branch was an example of how the wartime conditions and the presence of Greek government officials opened up the possibility of change in the relative standing of Greek ethnic organizations in Egypt. The patriarch had taken up his post in Alexandria on the eve of the Second World War, having served as the bishop of a province of the patriarchate, which encompassed Ismailiya, Suez, and Zagazig. Maybe there he had observed the ways the patriarchate was beholden to the community organizations and decided to try and do something about it when he became patriarch. He was quick to make his own political views known when the Greek government arrived in Egypt and distanced himself from the general attitude of the community leadership by stating that only promonarchists should be serving in the government.[22] He began a legal dispute with the Cairo community organization over property claims, and he clashed with both the Alexandria and Cairo community leaders over the content of the school curricula. Christophoros was not shy to seize the initiative and convinced the Anglo–Egyptian authorities not to consider the ethnic Greeks of the Italian-occupied Dodecanese Islands as Italian subjects and intern them, pointing out that they were Greek Orthodox. He chaired a committee, which raised almost LE15,000 for the Dodecanese Greeks in need and was involved in several other relief initiatives. He saw the war through a religious prism. In blessing an assembly of new recruits to the Greek Army in Alexandria in 1942, he told them to defend at all costs the religion of their fathers and secondly their country, and speaking about the enemy he said the Germans were idolaters and the Italians "if not idolaters" were "Catholics."[23]

Finally, in February 1942 the king and the Greek government officially revoked Metaxas's August 4 regime and restored the democratic constitution the dictator had abolished. The trouble was that Greek politics were shifting dramatically leftward and many liberals joined the communists and their supporters in expressing doubts that the king would automatically return to Greece in the postwar era. British reports that there were deep Venizelist–royalist divisions among the Greek forces stationed in Egypt and elsewhere in the Middle East persuaded the king and the prime minister to leave London and travel to Cairo. One of the three battalions that made up the First Greek Army Brigade in the Middle East included Greeks of Egypt who were either called up or volunteered. Much of the rest of the Greek community in Egypt was questioning whether a postwar Greece should include the king, who was tainted by his association with Metaxas and the anti-Venizelists. The Foreign Office still believed that Greek public opinion in Egypt was a gauge of the feelings within Greece itself, and continued to use its influence in order to persuade the monarch and the government to take steps to appear more democratic and inclusive. One such sign was the replacement of Sakellariou, the vice president of the government, by Panayotis Canellopoulos, a young liberal politician whom Tsouderos invited from Greece—assisting him to escape to Egypt.

Canellopoulos, having spent almost a year in occupied Greece, experienced somewhat of a culture shock when he arrived in Egypt. He had the same reaction as the officers and men who had experienced the difficult living conditions in wartime Britain and were shocked by the leisurely life they found in Egypt. The young Greek politician moreover did not belive that the views of the Greeks of Egypt were a more or less accurate reflection of those of the Greeks in occupied Greece. Instead, he found them somewhat spoilt and disengaged thanks to the security that Allied-controlled Egypt offered them. He also thought they were not sufficiently engaged politically. In his first public speech in Alexandria, at the Rialto Cinema, when he saw that only half the audience applauded his line that Greeks are friends of freedom, antidictatorial, and antifascist, he told them he would repeat it to give everyone the chance to applaud—and only then did he elicit cheers.

Canellopoulos was the nephew of a former prime minister and had studied law in Heidleberg and Munich and worked as a professor in the Athens Law School before becoming involved in politics. Thus when he met Greek community leaders, he left much less impressed than other visitors from Greece, who usually marveled at the leaders' wealth and the range of philanthropic institutions they had founded. Instead he regarded them as an oligarchy, which did not govern democratically and were not representative of all Alexandrian Greeks. When those same community leaders strongly protested the call-up of Greeks of Egypt to the Greek Armed Forces, Canellopoulos felt his view of them was confirmed. Many Greek residents in Egypt volunteered and joined the Greek forces. In December 1941, with the permission of the Egyptian authorities, the Greek military issued a call-up for all Greek males resident in Egypt. Over seven thousand Greeks enlisted, abandoning their studies and jobs. The Greek government made no provision for their families and ignored concerns about whether those called up would find their old jobs at the end of the war.[24] It was left to the community organizations to offer material and moral support, until the Greek government got round to offering monetary compensation to the families of all those who enlisted in 1943.

Canellopoulos and other Greek politicians assumed that fighting for Greece entailed sacrifices. But the community leaders insisted that their future in Egypt also be taken into account, especially since the contribution of the Greeks of Egypt was substantial. They staffed skilled positions, such as operators of radio communications, interpreters, clerks, engineers, gunners, and drivers. Had they not been part of the Greek units, as a character in Tsirkas's *Drifting Cities* solemnly declares, the units would have suffered "a complete breakdown."[25]

Canellopoulos's entry into the government was ultimately insufficient to stem the rising tide against right-wing officers in the Greek Armed Forces, a leftward tilt that was also reflected with the emergence of the Greek Liberation League, known by its Greek acronym EAS, by a group of communists and socialists within the Greek community. They had been part of international antifascist Marxist groups in Egypt in the 1930s. With the outbreak of the war the group broke up into national groups, even though internal debates had always raised the prospect of the 'Egyptianization' of the movement. The Greeks joined together to focus on Greece's affairs; others in the group, especially Jews such as Henri Curiel and Marcel Israël, remained committed to the cause of Egyptianization.[26] The members of the Greek EAS were lawyers such as Yanni Lachovaris, and teachers such as Giorgos Athanasiades, headmaster of Cairo's Xenakion School, and a poet, Theodosis Pierides, and others, all of whom the British intelligence report described as "near communists of the intellectual variety."[27] The organization's Greek-language monthly journal had existed before the war and was called Αιγυπτιώτης Ελλην and *al-Yunani al-mutamassir (The Egyptianized Greek)* in Arabic. In another sign of the absorption into Greek affairs its editors changed the name to Ελλην *(Hellene)* and stated its goals were to coordinate their struggle with that in Greece. Its circulation reached 2,500 in 1942, and copies were distributed not only throughout Egypt but also in Palestine, Syria, and Sudan.

In real terms the EAS's impact remained somewhat limited. It was the left-wing antifascist movement in the Greek Armed Forces that shook things up.[28] Initially it was royalist army officers who resigned in protest of actions taken by the republican commander. The Greek Brigade then participated in the Battle of al-Alamein in the summer of 1942 but after that it was brought back to the rear. By the end of the year left-wing agitation directed against royalist officers was on the rise. By March 1943 the brigade was riven by political demonstrations, and the Antifascist Organization of the Army (ASO), which had been formed by communists, orchestrated the submission of a set of demands addressed to the British government. There followed several days of confusion and uncertainty. The king arrived from London and Canellopoulos became the sacrificial lamb and was replaced by Georgios Roussos, the seventy-five-year-old Alexandrian lawyer who had served as a Greek government minister back in the 1920s under Venizelos.

The government had taken another, albeit small, step leftward, and it seemed—to British officials at least—that calm had been restored. The Greek Independence Day celebrations on March 25 took place with no trouble either among the community or the Armed Forces. "The King has been well received by the Egyptian Greeks and a number of loyal messages have been sent to him by Greek communities in various parts of Egypt," a British official in Cairo reported to the Foreign Office, explaining the political disturbances in the army were of an antifascist but not an antimonarchist nature. There were few genuine communists, the report noted, but the officers and men were "intensely politically minded" and communist propaganda gained some traction because some unattached Greek officers in Cairo were probably genuinely fascist.[29] But left-wing activities in the barracks would continue over the following months and the British began taking strict measures.

While the British tightened their control of left-wing activities in the Greek military units, the Greeks of Egypt continued to closely follow Greek politics in which the left-wing resistance organizations were gaining more influence from the summer of 1943 onward. By then, life had returned to normal, or at least its wartime normal, because the Allied troops, victorious in the North African front, were about to launch an attack on Italy. The war was moving further and further away from Egypt, but Greek politics were moving closer. The king had remained in London but Prime Minister Tsouderos and the rest of the government were now permanently based in Cairo, trying to monitor the situation in Greece and dealing with what had become the main issue to be decided upon when Greece was liberated: whether the king would return before or after a referendum was held on the monarchy.

The poet Georgios Seferis, who was awarded the Nobel Prize in

Literature in 1963, was serving as the government's press attaché at the time, and had a front seat to the swirl of Greek politicking that was going on behind the scenes. He excoriated the Greek politicians in and out of office who had congregated in Egypt, writing about the streets of Cairo littered with banana peels; "some dropped by Arabs, others by the politicians," whom he called "the whores of politics, who gathered in the evenings at the Shepheard's Hotel" in Cairo.[30] As part of the Foreign Office's interest in gauging the views of the resistance groups operating in Greece about the country's postwar future, it arranged for several representatives of those groups to be secretly flown out of Greece and brought to Cairo in August for talks. Inevitably, the representatives, who were engaged in fighting a guerilla war, initially thought they had landed in some sort of dreamland. One of them wrote subsequently that he felt that Cairo, along with the exiled government and the political intrigue going on far removed from the real developments in Greece, "resembled a large *café chantant*."[31] When those of them who belonged to the communist organizations met with the communist activists in the Armed Forces and the Greeks of Egypt who were in the pro-left-wing EAS, they were pleasantly surprised, though they advised them to be more moderate and include liberals who opposed the king's return to Greece. They repeated that message in the several public meetings they held before returning to Greece.

The EAS, accordingly, decided to mark the third anniversary of Greece's entry into the Second World War with public lectures and an exhibition that highlighted the suffering of the Greek people under Axis occupation and the work of the resistance organizations, both the communist-backed National Liberation Front (EAM), its military wing, the Greek Popular Liberation Army (ELAS), and the republican National Democractic Greek League (EDES). Seferis helped by providing them with photographs, documentary evidence, and clandestine resistance newspapers that had been smuggled out of Greece and kept at the government's press office. He also wrote the introduction to the exhibition's catalog. Prime Minister Tsouderos was invited and attended the opening in Cairo. After a few weeks the exhibit went on display at the Atelier des Beaux-Arts in Alexandria. EAS believed that the exhibit had succeeded in making the Greek resistance movement a source of pride for the Greeks of Egypt. It followed up within a few months with a successful drive to raise funds for vitamins for children in occupied Greece.[32]

There were moments of calm in the life of the Greek microcosm in

Egypt, as for example when Seferis and the English writer Lawrence Durrell, who was a British press officer in Egypt, were shown Cavafy's house and favorite haunts in Alexandria. But those occasions were not destined to last long.[33] As the end of the war approached, the Left versus the promonarchist Right tension in Greece escalated, with conservative liberals such as Tsouderos siding with the Right, and more radically minded liberals such as Roussos moving closer to the Left. Indeed, Roussos resigned from his post as vice premier because he felt Tsouderos was unable to persuade the king he should step aside and allow a referendum on the monarchy to be held immediately after the war. This was the beginning of a sharp polarization in Greek politics, with the king on one end and the communists on the other, a situation in which a liberal center would not hold.

The left-wing resistance organization in Greece decided to put pressure on the exiled government by forming a provisional government named the Political Committee for National Liberation (PEEA). Tsouderos thought he could ignore the news and did not mention that development in his speech to a large gathering of thirty thousand Greeks at the municipal stadium in Alexandria on the occasion of the commemoration of Greek Independence Day, March 25. The other main speaker, Mikés Salvago, mentioned the activities of the resistance groups in Greece, eliciting enthusiastic applause. At the gathering held in Cairo, the government speaker also chose not to mention the establishment of the PEEA.

EAS's reaction was to go ahead and hold meetings in Alexandria and Cairo, each attended by about two thousand persons, and triumphantly publicize PEAA's existence. Both meetings resolved to petition the government to begin negotiating with PEAA. It was a bold move by the left-wing leaders among the Greeks of Egypt.[34] Meanwhile, the left-wing leadership in the armed forces, mistaking the developments in Greece as a sign of an open confrontation, engineered public protests against the government and took action against the commanding officers who remained loyal to Tsouderos and the king. The events that unfolded in both the Greek military units and the warships, anchored in Alexandria, are described either as a pro-left-wing movement or as a series of mutinies. The seamen's union that represented the crews of the Greek merchant vessels that were in Alexandria at the time joined the protests.

In light of the critical situation, and upon Winston Churchill's instructions, British military and navy units intervened forcefully and restored order, and with Britain's backing the king arrived in Egypt to take control of his government, which was in disarray. Prime Minister Tsouderos resigned; Roussos was considered briefly as a possible replacement but Britain's influential ambassador to Greece, Reginald Leeper, rejected him as being too radical. Meanwhile the EAS dutifully came out in support of the uprisings in the armed forces although its leaders expressed concern about the wisdom of an open political challenge to the government on the part of the military. Soon the uprisings escalated with the occupation of the Greek military and naval headquarters in Cairo and Alexandria and the Greek Naval Cadet School in the Zizinia neighborhood of Alexandria. The leader of the seamen's union, Nikos Karayannis, barricaded himself along with two hundred seamen in the union's offices in Muhammad Ali Square in Alexandria.

The first moves by the British authorities were to arrest Karayannis and leading EAS members who had come out publicly in favor of the uprisings: Giorgos Athanasiades, Stratis Zerbinis, Yannis Lachovaris, and Michael Valtikos. This spelled the end of the EAS's activities even though those arrested were released within a few weeks, after British army and navy units ended the uprisings and restored order. While the operations were taking place, the British Army's Commander-in-Chief Henry "Jumbo" Wilson worried about possible support for the uprisings from Greeks in Alexandria and Cairo. But the Foreign Office, which in the past had considered the views of Greeks in Egypt as an indication of public opinion within occupied Greece, was no longer interested. Its instructions were, "Do not be influenced by possible anti-British sentiment among the local Greeks. It would be a grave mistake to end this grave business up in a pleasant kiss around."[35] This could serve as an epitaph not only for the end of the EAS's role but more generally on the ability of the Greeks of Egypt to shape Greek politics.

The end of the Second World War for Greece came in October 1944 and the exiled government made its way back to Athens via Italy—by the end of the year the Greek microcosm's sojourn in Egypt had come to an end. Liberated Greece did not return to normal. December witnessed bloody clashes between ELAS units and government forces backed by British troops. At the end of the month ELAS retreated northward; later a truce was agreed on, but it did not last and the clashes escalated into a civil war that ended in 1949 with the victory of the government. In the meantime, the so-called red terror of the Left was replaced by the white terror of the Right. Elections were held with the Left abstaining, and the right-wing victors organized a referendum on the monarchy, which predictably produced a result that brought the king back to Greece.

With Britain unable to continue its military backup of the Greek government, in 1947 President Truman announced his doctrine of US assistance to Greece and Turkey to help them fight international communism. Greece had become part of the Cold War under American tutelage, and its right-wing government managed to emerge victorious from the civil war in August 1949. Most of the liberals and republicans among the Greeks of Egypt could do nothing more than watch in horror as violent polarization ripped through Greek society. Conservatives, promonarchists, and moderates worried about the growth of the communist party supported the government side during the civil war. The radicals, after the end of the EAS, reorganized and became the Antifasistiki Protoporia (Antifascist Vanguard). It supported the Left, though like all Greeks of Egypt, it could now only follow events from a distance.

Postwar Attachment to the Homeland

Two hundred persons gathered at the Chatby Casino, a large dance hall and restaurant overlooking the sea in Alexandria, to honor the twenty-five-year tenure of Mikés Salvago as president of the Greek community organization. It was 1944, and the Greek government-in-exile was still in Egypt, so Prime Minister Georgios Papandreou attended. Also present were the minster for naval affairs, the Greek ambassador, Christophoros II, the Greek Orthodox Patriarch of Alexandria, and the three Greek judges at the Mixed Courts. The rest of the guests were a who's who list of the prominent Greeks of Alexandria and the rest of Egypt. In his speech, the prime minister mentioned that while Greece remained occupied, the Greeks of Egypt were the free part of Greece.

The rest of the event unfolded in a similarly patriotic tone with a celebration of Salvago's contributions and the achievements of the community in supporting the Greek presence in Egypt. Salvago in his speech expressed his confidence that the Greeks would remain the strongest foreign community in Egypt and continue to support Greece. He qualified that statement by mentioning that the community would be able to maintain itself as long as it adapted to postwar conditions. It was the only reference to the ominous developments that lay ahead for the Greeks in Egypt—the imposition of Egyptianization measures and the end of the Mixed Courts. Otherwise, the event, at which only Greeks were present, was a wholly hellenocentric affair. Yet many of those who were there to pay homage to Salvago and the achievements of the Greek community organization of Alexandria would soon be arguing that the Greeks enjoyed a close and special relationship with Egypt and should be spared the worst of the measures hanging over the heads of foreign communities.

One cannot help wondering whether the presence of the exiled government, the troops, and other civilians from Greece who sought refuge in Egypt somehow created a false sense of complacency among the Greeks of Egypt. The war years had turned the clock back and restored British control over Egypt. After a long period of hands-off policy toward the Greeks of Egypt, the government had come and settled in their midst. Yet it had no time to raise any issues related to their future with the Egyptian government. British troops escorted the Greek government back to Greece in October 1944, and in the civil war between government forces and left-wing guerilla units that broke out in Athens in December, the involvement of the British forces brought victory for the government. Churchill visited Athens; he had been in Cairo just over a year earlier. Was there not a new version of Pax Britannica being established in the eastern Mediterranean? And if so, was it not reasonable to assume that the reinforced bonds between Britain and Greece proved beneficial to the Greeks of Egypt? Yet such questions were not being raised in the ethnic press. The reason was that the rift between right and left that was polarizing Greek society was already being reproduced among the Greeks in Egypt.

In January 1945 the *Tachydromos* was warning that the leaders of the Greek ethnic associations in Egypt had not been elected so as to advocate for one or the other side of the Greek political divide. They had been put in office in order to defend the interests of the community, which required constant vigilance in the period of transition that Egypt would be entering.[36] A week later, the same newspaper was proclaiming the end of the Right versus Left clashes in Greece, and carried a front-page article discussing the territorial claims Greece would be putting forward at the postwar peace conference. As the conflict in Greece resumed, the *Tachydromos* and other Greek newspapers provided full coverage of the events in Greece. The umbilical cord between the Greeks of Egypt and their homeland across the Mediterranean remained as strong as ever in the late 1940s.

6

From the Cosmopolitan
to the Egyptian World

I n pre-1952 Egypt, the resident Greeks easily adapted to their surroundings. Above all, the Greeks easily interacted with the other
European and foreign communities living around them. But contacts
with the Egyptians were quite another matter. The elite and the political
class were accorded the respect that wealth and power earned, and those
who were Europeanized and educated were also treated decently. But for
many Greeks, the rest of the Egyptians were the 'arapáthes,' a term that
can be best described as a vernacularized version of the word 'Arabs,' and
which had a deliberately contemptuous meaning. Though the term is still
in use, there was a growing appreciation of Egyptians, and even in many
cases a feeling of empathy with their plight, which evolved steadily during
the twentieth century. Back in 1882 during the 'Urabi uprising, Benachi's
daughter Penelope, still a child and perhaps especially fearful and insecure,
described the fellahin as inferior beings. "We 'whites,'" she wrote, "thought
of the fellahin almost like animals and that one white could chase away ten
blacks . . . to beat an Arab was not only permissible but obligatory."[1] Such
attitudes still existed in the interwar period but were becoming much less
prevalent.

Thus, when the nationalists began to gradually enact Egyptianization
measures, all the Greek leadership could think of doing was to reiterate the
claim that the Greeks had and continued to contribute to Egypt's process
of civilization and modernization. They called for closer cooperation and
for Arabic to be taught in the Greek schools, while trying to negotiate
the preservation of at least some of their privileges in the name of the
close relationship between the two peoples. Yet there was a small group of
Greek intellectuals who thought all this was quite inadequate and began
advocating for a more authentic, equitable, and mutually respectful bond
between Greeks and Egyptians. Their voices gradually grew stronger, but

the Greek elites were unable or unwilling to listen. The contrast between the effortless way Greeks became part of Egypt's cosmopolitan environment and the difficulties they had in approaching Egyptians speaks to how deeply engrained the sense of entitlement Britain's hegemony had generated among the country's European residents was.

European Cosmopolitanism

The multiple nationalities living in Alexandria always impressed visitors. In a letter sent from Cairo in 1866 a traveler from France thought that Egypt was a wonderful place where one could study "races." Next to the son of "pharaonic Egypt" one could observe the "sedentary Arab" as well as the Bedouin, the Syrian, the Jew, the Turk, the Persian, the Circassian, the "negro of Soudan," the person from the Barbary Coast, the Greek, the Armenian, the Maltese, the Italian, the Englishman, the German, and the Frenchman. The most common European languages being used were Greek, Italian, and French. One could find a multiplicity of names for street signs such as Rue du Pirée, Lombart Street, and Via Garibaldi—it is a Tower of Babel, the visitor remarked.[2] One of the earliest tourist guides to Alexandria, published by its Municipal Council in 1911, declared, "Truly it has been said of Alexandria that it is the most cosmopolitan city in existence, for from your stand point of vantage you can watch passing in review before you the natives of nearly every nation in the world, Esquimaux perhaps excepted."[3] On the first page of his *Alexandria Quartet*, Lawrence Durrell wrote about "five races, five languages, a dozen creeds . . . but there are more than five sexes and only demotic Greek seems to distinguish among them."[4] Since then the description of the city as being cosmopolitan became commonplace.

But the image of a cosmopolitan Alexandria present in many historical studies and many more works of fiction has come under increasing scrutiny. Critics claim that to describe the city as cosmopolitan at best speaks of the experiences of the wealthiest foreigners. By the same token, it ignores the vast majority of Alexandria's Egyptian inhabitants, relegating them into a "faceless, voiceless non-cosmopolitan mainstream of poor Muslim Arab Egyptians who, by definition, cannot be cosmopolitans" who exist "submerged as a sort of human ballast, in order to elevate the cosmopolitan pinnacle."[5] The target of these critiques is a large corpus of work that addresses Alexandrian cultural and social life in the city during the first half of the twentieth century and includes histories that focus on all or one of the foreign communities that wrongly assume they are telling the story of the entire city. Even stronger criticism is reserved for novels set in an entirely Europeanized Alexandria as well as accounts that use that literary Alexandria to speak of a city dominated by memories and nostalgia for a lost cosmopolitan past. The Greeks of Egypt who have written about Alexandria have tended to discount evocations of its cosmopolitan character, favoring instead descriptions that portray it as a Greek city. Wherever reference is made to its cosmopolitanism appears as a secondary characteristic. When they do discuss cosmopolitanism, at least some of the Greek authors tend to speak of it not only as a relationship between the Greek and European elites but also a street-level relationship between the poorer Greeks, other Europeans, and sometimes Egyptians as well.

The remedies to the lopsided treatment of cosmopolitanism and its *par excellence* manifestions in Alexandria include treating it as a carefully circumscribed phenomenon, even discounting its significance, or rethinking Alexandria's history by delving into its daily life and studying how *all* Alexandrians experienced their city and interacted with each other. This offers "a picture of daily life that is not opposed to the cosmopolitan picture . . . but invests it with a new quotidian, non-elitist dimension."[6] Another approach has suggested that cosmopolitanism should be examined against the background of all periods of Egypt's history, as a legacy of the Ottoman era as well as a function of colonialism. By the same token its demise should be weighed against the rise of parochial nationalisms that took its place.[7]

The late Robert Mabro, who was born in Alexandria to Lebanese parents and grew up there before becoming an academic, and whose expertise included the Egyptian economy, has made a strong argument in favor of a cautious approach to the overall existence of cosmopolitanism in the city. He cites studies that suggest that phenomenon was linked to the city's existence on the Mediterranean,[8] and argues that various communities existed independently thanks to "a hard core of strongly felt beliefs and dearly cherished personal interests at the center and an ill-defined fringe all around." Significantly, "it was the fringe that related the members of the cosmopolitan group to another."[9] Interestingly, in listing the communities with the fringes that produced cosmopolitanism, Mabro discounts the role of the Greeks—whom he knew well because he spoke Greek—because of their strong sense of Greekness.

Indeed, Greekness was predominant, but the Greeks were also part of Alexandria's and even Cairo's cosmopolitan climate. To be cosmopolitan was to be European and that was something all Greeks, not only those in Egypt, have aspired to in the modern era. Cosmopolitanism was generated in practical terms by the residential patterns in Egypt's main cities and also found in economic activities, municipal level politics, education, and social and cultural life. In Alexandria the Greeks "had the tendency to group together in certain areas, as in Attarine and later Ibrahimieh . . . while poorer families lived in the 'Arab' quarters alongside Levantines, Italians and Egyptians," and spoke several languages—French, Italian, and later on in the 1950s, English "learned 'on the streets,' thanks to neighborhood relationships and the necessities of daily life."[10]

Cosmopolitan Spaces

The affluence and privilege Europeans enjoyed in Egypt meant that they inhabited the wealthier neighborhoods in Alexandria, Cairo, and the towns along the Suez Canal and by the same token banished the Egyptian population, with the exception of the elite, to the poorer neighborhoods of their cities. Ottoman cities were frequently divided into separate quarters in which ethnic or religious groups lived. These types of quarters were less formally established. It was economics and real estate prices that created those different spaces, and most observers spoke of cities in Egypt having either European or Arab quarters. The existence of those European quarters provided spaces in which the various foreign communities could intermingle formally and informally, creating the impression that the city was cosmopolitan. A visitor to Cairo in the late nineteenth century remarked that there was a new and an old Cairo, the new one consisted of the Ismailiya and Abbasiya quarters, where the thousands of Greeks, Italians, and Frenchmen lived and had their shops. Another visitor to Egypt around the same time saw Alexandria as divided into two completely separated Arab and European sections.[11] Similar divisions existed in towns in the Delta and along the Suez Canal.

In the early twentieth century, when the city had fully recovered from the serious damage British bombardment had inflicted in 1882, Alexandria appeared to most of its visitors as a modern city founded on banking, commerce, and cotton. Many western observers had their prejudices of what a Middle Eastern city would look like confounded by Alexandria's 'European look.' Indeed, if one made one's way up from the port, one encountered buildings and people that many described as resembling Marseilles or Naples. That was the effect Alexandria had on Martin Briggs, an architect and architectural historian who served as a non-combatant in the British Army in Egypt and Palestine during the First World War, as he noted when he published his impressions. The center of Alexandria, which he calls the eastern half, he writes, "is not really Oriental at all. It differs only in matters of detail from the quarters of other modern seaports across the Mediterranean. The streets are labeled with French names, while on the pavement one seems to meet far more English and French and Italians and Greeks than Egyptians," while "in the Rue Cherif Pasha at Alexandria one might imagine oneself in the Via Roma in Genoa or in the Toledo in Naples."[12]

To find "Oriental life," Briggs explained, one had to traverse Muhammad Ali Square, which functioned as the natural division among the city's European and Muslim quarters. There, proceeding southward toward the docks "there is hardly a single picturesque feature to relieve the dismal squalor of the Rue des Soeurs," while "half the frontage is occupied by shabby little restaurants." The alleys in-between were "decorated" with signs declaring them "Out of Bounds to Troops" and, he concluded, "in this quarter one may find everything that is least attractive in the cosmopolitan life of a great seaport."[13] Briggs also saw several of the more exclusive parts of the city. An avid swimmer, he enjoyed the water at Stanley Bay—favored among Europeans—a small sandy beach ringed by bath cabins, later to be replaced by terraced concrete cabins.

He does not record having visited the Quartier Grec, a residential enclave just off Rue Fu'ad, which contained the most impressive houses built in neoclassical, fin-de-siècle Italian, or French architectural style and surrounded by beautifully kept gardens. That was where the wealthy Britons, Greeks, Jews, and Syrians had their homes. Needless to say, the Benachis, Choremis, and Salvagos all lived there. Many of them also had villas in Ramla, which was further east and had been gifted by Muhammad Ali to one of the early Greek settlers, Stephanos Zizinia, in return for his services. In the rest of the city the various national groups mingled. In Tsirkas's *Drifting Cities*, trips on the Alexandria tramway meant hearing "people speaking Greek, Arabic, French" and at the Bacos neighborhood stop one noticed its cathedral, Notre-Dame, and around the station "a mixed crowd, some Arabs and Greeks, but mostly Italians and Maltese."[14]

In Alexandria the Municipal Council, established in 1890, was another space that fostered collaboration among the Europeans. For example, in 1909, when Benachi and Zervoudachi were sitting on the council, one source described the Greeks, Jews, and Egyptians as the ones with influence. In fact, the law that established the council decreed that not more than three elected members were allowed to belong to the same nationality, local or foreign.[15] In any case, the foreigners, usually among the most prominent of each community, predominated over the Egyptians on the Municipal Council of Alexandria. This was a quid pro quo for the foreigners agreeing to pay municipal taxes. The creation of the council had been preceded by voluntary contributions by foreign merchants designed to pave roads in the business quarters and improve the Mahmudiya Canal.

A British visitor with knowledge of the city's rich history, E.M. Forster, grumbled at some of the cosmetic changes the council had introduced, such as renaming the Rue Rosette to the "meaningless" Rue Fu'ad Premier and destroying a "charming" covered bazaar near the Rue de France.[16] But the Egyptian majority of Alexandria's population had much more to complain about, given that the foreign domination of the council was a gross misrepresentation of the ratio of Egyptian to foreign residents in the city. While the foreigners happily collaborated on the council, it became increasingly unpopular with Egyptian residents, who regarded it as a symbol of foreign domination. One of the first poems of Bayram al-Tunisi, a popular poet in twentieth-century Egypt, satirized the Alexandria Municipality.

In the 1920s Egyptian governments took steps to diminish the council's autonomy and increase the numbers of Egyptian members. At the same time there were signs of cooperation between foreigners and Egyptians. The seats allocated to foreign and Egyptian councilors came up for election at the same time and each candidate depended on both foreign and Egyptian votes. In February 1924, three foreigners ran as Wafd-supported candidates and were elected. Two of them were Greek: journalist Nikolaos Caravias and Nikolaos Nicolaou, an architect and member of the community organization's executive committee. In 1926 two Greeks and an Italian were elected with the Wafd's backing. By that time, measures to curtail the overall influence of foreigners were underway, and their collaboration on the council diminished as well.[17]

Private clubs, located, naturally, in the European business or residential quarters and with a multinational membership, were another significant cosmopolitan breeding ground. As was the case with schools, the foreigners in Egypt formed nationally focused clubs and semiformal groups known as cercles, but there soon emerged more inclusive clubs in terms of the ethnic and national origins of the members. Such clubs were a bastion of privilege, very much like the fee-paying schools. They also carried the imprimatur of a close connection to the British, signaling their connections to colonial power and social elitism.

The prime example was the Alexandria Sporting Club, founded in 1890 and commonly known as the 'Sporting.' It was a typically British club with "a blend of social and sports activities," which "provided a setting in which Britons could give themselves over to activities that reflected their insularity and their ethos: controlled entry into the institution and activities prescribed by their priorities and interests." The club "revolved primarily around horses, golf and similar activities" and included events designed to celebrate "Empire Day" and other British national events. The club was open to foreign elites because it was an institution "that would reinforce existing class structure and provide a setting in which to emulate the habits of the insular colonizer." It included, from its start, "patrician representatives of the city's diverse communities . . . affluent Greeks, Italians, Levantine Jews, and Christians as well as representatives of half a dozen European nations . . . missing from the equation were the Egyptians."[18]

A bit like Victoria College, it created a cosmopolitanism inflected by acknowledgment of Britain's hegemony in Egypt and Egypt's subordinate position. The Muhammad Ali Club in the heart of Alexandria, at the beginning of Rue Rosette (that became Avenue Fu'ad Premier), was another popular venue for the city's European residents: "smart and cosmopolitan, the club was the haunt of bankers, cotton brokers and *rentiers* who would sit on its verandah admiring the stylish women out shopping along the Rue Chérif Pasha, while inside there were comfortable lounges, a library, reading and music rooms and gaming tables at which there was high play." It was there that Cavafy met E.M. Forster, a meeting that "was to be of primary importance to twentieth century literature."[19]

The final resting place for the foreigners, a keen observer of cosmopolitanism in the Levant reminds us, could be described as "the most compelling relics of Alexandria's cosmopolitan century." Indeed, cemeteries for the Armenian, Catholic, Coptic, Greek Orthodox, Greek Catholic, Jewish, Protestant, and Free Thinkers communities occupy a large area in Alexandria's Chatby district, in the eastern part of the city. Like other cemeteries in major cities around the world, those cemeteries and especially the tombs of the notables speak volumes about the city's past. At Chatby, the mausoleums of the Sivitanidi, Aghion, Zervoudachi, and Cordahi families "are extravagant assertions of wealth and grief."[20]

European residential enclaves existed in Cairo and in the towns along the Suez Canal. The Khedive Ismail had envisioned making Cairo a Paris by the Nile and by the late nineteenth century European architects and contractors had given the center of the city a remarkably European look. By 1910 an eighth of the city's population was foreign born and they were well on their way to imposing their cultural hegemony. In 1925 a third of Cairo's schoolchildren were enrolled in foreign schools "taught in a score of religious persuasions and half a dozen languages."[21] Briggs found Cairo much more "Oriental" because of the numerous mosques and other examples of Islamic architecture he greatly admired. But there was, he noted, an upper-class quarter, Heliopolis, and an "English quarter" on the island of Gezira, where "some of the roads with their neat tree-lined pavements, their wooden garden gates and 'tradesman entrance' might be in Wimbledon or Beckenham or some other prosperous London suburb." Just over the Nile in the city's center "French, Belgians and Italians are very numerous," while "the Greek swarms everywhere."[22]

A decade later, according to the 1927 census, a fifth of the city's population belonged to minorities: thus, one could conclude "Cairo no longer aspired to be cosmopolitan; it already was."[23] The Sporting and Muhammad Ali equivalent in Cairo was the Tawfiqiya Club—the one in Gezira was the exclusively British club. Edward Said, the Palestinian-American academic who spent his boyhood between Cairo and Jerusalem, recalls that in 1949 the Tawfiqiya had an "extraordinary varied, a bewildering Levantine *mélange* of Greek, French, Italian, Muslim, Armenian, Lebanese, Circassian and Jewish members." Much later in life Said would produce an acclaimed critique of the West's privileged gaze on the Arab Middle East, but he was evidently already aware of the incongruity of "privileged enclaves like Tewfiqya, where an extroverted non-Arab, non-Muslim life that was not quite European, because tied to Oriental luxury, service and sensuality, could take place with relative freedom from outside interference."[24]

Briggs left Cairo when he was posted to the canal town of Ismailiya, which he described as very pleasant, and noted, "One might almost say Ismailia appeals to a traveler in Egypt just because it is so un-Egyptian . . . its character is essentially French or Italian rather than Arab."[25] Ibrahimiya, Port Said, and Suez were all built during the digging of the Suez Canal. Its subsequent administration was carried out by Europeans, so perhaps it is not as surprising to learn that many visitors to Port Said reported that the town was clearly divided into European and Arab quarters.[26] Crusading European moral reformers who visited the Canal region in the early twentieth century wishing to put a stop to prostitution and the trafficking of women blamed those activities not on them being busy port cities but on their "highly cosmopolitan population," which included Greeks as well as "bloodthirsty islanders from the Aegean sea."[27]

Decades later, life in these towns was considerably tamer, but the cosmopolitan climate remained. A Greek who grew up in Port Fouad, the town across the Canal from Port Said, remembers that during Christmas and Ramadan in the 1950s, Christians and Egyptians would exchange well-wishes and thought it natural to celebrate each other's festivities. It was the Greeks and the Maltese who were closer to the Egyptians, the British and French more distant.[28] At the southern tip of the Canal, at Port Tawfiq, next to the town of Suez, there was also a cosmopolitan environment, though there were two beaches, the 'French' one for the senior employees and the 'Greek' one for lower level staff of the Canal Company.[29]

The divisions outsiders were quick to confirm were by no means set in stone. In real life the boundaries were crossed in terms of residence, with wealthy Egyptians having homes in the so-called European quarter and poorer Europeans either living or working in the Arab quarter. The division was also porous in terms of where residents spent time or visited. There were working-class neighborhoods in both Alexandria and Cairo where Europeans, especially Greeks, Italians, Maltese, and Egyptians lived side by side. In pre-1952 Egypt "tongues and races mingled amid the tight ranks of working-class districts—Shubra, Abbasiyya, Bulaq . . . they mixed happily on the whole, even if the influence was mostly one-way, and even if marriage across religions remained rare."[30] This was a different, "street-level" cosmopolitanism, just as evident as in other parts of the city.

In Lawrence Durrell's words, one could catch "fragments of every language—Armenian, Greek, Moroccan Arabic" and encounter "Jews from Asia Minor, Pontus, Georgia: mothers born in Greek settlements on the Black Sea . . . these are the poor quarters of the white city" that "bear no resemblance to those lovely streets built and decorated by foreigners where the brokers sit and sip their morning papers."[31] And there, not surprisingly, communication that entailed cursing deployed a foreign language for effect. A careful and creative reading of late nineteenth-century Alexandria's legal records has shown that "cursing in the streets reveals the practical poly-glossia that was the medium of everyday communication . . . cosmopolitan insults emerged from their linguistic context to assume a place in the shared language of the city."[32] There was also polyglot cursing in higher places as well. Said learned how to curse in French with scraps of English and Arabic at the Tawfiqiya.

Boardroom Cosmopolitanism

Wealthy elites among the foreign communities lived cosmopolitan lives to the extent that they collaborated and shared the same pro-European orientation and values. They resembled another privileged minority in the Middle East, the Levantine bourgeoisie, who were based in port cities such as Beirut and Smyrna and were "slavishly imitative of Europe, at least on the surface and more often than not despised the Oriental life around them." They imitated "the French or English way of life" and "many of them adopted the French language as their own, and conceived a hopeless love for the French civilization."[33] In the case of the Greeks and other foreigners, the cornerstone of their cosmopolitan existence was their role linking Egypt with the global economy through their ties with European firms, know-how, and cultural skills that required a knowledge of English and French, if not other languages. In pursuing their economic role in Egypt, foreigners tended to establish family and ethnic-based firms. In the twentieth century and especially after the First World War many firms had multiethnic owners and boards of directors.

Of the 112 companies described in the *Annuaire Financier de l'Egypte*, published in 1907, no fewer than fifty-four could be described as having an internationally mixed directorate, and of this number at least twenty-nine had a number of local residents on the board—the Greek names that appeared more frequently were Benachi, Ralli, Salvago, and Zervoudachi.[34] A study of boards of directors of companies in Egypt published in 1923 found that twenty-one firms had boards that included a mixture of foreigners resident in Egypt. Not surprisingly, it noted that the name Salvago appeared in seven of the mixed boards, but as one scholar noted, "the Salvagos were ably assisted by H.E. of the famous Anglo-Levantine Barker family, who had resided in the Middle East since the middle of the eighteenth century."[35]

The *Annuaire des Sociétés Egyptiennes Par Actions* published in 1938 shows that there were Greeks sitting on thirty company boards with other foreigners, including of the one of the biggest firms in Egypt, the Choremi, Benachi Cotton Company, as well as fifteen manufacturing firms (Associated Cotton Ginners of Egypt, Cigarettes Nestor Gianaclis, Crown Brewery, Egyptian Copper Works, Filature Nationale d'Egypte,

Garbieh Ginning Company, Kafr al-Zayat Cotton Company, Société Anonyme Egyptienne Carba, Société An. de Nettoyage et Pressage de Cotton, S.A. des Presses Libres Egyptiennes, Société Egyptienne des Industries Textiles, Soc. Générale de Pressage et de Dépôts, Société Générale des Sucreries et de la Raffinerie d'Egypte, Société Nationale du Papier, and Société Viticole et Vinicole d'Egypte); six real estate companies (Alexandria Exchange, Building Lands of Egypt, Gabbari Land Company, Société Anonyme des Immeubles d'Egypte, Société Anonyme Immobilière des Terrains Ghizeh & Rodah, and Société Egyptienne de la Bourse Commerciale de Minat al-Basal); five transport companies (Alexandria and Ramla Railway Company, Alexandria Transport Company, Egyptian Motor Transport Company, Compagnie Egyptienne de Navigation "Le Dodécanese," and United Egyptian Nile Transport Company); three banks (the Commercial Bank of the Near East, Crédit Agricole d'Egypte, and the Crédit Foncier Egyptien); three insurance companies (Al-Chark – L'Orient, National Insurance Company of Egypt, and National Insurance Company of Egypt – Life Insurance); three petroleum companies (Egyptian Independent Oil Company, National Petroleum Company, and Société Egyptienne des Pétroles); one landowning company (Kafr al-Zayat Land); one public utility (Alexandria Water Company); one hotel company (Upper Egypt Hotels Company); one company promoting a type of cotton (Société Cottonière Maarad); Alexandria Racing Club; Société Egyptienne pour l'exploitation de Mines et Carrières; Société Egyptienne Financière pour le Commerce et l'Industrie "Sefina"; Société des Entreprises M. Cockinos, and Société Franco-Egyptienne d'Importation.[36]

By the end of the Second World War, the companies run primarily by directors representing a single foreign country or ethnic community constituted a much smaller proportion of the total than they had prior to the First World War—thirty-eight firms were run by Jewish directors, twenty-two by Greeks, eighteen by British, eighteen by Belgians, eighteen by Syrians, and sixty firms run by Egyptians. The Egyptians and the Syrians were the two groups that had expanded the most, but the greatest expansion of all occurred among mixed nationality firms. By 1946 there were 163 of them. These locally resident mixed companies included some of the most important industrial and commercial enterprises in Egypt.

The growing number of nationally mixed board companies functioned as the economic base on which a cosmopolitan superstructure emerged beginning in the 1920s. It was restricted to the wealthiest stratum that has been described as the "haute bourgeoisie." This stratum coalesced into a cosmopolitan class for itself, conscious of its affinities and its class interests. Accordingly, it used bodies that represented its collective interests such as the Egyptian Federation of Industries to block attempts to introduce legislation that would ameliorate employees' abysmal working conditions.[37]

Foreign Schools and Languages

The foreign schools in Alexandria and Cairo were the crucible that produced a cosmopolitan outlook among the younger generations of Europeans. The British-run private school Victoria College in Alexandria, which opened in 1902, was the archetype, fostering cosmopolitanism under the aegis of British power and influence. As the school's official history put it, "no institution can be a better reflection of the cosmopolitan nature of Alexandria."[38] Lord and Lady Cromer were the guests of honor at the official inauguration of a new building in 1906. Lady Cromer laid the foundation stone, with Greek Orthodox Patriarch Photios II and community organization president Mikés Sinadino in attendance. Cromer made the official address and expressed the hope that the school would "help in some degree towards the political and social fusion of the various nations who inhabit the valley of the Nile."

That year the school had 196 students of whom ninety were Christians, sixty-seven were Jews, and nineteen were Muslims. The national and ethnic groups represented were Egyptian, Armenian, Belgian, Dutch, English, French, Greek, Italian, Maltese, Spanish, Swiss, Syrian, and Turkish. The school's official history mentions that from the beginning Syrian Christians and Jews sent their children to Victoria College and "well known Greek families also preferred the new English school to their community schools." Among the first Greek families to send their sons there were the Lagonicos, Valassopoulos, and Rallis.[39] There were other international schools in Egypt, for example the Gezira Preparatory School in Cairo, where the young Edward Said encountered "Armenians, Greeks, Egyptian Jews, and Copts as well as a substantial number of English children."[40] Said went on to study at the Victoria College campus established in 1948 in Cairo, where he "entered a mongrel world made up of miscellaneous last names" and was intrigued that the various nationally based social groupings of students were not "exclusive or watertight" and this produced "a dancelike maze of personalities, modes of speech, backgrounds, religions and nationalities."[41]

Knowledge of several languages, not necessarily very well, was another sign of cosmopolitanism and it was true not only of the wealthy but almost all foreigners. Cavafy treated Forster to long, complicated sentences, which he could deliver with equal ease in Greek, French, or English.[42] Those who were able to attend a British or French school were obviously at an advantage and learned those languages well, but both were a kind of lingua franca. By the same token, Arabic was purposely not used, aside from its 'kitchen' version when speaking with domestic servants. Said remembers the Egyptian and Greek employees at Groppi's, Cairo's landmark chic café and pastry shop, addressing customers in "jaw-shattering French" when it was clear that communication in Arabic would have been more effective. The same happened in the workplace almost everywhere. A young Alexandrian remembered that when his uncle took him along to the cotton warehouses of Minat al-Basal and Gabbari, "the Egyptian workers would address him in a Graeco-Arabic patois while the office staff spoke Arabo-Franglais."[43]

Reaching Out to Egyptians

Briggs, the British architect who visited Egypt during the First World War, wrote that in Cairo the Greek "swarms everywhere" and in doing so he links East and West. Compared to other foreign communities, the Greeks had spread out the most throughout the country and could be found in poor urban neighborhoods and the smallest villages. This meant that many of them had regular if not daily contact with Egyptians. Yet this did not necessarily bring Greeks and Egyptians closer to each other because the ubiquitous Greek, whether a grocer, a food vendor, or other retail trader, was often exploiting his local customers or lending them money at exorbitant rates. Or worse, he or she was engaging in illegal activities such as prostitution or selling alcohol or drugs.

Nonetheless, as Egyptian nationalism gathered momentum in the interwar years, several members of the community regarded the contacts of Greeks with ordinary Egyptians as the basis on which Greeks could begin to redefine their relationship with Egyptians and cast it on a more equitable basis. This was a challenging task because it required an abandonment of the standard claim that the Greeks were in Egypt as pioneers of civilization who contributed to the country's modernization. It meant going much further than merely responding to Egyptianization measures by including Egyptians on the boards of Greek-owned companies, coordinating the activities of Greek small business owners, or proposing that Greek schools introduce more hours of Arabic instruction. It entailed an effort to stop viewing Egyptians from a superior vantage point. As easy as it had been to reconcile the attachment to Greekness with membership in Egypt's cosmopolitan world, it was so much more difficult to become part of a new Egypt.

Prior to the 1930s, when attempts to go beyond the portrayal of Greeks as pioneers of civilization in Egypt began, there had been moments of a more equitable relationship between Greeks and Egyptians in labor unionism. The earliest forms of union organization and strike action involving Greek workers occurred in cigarette factories and among employees at the Suez Canal in the 1890s. A strike spearheaded by Greek cigarette rollers in 1899 appeared to entail a clash between Greek workers and Greek factory owners but the union organization that eventually emerged also included Armenians, Italians, and other nationalities including Egyptians. In Stratis Tsirkas's three-part novel *Drifting Cities*, set in the 1940s, a newcomer to Egypt proudly tells a Greek living in Egypt that he knows about Greek involvement in the labor movement there, remarking, "wasn't it back in 1899 that the cigarette workers in the Vafiadis and Melachrino came down on strike, both Arabs and whites together . . . and then in 1911 didn't the cigarette workers in Alexandria get what they want because they refused to split the strikers into locals and Europeans?"[44] There was strike activity among employees of the Suez Canal Company and in May 1918 a strike committee included two Greeks, two Italians, an Austrian, and an Egyptian. In the 1920s there were several international labor unions appearing in Egypt; the seamens' union included Greeks and Egyptians.[45]

During the 1920s, Greek intellectuals collaborated with other foreigners to propagate socialist ideas, for example with the formation of the Groupe d'Etudes Sociales in Alexandria. They then established a socialist party. Among them were Iordanis Iordanidis, a teacher at Victoria College, his future wife Maria Kriezi, and Sakellaris Yannakakis, a self-educated sponge merchant from the Aegean island of Kalymnos. Both Iordanidis and Yannakakis had close contact with the Greek literati in Alexandria; Yannakakis unsuccessfully tried to persuade Cavafy of the value of historical materialism. Those Greeks collaborated, among others, with Joseph Rosenthal, a German Jew considered the founder of the communist movement in Egypt. He had arrived there in 1899 and although reportedly he was a jeweler, he had been involved in several labor unions and strikes. The socialist party they founded in 1921 had a small membership made up of Armenians, Greeks, Italians, Russians, and a few Egyptians.

The party decided to adhere to the Comintern's conditions and changed its name to the Egyptian Communist Party with one of its Egyptian members, Husni al-'Arabi, as its secretary. Rosenthal, whose wordview included a strong anarcho-syndicalist streak, opposed the party's affiliation with Moscow and was expelled. In any case, the foreigners, aware that the party needed a strong Egyptian profile, tended to hold back on assuming leadership positions and tried to balance recruitment strategies so as not to attract more foreigners than Egyptians.

Yannakakis would remain active in the 1920s and 1930s but mainly in the small socialist circles of the European communities.[46] Inevitably, the collaboration between Greeks and Egyptians in the small communist party and socialist circles would have a correspondingly small impact on Greek–Egyptian relations writ large.

The artistic world of Egypt was another very particular sphere in which a few Greeks interacted with foreigners and Egyptians, of which the Egyptian surrealist movement that appeared in the late 1930s is a good example. There were three Greeks among the thirty-one persons who signed the manifesto entitled "Long Live Degenerate Art" that announced surrealism's arrival in Egypt. They were the painter Aristomenis Angelopoulos, the literary critic Timos Malanos, and Athanasios Politis, the diplomat and author of the two-volume history of the Greeks in Egypt. The painter Antonis Malliarakis, who was born in Port Said in 1905 and went by the artistic name of Mayo, was a significant figure in the surrealist art scene in Cairo. He spent most of the 1920s in Paris but from then on divided his time between European cities and Cairo. His first exhibition there took place at the Cercle du Canal du Suez in Ismailiya in 1933 and continued to exhibit his work in Cairo throughout the 1930s. After the Second World War he remained in France and later on moved to Italy.[47]

A few Greeks were able to join the world of Egyptian performing arts. Nelly Mazloum, born in Alexandria of an Italian father and a Greek mother, became an accomplished dancer, choreographer, and dance teacher, and is credited with founding the first Egyptian folk dance troupe. Kitty Fotsaty, born of Greek parents in Alexandria, was one of the best-known belly dancers in Egypt and performed in several feature films, in some of which she starred alongside Isma'il Yassin, a popular comedian.

Sport was one area where contacts between Greeks and Egyptians were easy, and despite the popularity and spread of sporting activities, these contacts ultimately were self-contained and did not affect relations beyond the sporting arena. The British introduced modern organized sports in Egypt but unlike countries where colonial rule was formal and upper-class sports such as cricket and polo would filter through the local elite and become popular sports, the British in Egypt reserved those pastimes for themselves, meaning that football and track and field would become the major sports taken up by Egyptians. The anglophile foreign residents also took up those sports and thus helped their spread throughout the country.

Sports clubs focused mainly on football (soccer) and track and field began appearing from the early twentieth century onwards. The Greeks formed their own clubs, as did the Armenians, the British, the Italians, and the Jews; some of these were short lived but many were active for several decades. A total of about twenty-five Greek sports clubs were formed in Alexandria, about the same number in Cairo, eight in Port Said, seven in Mansura, and there was at least one in most of the smaller towns. These clubs competed in Greek tournaments and also played against other foreign and Egyptian clubs, and the top athletes competed in the Egyptian national championships, and several of the best produced record performances. Several athletes and coaches who worked with Egyptian athletes received awards for their contributions from the Egyptian sports authorities. When the Greeks began leaving gradually in the post-Second World War era, several clubs merged together before eventually closing down. Several Greek athletes were able to continue their careers in Greece, for example football player Yannis Komianidis, while the women's table tennis players pair of Laitou and Kardia went to the big Athens sports association Panathinaikos.[48]

Angelo Bolanachi was born in Alexandria in 1880 and studied in England and France, where he took up sports that he continued practicing when he returned to work in his father's alcohol distillery. He took up the cause of connecting Egypt with the nascent Olympic Games, and his well-meaning efforts throughout the rest of his life illustrate the difficulties created when foreign residents become involved in sports in Egypt. Bolanachi worked toward the establishment of sporting organizations such as the Fédération Sportive d'Egypte, which included both Egyptians and foreign residents. Thanks to his international connections, the International Olympic Committee appointed him as its representative in Egypt and with their blessing he went ahead and created the Egyptian Olympic Committee, which had Prince Omar Toussoun, a great-grandson of Muhammad Ali, as its president and Bolanachi as treasurer.

Bolanachi was a major advocate for the construction of a modern stadium in Alexandria and of the city hosting the First African Games. The concept of those games was supported by Baron Pierre de Coubertin, the founder of the Olympic Games, as a form of satellite tournament of the Olympics. Britain or France, the continent's overlords, were concerned they may trigger or encourage local nationalist sentiment. Accordingly, France saw to it that the games, planned for 1925 in Algeria, were never held, and to Bolanachi's dismay Britain blocked the rescheduled games, which were to be held in April 1929 in Alexandria.

Ironically, by that time growing national sentiment in Egypt meant that having a non-Egyptian as the country's representative was regarded as incompatible with Egypt's dignified standing as a nation. Bolanachi resigned even though the International Olympic Committee dug its heels in, claiming that its members did not represent a country but represented the committee to a particular country. Tensions escalated and Egypt refused to participate in the Los Angeles Olympics of 1932. In the end, the International Olympic Committee reassigned Bolanachi as one of its representatives of Greece and appointed an Egyptian, Muhammed Tahir Pasha, a nephew of King Fu'ad, as its member for Egypt.[49]

The Egyptianization of the nation's Olympic Committee—the respective federations that ran individual sports had already undergone that process—left Greco–Egyptian cooperation on an ad hoc basis. For example, in 1928 a football team of mostly Egyptians representing Alexandria also included several Greek players in its lineup when it met a visiting Hungarian team. Individual club teams were primarily nationally focused, either Egyptian or Greek, but would include players of different nationalities.[50] But when it came to the team representing Egypt, for example, the World Cup tournament of 1934 in Italy, then all the players were Egyptian. When Alexandria bid successfully to host the First Mediterranean Games, Bolanachi and Tahir worked closely together, and Bolanachi ensured that Greece's Olympic Committee supported the project. During the games that took place in October 1951, the *Tachydromos* noted with pride that many of the technical committees involved in running the games were Greeks of Egypt.[51] When the games got underway, naturally, the Alexandrian daily gave its full support for the Greek teams. Sports brought the Greeks and the Egyptians in close contact throughout the twentieth century, but national allegiances remained when it came to the Greek national team competing with the Egyptian team.

The Intellectuals Intervene

It was left to Greek intellectuals, either liberal or socialist, to take on the responsibility of implicitly or explicitly articulating a vision of a world in which Greeks would treat Egyptians as their equals. Those initiatives unfolded beginning in the 1920s, a time when the concept of the Greeks as the pioneers of civilization and agents of modernity was in full swing. Among those indirectly undermining the master narrative was Christophoros Nomikos, a historian interested in the history of the Arabs in the Middle Ages and Arabic pottery and ceramics, which he collected. He lived in the Quartier Grec, born into a family with origins in Istanbul but is recorded to have moved to Alexandria in 1907 to work in banking and the cotton business. He became a member of the Greek literary circle and eventually became president of the Amis de l'Art, the Alexandrian branch of the prestigious arts lovers club established in Cairo, which included members of the Egyptian and European elite.

In 1919 Nomikos was one of the first scholars to discredit the theory that Iznik ceramics originated in Rhodes. He was also the author of several books on Iznik and Kutahya pottery published in the 1920s. Nomikos shared his interest in Islamic pottery and ceramics with Alexander "Alec" Benachi, one of Emmanuel's sons. Alexander died unexpectedly of a heart attack in 1922 while playing polo in Alexandria, and his collection passed into the hands of his brother Antonis, who was also a member of the Amis de l'Art. In 1925 Nomikos and Antonis were the driving force behind a major exhibition of 370 Islamic artifacts from personal collections that was hosted by the Amis de l'Art in Alexandria. Antonis left Alexandria and settled in Athens in 1926 and when his father Emmanuel died three years later, he and his sisters decided to donate the family-owned neoclassical mansion in central Athens to the Greek state to use as a museum that would house Antonis's collection of Islamic and Byzantine artifacts that were brought over from Alexandria. Today, the Benaki Museum is one of Greece's foremost cultural institutions.

Two years later, Nomikos would publish his major work, a book-length study in Greek on the history of the Arabs. In the introduction he expressed the hope that historical studies written objectively could persuade people that "no one should be proud only of their own race and be contemptuous of others because we are all human beings trying to find some happiness in the course of our lives."[52] It was a genteel rebuke to the advocates of the idea that Greeks rescued the helpless Egyptians. Nomikos's contribution to the project of familiarizing the Greeks in Egypt with the history of the people among whom they were living, an insightful reader of his texts has suggested, was qualitatively more refined than the other initiatives being taken at the time. Those included Evgenios Michaelides's prodigious writings on Arab and Egyptian history in the 1920s and 1930s. Impressive in their number and scope, his works most certainly enlightened many readers but tended to consider the impact of the West, including the Greeks as positive. The corollary was the assumption that any movement to realize Egyptianness (al-misriya) should recognize the contributions of those others. In contrast, Nomikos treated western intervention, especially the Crusades, as a negative phenomenon. Thus he offers the means for his readers to think critically about the triangular relationship between western powers (and the Greek state that was under their sway), the subservient status of the Arab East, and foreign residents in the countries of the Middle East.[53]

A more direct and more accessible cluster of voices calling for an authentic cooperation with Egyptians appeared in the columns of the Alexandrian daily Tachydromos around the same time that Nomikos published his book. The newspaper ran a column devoted to views of prominent— mostly professional—Alexandrian Greeks about what the Greeks of Egypt should do to deal with the issues they were facing. Those were not set out explicitly, presumably because everyone knew what they were: the erosion of foreign privileges and growing economic competition from Egyptians. Three years earlier, just before the Greeks began experiencing widespread setbacks, Ioannis Kasimatis, the reporter in charge of the column, had proudly described the Greeks in Egypt as "a small Greece, integral, strongly constructed and prospering."[54] Inevitably, the way the newspaper and Kasimatis framed the survey solicited introspective recommendations. Most responses focused on the need to strengthen the collaboration among Greek businessmen, increasing Greco–Egyptian trade enacted by Greeks in Egypt, reforming the educational system, and the necessity for the wealthy to stand by the rest of the community.

A few thought the Greeks were not really facing a crisis but the effects of inevitable changes, while others acknowledged it was the small businessmen and shop owners who were succumbing to competition and wondered whether they might no longer have a place in Egypt. These suggestions or versions of them kept being repeated in the column that began on January 3, 1928 and concluded on March 1 with a series of columns by Kasimatis, who summed up the recommendations and identified those he considered more useful. Significantly, the column appeared daily on the front page.[55] One of the respondents early on in the series came up with what turned out to be an almost unique take on the crisis. It came from Georgios Petridis, a chemist born in Alexandria, who had participated in the activities of the literary and socialist groups in Alexandria. As a Marxist he had represented Greece at the Fourth Inter-Allied Socialist Conference that took place in 1918 in London and the Socialist Being Conference held in 1919 in Berne.

Petridis, examining the issues through a Marxist lens, argued that the workers, professionals, and petit bourgeois were the ones losing ground, not the bourgeois and the capitalists. He launched an attack on the very core of the Greek self-justification of being in Egypt. The Greeks had not anticipated the changes that had created this situation, he said bluntly, because they had been hiding complacently behind the views that they were a "chosen people," "the bright light of civilization in the East" and the "pioneers and civilizers" and, he added, they thought the natives would always remain "uncivilized, always sheep ready to be shorn, always slaves, always inferior." But the reality of life, he continued, opens our eyes and makes us think. He went on to offer his own solutions. These included various forms of reorganization, which one would have expected from someone speaking from a Marxist standpoint, pursuing "productive" forms of economic activity such as manufacturing, establishing cooperatives, creating a "popular" bank that would support small businesses, and more active participation in the Greek community organizations.

Third on his list was a truly radical proposal, namely "an authentic blending in with the native population, intellectual, economic and social," which would bring about a better understanding between the two sides. "None of us has native friends" he continued, "we are ignorant of everything about their lives." He added, "now that Egypt is awakening we ought to closely observe their intellectual, economic and political lives." This was certainly one of the most clearly articulated critiques of the status quo of Greek–Egyptian relations and a public appeal for a more egalitarian and respectful approach on the part of Greeks. In the standard prefatory note Kasimatis inserted to provide some background to each person whose views were presented, he mentioned Petridis's socialist credentials and added that he would be commenting on those suggestions when he presented his conclusion at the end of the series.[56]

Petridis's trenchant critique and his call for more authentic relations between the Greeks and the Egyptians went unanswered, at least on the part of the community's decision-makers. Cast as it was in the language of class, it resonated with a relatively small audience since Marxist ideas were of limited appeal to the Greeks in Egypt as a whole. But if one sidestepped his vision of a community divided by class, his call for a new relationship remained valid. While the survey continued, one of the regular contributors to the newspaper, the Cypriot novelist Yangos Pieridis, writing under the pseudonym 'Scaravaios,' supported Petridis's point that the Greeks had remained willfully ignorant of the lives of Egyptians. He lamented the way Greeks focused their attention on money and regarded Egyptians as part of the decorative background, and asked, What did Greeks really know about the lives of Egyptians? For too long, he concluded, Greeks had considered themselves temporary residents in Egypt and had ignored the very places they were living in—"gypsies and travelers have shown more interest in the villages they stay in," he declared.[57]

When the time came for Kasimatis to present his conclusions at the end of the survey, the closest he got to endorsing Petridis's recommendations was to call for the community's leaders to pay more attention to the "popular classes." He chose not to discuss Petridis's appeal for a new relationship between Greeks and Egyptians. Perhaps that appeal would have resonated more without its class dimension. Petridis seemed primarily interested in launching a conflict among the community's lower class by galvanizing it to challenge the dominant Greek mentality in Egypt and its economic practices that "objectified" the native Egyptian. To challenge the hegemony of the wealthy and redefine the relationship between Greek and Egyptian proved to be too enormous a task. As Manolis Marangoulis has suggested, the dominant Greek ideology was successful in ignoring the Egyptians but also the poorer Greeks, who were something akin to the underprivileged "petits blancs" in French colonial structures, so the status quo remained in place.[58]

The prospect of an inner Greek class struggle remained dormant, but Petridis's call for closer Greco–Egyptian contacts was picked up by a small group of intellectuals based in Alexandria. There was an attempt to begin publishing Greek-literature in Arabic, led by Stefanos Pargas (the pseudonym of Nikos Zelitas), a mainstay of Alexandria's Greek literary circles and publisher of the Greek-language magazine Παναιγύπτια (Panegyptian) that enjoyed a wide circulation until it closed with his death in 1938. The project never materialized because of a lack of funds, but the cause was continued by Angelos Kasigonis, a publisher of Greek-language books and magazines who had moved to Alexandria from his birthplace Edirne in eastern Thrace, after being educated in Constantinople and the law school of the University of Athens. Kasigonis began producing a monthly bilingual newspaper entitled Αιγυπτιώτης Ελλην / al-Yunani al-mutamassir (The Greek of Egypt, rendered in Arabic as the Egyptianized Greek). When it first came out in 1932 it was warmly received, with the Greek minister of foreign affairs contributing an article on the lessons learned from Greco–Egyptian relations. The articles published in its eight years offered a positive portrayal of relations between the Greeks of Egypt and Egyptians. In one case an article written by an Egyptian contributor, Mahmud Ibrahim, the Alexandria reporter of the Wafdist al-Balagh newspaper, spoke warmly of a Greek grocer and moneylender in a village in Sharqiya province and his popularity with the villagers. But the magazine never caught on with Greeks and Kasigonis was always scraping around for funds and subscriptions, too independently minded to accept monetary assistance from the Greek embassy.

With the advent of the war and the arrival of the Greek exiled government in Egypt, Kasigonis got caught up in the community's headlong involvement in all things Greek. He changed the title of the newspaper to The Greek and the Greco–Egyptian character of the publication came to an abrupt end.[59] The limited steps toward becoming more integrated in Egypt are most clearly evident in the relatively small numbers of Greeks who acquired Egyptian citizenship. Egypt's official statistical data for 1942–43 reported that only 17 percent or just over fifteen thousand Greeks had acquired Egyptian citizenship. This is low for a national group that claimed to have such close affinity with Egypt and the Egyptians. In contrast, about 90 percent of the Syrians in Egypt who were Arab and Christian—specifically Greek Catholics—had Egyptian citizenship.[60]

Literary Images

The town of Asyut in Upper Egypt, more than 600 kilometers south of Alexandria, was an unlikely location to find a Greek novelist and short story writer. Yet many of the Greek literati—men and a few women—whose works populated the pages of the many Greek-language literary magazines published in Alexandria had regular jobs as merchants or white-collar workers. Kostas Tsangaradas spent part of his boyhood a little further north in Minya, where his father worked in the 1890s. At the Greek community school there he learned English and Arabic. He then spent some time in Alexandria where he worked at the Greek-language literary magazine *Serapeion (Serapeum)*. He went to Greece to fight in the Balkan Wars of 1912–13 and returned to settle in Asyut, where he worked as a cotton merchant and pursued his literary interests. In 1924 he published a novel entitled Ναμπία *(Nampia)*, a love story with a strong dose of eroticism set in Asyut against the backdrop of the nationalist uprising of 1919.

Thirty years later it became the first novel written by a Greek of Egypt to be published in Arabic and appeared under the title *'Adhra' Asyut (The Virgin of Asyut)*. As importantly, Tsangaradas's novel was the first by a Greek of Egypt to be focused entirely on Egyptians and their lives. A detailed, exhaustive critique of the novel has highlighted its orientalist tone, yet in terms of the subject matter of Greek literature produced in Egypt, Tsangaradas signaled a new trend: a focus on Egypt and the Egyptians, albeit from a vantage point of privilege. Tsangaradas helped this trend develop by publishing a collection of short stories the following year about Egypt in Greek. He gave the collection an Arabic title, *Hikayat (Stories)*, rendered in Greek as Χικαγιάτ.

There were others who followed Tsangaradas's footsteps. In most cases it was Greeks with literary ambitions living, working, or visiting the provinces who published stories focusing on the life of Egyptians. The lives of the fellahin were of particular interest to Arga Peleia (the pseudonym of Maria Voltou), who visited a Greek-owned *'izba* (farm) in Upper Egypt. Georgios Vrisimitzakis spent a few weeks in a village at the Delta Barrage, a dam at the point where the Nile divides north of Cairo into the two branches that form the Delta. He published a collection of poetry in Greek entitled *The Songs of the Fellah*.

In 1930 Yannis Hadjiandreas, a nineteen-year-old graduate of the Ambetios Commercial School of Cairo, got a job as an accountant at a Greek cotton firm in Abu Tig, a town in the Asyut governorate. It was his first encounter with the fellahin, which he built upon when he moved to a similar job in Dayrut, another town in Asyut, where he stayed for a decade before moving to Alexandria where he became the manager of a tanning factory. While still in Upper Egypt he published a collection of poems in Greek entitled *The Fellahin*, inspired by his life in rural Egypt. He used the pseudonym Stratis Tsirkas. He was already in contact with socialist intellectuals in Alexandria and would become actively involved in Greek political activity during the war years. After the war he would leave poetry behind and focus on prose. Among his major works would be a comprehensive study on Cavafy and a three-part novel set in Egypt and Palestine during the war, a fictional account of the left-wing movement that had developed within the Greek Armed Forces. Years later he would recount that his stay in Asyut brought entirely new experiences. He mentioned that the fellahin had a sense of dignity and courage about them and their manner reminded him of the Souliots, mountain dwellers of a legendary bravery who had fought in the Greek revolution of 1821.[61]

In Tsirkas's attempt to represent the life of the fellahin we have the literary version of Petridis's call in 1928 for greater involvement with Egyptians and their lives, its strengths and weaknesses. The Greek intellectuals who subscribed to a Marxist class analysis used it as a springboard to bridge the gap between Greeks and Egyptians. Placing themselves on the side of the ordinary Greeks of Egypt, they drew a distinction between their underprivileged status and that of the privileged Greek elite who saw themselves as pioneers of civilization, modernizers of Egypt, and by the same token superior to Egyptians. Their ideological lens made that approach easier but only in theory or through literary representations.

In practice little was achieved through the end of the interwar period. In his comprehensive study of intellectual thought among the Greeks of Egypt, Manolis Marangoulis suggested that the colonial structures were simply too ingrained in Egyptian society for even the "underprivileged" Greeks or their Marxist spokesmen to make meaningful contact with the other side. They remained "petits blancs"; certainly poor and subordinate, but still benefiting from Egypt's colonial status quo. Moreover, Greek socialists were more focused on Greece than Egypt. Granted, the arrival of the Greek government and armed forces, and the extraordinarily high political and ideological stakes of the conflict between the Greek Right and Left would have sucked them in anyway. But when the war was over and the Greeks from Greece took all their ideological baggage with them, the Greeks left in Egypt, not to mention the rest of the community, had to scramble to redirect their attention to the new round of Egyptianization measures.

The Eleventh Hour

There was little time left for Greeks to refocus on the situation in Egypt, the scheduled end of the Mixed Courts, and what many hoped would be a favorable agreement between Greece and Egypt concerning the 'establishment,' that is, the status of Greeks in the country. What had been an almost perennial debate about the future of the Greeks in Egypt seemed to be in abeyance. Many regarded the impending treaty of establishment as enough of a guarantee, and calls for adaptation and reaching out to Egyptians lost their urgency. What had become "an entrenched belief that the future of the Greeks in Egypt almost exclusively depended on the treaty" became the reason for the community's inertia, interrupted by very few voices warning the Greeks they had to do much more than rely on negotiations between the Greek and Egyptian governments.[62]

Of the fifty Greek-language books published in Egypt in 1946, only two addressed the present and future of Greeks, while one was on reforming Greek schools.[63] One of those two books was by Tsangaradas who, from his southern outpost of Asyut, made one last effort to mobilize his fellow Greeks in the rest of Egypt. Two decades after he had written about ordinary Egyptians, Tsangaradas spoke about how the few remaining Greeks in Upper Egypt were being assimilated by their Egyptian environment. Unlike the socialist writers he saw that as a negative development and suggested that maybe the Greeks of Egypt should begin to "repatriate" to Greece.[64] It represented a dramatic turnaround in Tsangaradas's thought and reflected the narrowing constituency of those who believed Greeks should try and integrate into Egyptian society. The numbers of those doing so were small but not insignificant, as Tsangaradas implied.

Official statistics show that 771 students with Greek citizenship attended Egyptian schools during the 1948–49 school year and it is certain that children whose Greek parents had obtained Egyptian citizenship would also have attended Egyptian schools. There were probably a number of practical reasons for choosing an Egyptian school, such as the availability of other options (Greek or foreign schools), and the costs involved—community organization schools did not provide free education to students whose parents had Egyptian citizenship and indeed many of those families would have lived in Asyut and other towns in Upper Egypt.

The apparent eleventh hour of the Greeks in Egypt had its contradictions. In 1944 the community organization in Cairo decided that the many Greek sporting clubs needed their own sports stadium, and it began fundraising toward that purpose. Ultimately, after its completion, the venue was open to the entire community and several festive and cultural events were held there as well as school parades along with a number of sports events. Significantly, the stadium was inaugurated on March 25, 1947, Greece's national independence day. The guest of honor was Apostolos Nikolaidis, the president of the Greek Association of Sports Clubs, who came over from

Athens for the occasion, bringing with him earth from the Panathenaic stadium in Athens where the 1896 Olympics were held, which was scattered on the surface of the stadium in Cairo. There were about seven thousand people in attendance. The project cost a total of LE31,000, but more importantly it stood as a symbol of the confidence the Greeks of Cairo obviously had about their long-term prospects in Egypt.[65]

A speech Nikos Tsaravopoulos delivered in Cairo in December 1947 represented one of the final appeals by the socialists for Greeks to throw their lot in with Egyptians. Tsaravopoulos had been born in Cairo and encountered radical ideas at the city's Greek Ambetios School in the 1930s. After he was drafted into the Greek Army he participated in the left-wing movement and was interned by the British. He returned to Cairo and was working at a Greek Bank when he was invited to speak about the presence of Greeks in Egypt. He began by discussing the history of their establishment in Egypt and concluded by addressing the issues they were facing by offering three strategies. The first was for the Greeks to populate their community organizations, become more active, and make them truly representative and democratic bodies. The second was the reactivation of the philanthropic spirit of wealthy Greeks, which he felt had atrophied at a time when there was great need. Thirdly, he said, "we have to feel for Egyptian reality and to stop having self-deceiving notions that we can remain here as a privileged minority and understand that our future depends on our professional qualifications, the extent to which we can develop ties of friendship with the Egyptian people and the appreciation and respect we can inspire in them as their friends."[66]

During the following months Tsaravopoulos disappeared from Cairo and in late 1949 he sent word to his family to come and join him in Hungary. He had decided to go and fight for the communist-led Democratic Army in the Greek civil war and had somehow made his way to Greece and saw combat in the final phase of the fighting that ended with the victory of the government forces. The defeated Democratic Army fighters fled across the border, seeking asylum in Eastern Europe. Tsaravopoulos and his family ended up in Bucharest, "a village" compared to Cairo and Budapest, his son recalled.[67] The lure of the Greek homeland, albeit for the purpose of turning it into a socialist or communist country, had gotten the better of Tsaravopoulos. The choices he exercised are a sharp reminder that even those who had called for some form of Greek integration into Egyptian society in practice prioritized Greece over Egypt.

7

In-between Revolutionary Egypt and Greece

In 1954 Antigone Costanda won the Miss Egypt beauty contest and went on to represent Egypt at the Miss World beauty pageant. Costanda was born in Egypt of Greek parents and grew up in Ibrahimiya, a neighborhood of Alexandria where many Greeks lived through the early 1960s. Like many young Greek girls she completed her high school education by attending a French lycée. Costanda had first won the Miss Alexandria contest before becoming Miss Egypt. In London she was crowned Miss World for 1954. The Greek press in Alexandria covered her triumphant return to her hometown, describing her as a Greek beauty even though she was officially Egypt's contestant—in fact that year Greece's entrant in the Miss World pageant came in third. Costanda did not travel to London for the 1955 pageant to crown her successor as was the custom because of escalating tensions between Egypt and Britain over the Suez Canal.

She remained in Egypt and pursued a successful modeling career until she went into interior design, running a company that focused on commercial properties. Costanda's life was certainly not typical of the lives of the Greeks of Egypt but her experiences were representative of what many went through in the 1950s. The new regime in Egypt that took power in 1952 embarked on a series of conflicts with Britain while pursuing vigorous Egyptianization policies that raised the question of whether the Greeks could survive in the new Egypt or if they would have to leave.

The 1950s would turn out to be an especially challenging time for the Greeks of Egypt. It stretched their ability to adapt to changing circumstances while continuing to play a role in Egypt's development. Although the left-wing organization Antifascistiki Protoporia was not representative of the majority despite its growing influence in the 1950s, eventually stymied by the Greek consular authorities, its predicament during this period reflected those of the Greeks as a whole. The organization was trying to balance three goals at the same time: support the left-wing movement back in Greece; challenge the conservative leadership of the community organizations; and reach out to the Egyptian radical movement. Often those goals contradicted each other, and raised the question of whether the organization was Greek or Egyptian. But the organization marched on as best it could, trying to fulfill all three tasks while reflecting "the complexities and contradictions both within the Greek community and Egyptian society."[1]

The Greeks and the 1952 Revolution
The front page of the *Tachydromos* on January 1, 1951 carried an article by one of its columnists complaining that hearing New Year's Day wishes in Arabic meant that someone was asking for a tip.[2] It was an odd way to start the particular year, given that Greeks were beginning to feel the pinch of Egyptianization measures. But outwardly there were few signs that things had really changed for the Greeks in Egypt. The January 1 issue of the Réforme Illustrée, a magazine that came with the Sunday edition of the Alexandrian French-language newspaper Réforme, provided no clues that things were changing in Egypt. The advertisements section showed that Paul Zervoudachi & Company were the general agents of the Fiat motor company in Egypt. The National Bank of Greece informed readers it had branches in both Alexandria and Cairo, as did the Bank of Athens, which also had a branch in Port Said. P. Demetrio & Company announced a most brilliant upcoming season at the Théâtre Muhammad Ali and the Cinéma Royal. Tommy Christou & Company announced a series of Italian films at the Strand Cinema. There were also advertisements for furs at Sistovaris (with branches in Alexandria and Cairo), a "haute coiffure" owned by Mrs. Suzy Grivas, and familiar brand names such as the cotton brokerage firm of J.P. Salvago & Company and the Pastroudis teahouse and patisserie. Miss Lena Christou and Mrs. Georges Choremi were among the society ladies photographed wearing evening dresses. There were also changes afoot. That year Theodore Cozzika, the president of the Greek community in Cairo, moved to France, where he owned a stud farm southwest of Paris. Community organization vice president Georgios Roilos tried to persuade him to return to Egypt but Cozzika refused, remaining there until his death.

But in October 1951 no one would miss that things were changing in Egypt. The Greek press in Alexandria was busy reporting on the First Mediterranean Games that were taking place in the city, giving a lot of coverage to the performances of athletes from Greece. Suddenly a major event pushed the sports off the front pages. The Egyptian government unilaterally abrogated the Anglo–Egyptian Treaty of 1936 and demanded the British withdraw immediately from the Suez Canal area. Demonstrations were held throughout Egypt in support of this demand and against Britain. Egyptian and foreign workers, including Greeks, abandoned their positions in the canal-related services and guerilla fighters called fedayeen launched attacks on British military facilities. The British responded by sealing off the Canal Zone from the rest of Egypt and taking steps to put down demonstrations and defend against armed attacks. The canal town of Ismailiya became one of the flashpoints of the Anglo–Egyptian clashes. Foreign nationals 'collaborating' with the British were also targeted. In January the Egyptian government rescinded the residence permits of Nikolaos Papastratis and two other Greek shopkeepers with British passports because they were supplying an army hostile "to the country that had offered them a welcome home."[3]

As the clashes escalated the British forces attacked the police station considered as one of the centers fomenting unrest. The next day the *Tachydromos* reported that the assault resulted in forty-six Egyptians dead and twice as many casualties, as well as three British deaths and sixteen casualties. In response there were massive demonstrations in Cairo that degenerated into riots and the burning of buildings. The events, which took place on Saturday, January 26, became known as the Cairo fire or "Black Saturday." Two Greeks lost their lives, a personnel manager at Barclays Bank and the treasurer of the Greek community organization of Cairo. The rioters looted and destroyed 463 foreign-owned stores, 157 of them Greek-owned. Early estimates of the cost of damages the Greeks suffered placed them at LE1 million. One large Greek-owned grocery survived because a salesman "cunningly gave out handfuls of piasters and turned away the mob." Greek-Cypriot owners of small businesses burnt in the fire—their bars and cafés were one of the main targets of the rioters—made their claims for compensation to the British authorities on the island.[4]

The community organization and the Greek press in Cairo put on a brave face in the wake of the fire. But many observers believe that in retrospect the fire was another turning point for the foreigners and that Cairo "may have swiftly rebuilt its European-looking façade after Black Saturday's fire, but for most of the city's Europeans it was now just that: a façade . . . they could feel their place in the country's future shrinking by the day . . . at the Hellenic Club, the Circolo Italiano, and the Alliance Israelite the talk was of timetables, of cousins in Montreal, and—*sotto voce*—of false bottomed suitcases."[5]

The Greek reactions to Egypt's repudiation of the Anglo–Egyptian Treaty were mixed, and complicated by political realignments within the community organizations, especially in Alexandria. The community organizations and the press expressed their support for Egypt's wish to gain more independence, but also counseled Egyptians to remain focused on negotiations rather than demonstrations and attacks by fedayeen in the Canal Zone. There were a few left-wing Greeks who actively assisted the fedayeen. Many other Greeks were sympathetic to their ends, not their means. In the Nile Delta towns such as Mansura and Zagazig, the Greeks publicly supported Egyptian moves against the British but were also fearful of a backlash against them. In Alexandria the Greek community organization participated in an anti-British demonstration, as did other Greek organizations. But Alexios Liatis, the Greek consul in Alexandria, opposed such moves and tried to take down names and even photograph those Greeks openly supporting the Egyptian cause, assuming they were communists.

In the wake of the end of the Greek civil war, which pitted British and then US-backed government forces against a communist-led guerilla army, Greek diplomats in Egypt throughout the 1950s would be on the lookout for Greek communists and other subversives. In upholding Greece's pro-Western and anticommunist policy they overlooked the fact that left-wing Greeks in Egypt were often at the forefront of forging close relations with Egyptian nationalists and were committed to finding ways that would ensure a future presence of Greeks in Egypt. Dimitris Zerbinis, the politically conservative industrialist who had been elected president of the Greek community organization in 1948, did not go along with the anticommunist hunts of Greek diplomats throughout his tenure, which ended in 1954. In return, the left-wing Greeks supported Zerbinis, and although they made for strange bedfellows, both sides shared a common cause: to prevent the old elite from controlling the Alexandria community organization. In contrast to Zerbinis, the president of the Greek Chamber of Commerce in Alexandria, Nikolaos Sakellarios, spoke openly about the danger of the Suez Canal falling into the hands of communists.

Meanwhile, undaunted by the attempts of diplomats to discourage them, liberal and mostly left-wing Greeks formed the Council of Greek-Egyptian Friendship and Cooperation, which as its name implied, aimed at bringing Greeks closer to the Egyptian nationalist cause.[6] There were clearly two different sets of attitudes crystallizing among the Greek leadership in Egypt. Some favored moves that would bring the Greeks closer to Egyptians. But others stuck to the hope that a treaty of establishment giving Greeks some rights would be implemented. Expressing that wish, Sakellarios reiterated the desire of the Greeks to stay in Egypt where they and their fathers had been born and "to find again the old familiar face of Egypt." Those words were spoken in early 1952. Within a few months, Egypt would take a huge step toward independence and the possibility of retaining any special status for the foreigners would become even more remote.

A few days after the Free Officers seized power on July 23, daily life went back to normal for most Egyptians, while the Greek organizations and newspapers were cautious but supportive of the new government. Three days later the *Tachydromos* would report that one of the leaders of the coup, General Muhammad Naguib, arrived in Alexandria and reassured foreigners they had nothing to fear. Naguib was there to oversee King Faruq's departure from Egypt. That same day the scheduled horse racing took place at the city's sporting club, and a few days later tickets went on sale for the upcoming visit of the Harlem Globetrotters basketball team. But changes were taking place and the Greeks began adjusting. Over the next days the Greek newspapers expressed more support for the military and Naguib, whom the Greeks saw as a guarantee that the new regime would not turn against the foreigners. The Council of Greek-Egyptian Friendship and Cooperation congratulated Naguib on the magnificent new page of history he was opening. On August 1 the community organization of Alexandria also sent him an official congratulatory message. Later that year Naguib visited the Greek Orthodox Patriarchate of Alexandria and reiterated the view he had expressed in late July that the Greeks were welcome in Egypt and should not feel insecure.[7]

On the occasion of Greek Independence Day in March 1953, Naguib made another statement reassuring Greeks. Thus, the sense of confidence in the general continued and it strengthened when the monarchy was formally abolished the following year and Naguib became president. When in 1954 Nasser swept him aside and took over, the Greeks dutifully expressed their loyalty to the new leader. This was not an unreasonable reaction. Until that point the regime did not wish to alienate foreigners, who it regarded as sources of investment, which would improve Egypt's international standing. Nasser also did not want to offer Britain a pretext to intervene by mistreating foreign residents. The only 'radical' measure the new government took was introducing an agrarian reform law that limited agricultural holdings to a maximum of two hundred feddans and required that holdings above that limit be expropriated and distributed to the fellahin. That was the only measure that directly affected Greeks and other foreigners, but only very few of them.

The expressions of loyalty and support notwithstanding, the Greeks were experiencing growing alarm about their future prospects in Egypt in the wake of the events of 1952. The lack of the so-called treaty of establishment that would have made the presence of the Greeks more 'official' and the requirements for acquiring a residency permit were a continuing source of concern. In 1952, the *Tachydromos* complained that government authorities had barricaded themselves behind "barbed wire" and red tape, making the process of acquiring a residency permit all the more arduous, slow, and frustrating. In the meantime, the Egyptianization measures introduced in 1947 were gradually being implemented. In the case of the Suez Canal Company, where the type of skills required and its status had traditionally favored foreigners, the Free Officers were especially eager to reduce the number of foreigners and increase the numbers of Egyptians employed. For example, the number of Egyptian employees hired as contractors almost doubled between 1949 and 1955, while the corresponding number of foreigners dropped by over 20 percent, many of them choosing early retirement. Reports spoke of low morale caused by the prospect of a British withdrawal.

In early 1956 foreign workers, a majority of whom were Greeks, petitioned the company to be given a favorable allowance if they resigned for the purposes of emigrating. The reason they gave was the increasingly unfavorable employment laws in Egypt, their reduced prospects of being promoted, and that their children had "practically no chance for a future." The management was unsympathetic to that and other complaints of Greek workers, noting that they had enjoyed a privileged position in the company for many years and could not admit that things were changing because of the increase in quality of the Egyptian labor force. Even Greek-owned companies had to dismiss Greek employees, either in order to comply with Egyptianization laws or using them as an excuse. This was not always easy in an environment in which traditionally Greeks had used national ties in business. The Société Viticole et Vinicole d'Egypte, the wine company which Gianaclis established between Alexandria and Cairo, did all it could to retain its Greek employees, and felt pressure from the community not to dismiss fellow Greeks.[8]

Beyond the continuation of Egyptianization measures there were other moves the new regime made that were worrying, such as limiting the amount of currency travelers could take when leaving Egypt and later imposing certain travel restrictions on Egyptian citizens. In May 1953 the regime announced an easier process for obtaining residency permits for foreigners willing to invest LE20,000 in new or existing firms, an admission that obtaining that permit was not easy. Some Greeks meanwhile saw tendencies among the leading cadres of the regime that could result in restrictions affecting foreigners. Therefore, there was no rush to invest in Egypt by Greeks or other resident foreigners. When Nasser displaced Naguib in 1954, those anxieties grew. Greek diplomats and the Greek press, which usually followed their lead, struck an optimistic tone and wealthy Greeks did not show outward signs of concern, but none of that could offset the unease that spread throughout the community. Only the left-wing *Paroikos* newspaper openly supported Nasser and reprimanded the Alexandria community organization for its lukewarm support of Egypt's leader. The *Tachydromos* warned against Greek public demonstrations in favor of the regime until the situation in Egypt had settled down. After all, the British still controlled the Suez Canal.

Many Greeks voted with their feet, leaving Egypt and trying to export or smuggle out as many of their liquid assets as possible. One indication of the numbers leaving was that in 1952 the Greek consul general in Alexandria issued 452 exit visas, among them 165 for Greece and 207 for Australia. Obtaining an exit visa was easier than going through the process of leaving the country permanently and it enabled a return to Egypt. The following year it issued a total of 341 exit visas, with the number for Australia again higher than that for Greece. In Cairo in 1952 the visas for Australia were three times more than those for Greece—180 compared to sixty-two. Australia, which was welcoming immigrants at the time, was a destination Athens strongly recommended that the poorer Greeks of Egypt choose to go because it feared that war-torn Greece would offer them little opportunity. If they arrived in Greece and became destitute, not only would they be a burden on the state, they may even be attracted to communism. In late 1951 the general consul in Alexandria established a fund through which it offered financial assistance to those Greeks unable to pay for their passage to Australia. The only objections came from the left-wing *Paroikos* that declared that the authorities should be encouraging either readjustment to Egypt or repatriation to Greece. Consul Liatis believed in the necessity of "decongesting" the Greek community, and that the communists opposed migration to Australia of poorer Greeks because that would deprive them of potential supporters. Another destination was Israel, the choice of the Greek Jews who were also leaving Egypt due to the increase in anti-Semitism after the Arab–Israeli war of 1948. That outflow would increase after the Suez Crisis.[9]

In September 1955, without warning, the government took another step that limited foreign privileges when it abolished all religious courts. The measure affected the *shari'a* Muslim courts and the *milliya*, the Christian ecclesiastical and Jewish rabbinical courts. All pending and future cases were to be transferred to the national Egyptian courts. The abolition was not straightforward, in that the government measures stipulated that the civil courts would apply the religious laws of the litigants. Yet additional steps, including a draft of a new constitution proclaiming Islam as the state religion in Egypt, a step probably designed with a view to increasing Egypt's influence over other Arab countries, raised another possibility. It was the old Islamic and Ottoman order that had originally offered privileges to the non-Muslims. Could a future Islamic status quo bring back the arrangements that had benefited non-Muslims?[10] Like most of the legislation of this era there was a great deal of ambiguity and the possibility of exceptions and loopholes. But it did nothing to reassure non-Muslim minorities that their future in Egypt was secure.

Help from the Homeland

The vast majority of Greeks who remained in Egypt after 1952 soon discovered that things were changing. The economic hardships they faced due to the Egyptianization measures and their inability to respond either by learning Arabic or acquiring Egyptian citizenship was putting enormous pressure on community organizations and the services they offered, such as free or reduced-fee education. But because of the uncertain circumstances, the big donations by wealthy Greeks that had kept those services going in the past were now drying up. Greek employers, under pressure to hire Egyptians, could not be relied upon to offer jobs to compatriots in need. Signs of trouble were everywhere. In 1952 the Greek community organization in Cairo decided to begin the sale of its real estate holdings in order to balance its budget. It also discovered that income from its lottery, which had always been a reliable source of funds, was substantially reduced.

In Alexandria, the largest institution run by the community organization, the hospital funded by Cozzikas, had a serious budget deficit. The
numbers of students, especially those paying full fees, began to decrease in
the community schools. On the day the newspapers announced Costanda's
big achievement at the Miss World contest in 1954, they also reported serious divisions within the community organization over administering grants
to students whose families could not pay full fees because the number of
claims had increased substantially. In Kafr al-Zayyat the number of students at the community school fell by two-thirds in the early 1950s.[11] The
steady decrease of Greek business in the interior gained pace in the 1950s.
One source estimated that only twenty of the 120 entirely Greek-owned
manufacturing plants were still in operation.[12]

Community organization leaders turned to the government in Athens
for help. Its envoy, representative, economist, and lawyer was Sotirios Agapitidis, a professor at the Athens Polytechnic who had been involved in the
initiative to direct the Greeks of Egypt wishing to emigrate to Australia.
Agapitidis arrived in Egypt in December 1954 and would make several
trips there over the next two years. At the core of his proposals were drastic,
across-the-board cuts in the expenditure of community institutions along
with financial help from the Greek government. His report targeted the
schools and recommended the abolition of free education, budget cuts
that would affect the overall running of the schools, a reduction in the
free meals the schools provided, and scholarships only for the most gifted
schoolchildren. Community organizations should coordinate their activities, the report proposed. Land holdings in rural areas should be sold off
and the old people's home in Alexandria should be absorbed by the hospital. The report dwelled at some length on the problems facing the Cozzika
Hospital in Alexandria due to its budget deficit. Agapitidis had a radical
proposal, either it became an independent organization or the Greek government took it over, but Athens ultimately rejected such a move and the
hospital continued to face difficulties, even though Theodore Cozzika
contributed generously in order to help its finances. Fortunately for the
Greeks of Egypt and their institutions, the Greek government agreed to
provide some monetary assistance.[13]

Significantly, Agapitidis submitted his report to the Greek government,
not the community organizations, although they were involved in the discussions and sent representatives to Athens to review the situation. It was a

sign that the leadership of the Greeks of Egypt put its hopes in the homeland rather than come to some arrangement with the Egyptian authorities.
The thinking was that the community organization existed to serve the
interests of Greeks and any approaches to the Egyptian authorities could
result in them losing that exclusive character. This attitude dovetailed with
the leadership's belief that the only way the Greeks could remain in Egypt
was to be recognized as an entity exempted from the restrictions imposed
on other foreign residents, and by the same token be given some leeway so
as not to become fully integrated into Egyptian society.

It was only left-wing Greeks, a significant but minority voice throughout the 1950s, who thought otherwise and called for some form of
integration. How that tactic would be effected, and whether it would be
allowed on the Egyptian side, was never explored. In any case the logic of
regarding the Greeks as a national group remained. It was up to the Greek
government to intervene, and in order to provoke it to act, Agapitidis concluded his report by noting that the unfolding events in Egypt threatened
to obliterate the Greek presence, whose total wealth he estimated at le160
million. If the government did not intervene, he added ominously, the consequences would be catastrophic.

In 1955 another report appeared about the state of the Greeks of
Egypt, this one by a Greek diplomat serving at the Greek embassy in Cairo,
who studied the situation of the Greek schools. It was a comprehensive
study published as a fifty-four-page booklet two years later. Most of it consists of painstakingly collected facts about the number and the location of
the Greek schools and the numbers of students in attendance. The report
showed there was an overall decrease in the total number of students in the
1954–55 school year compared with the number that attended in 1952–53.
The conclusions include a set of recommendations, which must have created a sense of déjà vu to any reader who had followed the debates over
Greek educational reform in Egypt over the previous twenty-five years.
The author of the report conceded that some reforms had been introduced,
but then went on to list a catalog of recommendations that had been voiced
in the past, designed to reorient the curriculum toward providing practical
skills to students as well as a greater proficiency in mathematics and the
natural sciences. There was an urgently worded call for an increase in the
number of hours of Arabic and other foreign languages. Had the Greek
embassy pushed for such a set of reforms twenty years earlier, the report
might have been more useful.[14]

The Suez Crisis

When Nasser nationalized the Suez Canal in July of 1956, a month after British troops officially evacuated the area, he came up against the combined force of Britain, France, and Israel. Greeks, who claimed a special relationship with Egypt, led by their diplomats under instructions by Athens, came out in support of Nasser's move. Two weeks after the nationalization and at a time when the outcome of Nasser's move was in the balance, the Greek vice consul in Port Said, speaking to Greeks in Ismailiya, declared that the Greek government put all its trust in Egypt's leader. Most Greek organizations came out in support of the canal's nationalization. Only the Greek community organization of Alexandria was slower to react, and privately many Greeks hoped the Anglo–French would force Egypt to reverse the nationalization of the Suez Canal Company.

The Greek government registered its support by declining an invitation to take part in an international conference of all states affected by the nationalization of the canal that was meeting without Egypt, to consider imposing international control over the canal. These expressions of support notwithstanding, all foreigners including Greeks felt a growing sense of alarm at what might happen and how they would be affected. The *New York Times* reported that foreigners were "afraid lest the British and the French take armed action. They feel foreigners in Egypt would be the first victims of the popular reaction."[15]

In September, when Nasser had not yielded to diplomatic pressures, Britain and France stepped up the pressure to make him rescind the canal's nationalization. One of the measures they agreed upon was to remove the official restraint on the old Suez Company's desire to withdraw its pilots from the nationalized canal. This was potentially a crippling blow because many of those employees were navigation pilots and without them the new Egyptian authority would be unable to operate the canal. At the time of nationalization in July, the company had 205 pilots, sixty-one Britons, fifty-three Frenchmen, forty Egyptians, fourteen Dutchmen, twelve Greeks, and fourteen more of several other nationalities. The company reported that almost all non-Egyptians with the exception of the Greeks had asked to be repatriated. Britain and France had told the company to ask the pilots to remain on the job pending the diplomatic initiatives taken in August and early September. The Greek government, eager to enlist Egypt's diplomatic support for the Greek–Cypriot struggle that had broken out on British-controlled Cyprus, ordered the Greek employees to stay in place.

In late August the Egyptian government claimed some foreign pilots (none of the Greeks) were feigning illness to undermine the smooth functioning of the Suez Canal, but they were effectively being replaced by Egyptian and Greek pilots, and that the new state company was hiring an additional twenty-seven Egyptians and three Greek pilots.[16]

Then in early September, Britain and France agreed to the withdrawal of the foreign pilots, triggering their departure and leaving only the Greeks. The Egyptian authorities rushed to replenish the numbers by training qualified volunteers. Of the foreign pilots only eleven Greeks and one Spaniard remained.[17] Egypt's response to the departure of the foreign pilots was to recruit and train Egyptians, Greeks, and others from several other countries. By late October there were 233 pilots working for the nationalized canal, 180 of them fully qualified, the others in training. There were one hundred Egyptian pilots. The next largest national group were thirty Greeks. In order to ensure the continued loyalty of the Greek pilots and administrative employees at the nationalized Canal Company, the local Greek consular officials declared they would not be providing those Greeks with exit visas and even threatened to pass on names of those making such requests to the Egyptian authorities. Undeterred, at least thirty-one Greeks somehow managed to obtain visas with the help of French authorities. Overall, beyond the official statements of support from Greek diplomats and the community organizations there was a wide range of attitudes toward the canal's nationalization. The Greek–Egyptian Cooperation Committee took a number of initiatives, from raising funds to enlisting volunteers to fight on the side of the Egyptians if the need arose.

The Greek contribution to the pressing need for navigation pilots in the nationalized canal was a symbolic gesture that set the Greeks on Egypt's side. Throughout the period of nationalization to the resolution of the crisis, Egyptian demonstrators and government officials acknowledged the help from Greeks. Nasser even decorated the Greek pilots who remained at their posts. It remained to be seen if that was enough to protect the Greeks from the consequences of the Suez Crisis for foreigners.

In the end, Egypt "won the peace" as one historian put it, because the tripartite attack of Britain, France, and Israel that began on October 29 aimed at regaining control of the canal ultimately ended in failure. Their combined force easily defeated the Egyptian army. Port Said was hit especially hard and four Greeks were among the dead from British aerial bombardment. The logistics of the invasion were badly bungled. The piecemeal process of the invasion enabled the Egyptians to block the canal, so the overall outcome was an impasse: Anglo–French occupation of the Canal Zone but with shipping unable to use the waterway. After pressure from the United States and the Soviet Union, the invading forces withdrew and United Nations forces arrived to take over control of the canal temporarily. Nasser survived, indeed his stature increased, and the canal remained nationalized and opened again in March of 1957.[18]

The Suez Crisis and the war would have a drastic effect on foreign residents in Egypt, including directly or indirectly on most Greeks. In the immediate aftermath of the crisis, and in retaliation against the tripartite attack, the regime targeted the British, French, and Jewish residents of Egypt. About one thousand Jews were detained, and thirteen thousand British and French citizens, some of them Jews, were expelled from Egypt. British-, French-, and Jewish-owned businesses and properties were nationalized. Over fourteen thousand Jews, a third of the total residing during the Suez Crisis, had left the country by March 1957. Many left as impoverished refugees, although the property of Jews who were not British or French citizens was returned.[19] Greek Jews were among the five hundred Jews not holding British or French nationality who were also expelled. The most famous Greek Jew from Egypt, the singer Georges Moustaki, had already left in 1951 for France. There he embarked on a spectacular career as a singer and songwriter, which included a close personal and professional relationship with Edif Piaf. His original name was Giuseppe Mustacchi; his parents had moved to Alexandria from the island of Corfu.

But agreeing to a request made by the Greek government, Greek Cypriots with British passports were excluded from the deportations and were recognized as Greek nationals.

Next to the planned expulsions there were foreigners who made the decision that their future in Egypt was no longer promising. This was especially true in Port Said, which was badly hit during the military operations. As these were taking place, Egyptian officials issued reassurances to the foreign residents in Port Said that the police would protect them from looters and any retaliation against them.[20] But the economic uncertainties and psychological effects of the war and destruction meant that many European residents, about 1,500, were on their way out; six hundred had already left by early December. Some feared reprisals because of the high number of casualties Egyptians suffered during the bombing and fighting in the city. Others, especially Italian laborers, were leaving because they were out of work due to the closing of the canal. About nine hundred Italians made plans to return to Italy. France granted asylum to two hundred stateless persons and 150 persons of different nationalities. Britons and Jews were also leaving. "A notable exception," one foreign correspondent noted, were the Greeks, "the largest of the foreign communities," adding, "of the 5,000 to 6,000 holders of Greek passports in the Port Said—Port Fu'ad area, only eighty had signed up at their consulate for repatriation."[21] Most, though not all, of the Greeks remained, even in Port Said. But the departure of other foreigners deprived many Greek shopkeepers of a large proportion of their regular customers as well as suppliers and business associates. Reports of mistreatment of those being forcibly expelled and the restrictions on those Britons and Frenchmen who remained in Egypt contributed to the growing sense of unease about what the future would bring.

In January 1957 the government announced the Egyptianization of all British and French banks and insurance companies, while all other foreign banks and insurance companies were given five years to undergo the same process. British and French banks had been sequestered during the Suez Crisis. This legislation made the changes permanent. Egyptianization in practice did not mean nationalization but that private shareholders who would retain their stocks had to be Egyptian citizens born in Egypt; company directors also had to be born in Egypt, and only a limited percentage of company profits could be invested abroad. Another law that was introduced stipulated that all agents representing foreign manufacturers in Egypt had to be native-born Egyptian citizens, though in some cases an exception was made and foreigners were allowed in those positions for another five years. While Greek banks were not immediately affected, there were many Greek employees in the British and French banks that were subject to the new measures.

The Greek leadership began to react when rumors of the impending measures became hard to ignore. Community organization president Anastasios Theodorakis, Greek Chamber of Commerce in Alexandria president Yagkos Chryssovergis, and Georgios Roilos, the president of the Greek community organization in Cairo, drafted a strongly worded message—a rare public criticism couched as an appeal—to Nasser to moderate his measures requiring that all banks, insurance companies, and foreign commercial concerns be placed under the control of Egyptians. Speaking for an estimated seventy thousand Greeks, the largest foreign community in Egypt, the signatories expressed their "bitterness, concern and confusion" over recent laws affecting foreign business interests. The new measures were, they stated ominously, "a deadly blow to a majority of the Greeks living in the country."[22]

The Athens–Cairo Connection

Nasser's rise to power in Egypt and his embrace of the movement of non-aligned states that coalesced around the Conference of African and Asian States held in 1955 in Bandung, Indonesia, coincided with the escalation of an anticolonial struggle by the Greeks on Cyprus, a British colony. The Greek–Cypriot struggle was aimed at ending British rule and realizing a longstanding demand that Cyprus be united with Greece. After the British rejected the outcome of a referendum held on the island in 1951 that produced an overwhelming vote in favor of union with Greece, the Greek–Cypriot leader Archbishop Makarios launched a diplomatic campaign to solicit support from the United Nations while a group of Greek Cypriots launched a guerilla struggle against the British in April 1955. That same month Makarios and Nasser attended the Bandung Conference.

Meanwhile in Athens, the Greek government was trying to balance between its status as a member of the western NATO alliance and support for fellow Greeks in Cyprus, whose struggle resonated with public opinion on the Greek mainland. Greece had already broken ranks once with its western allies when it voted against the plan to partition Palestine into two states, one Arab and the other Jewish, and two years later it offered Israel de facto but not de jure recognition. The reasoning behind that policy was the need to protect the Greeks in Egypt, Greek shipping's access to the Suez Canal in case Egypt retaliated against states recognizing Israel, and to protect the status of the Greek Orthodox Patriarchate in Jerusalem. With the United Nations becoming a venue where the Greek-Cypriot cause could gain international recognition, something that would require the votes of the Arab and non-aligned states, courting Nasser became a priority in Athens.

The status of the Greeks in Egypt became part of the conversation between Greece and Egypt, but significantly it was of secondary importance to the Cyprus issue. Community leaders assumed that close relations between Athens and Cairo would also mean favorable treatment of their demands by the Egyptian government. When a Greek government minister visited Egypt in March 1956 his report to the Cabinet explained that the goals of the trip were to secure Egypt's support for the Greek–Cypriot struggle, to meet with the Greek community organizations, and to convey to the Egyptian government that Greece was embarking on a policy designed to improve its relations with all Arab states. Indeed, in the ensuing months Greek foreign policy laid great stress on Greco–Arab relations. When the Suez Crisis came around, Greece was theoretically neutral. It declined to attend the meeting held by Britain and France, kept the Greek pilots at work, and openly supported Egypt during the debates and votes in the United Nations.[23]

Soon after the Egyptian government announced the new Egyptianization measures there was a range of reactions on the part of Greeks. Community leaders turned to the government in Athens. Greece's ambassador to Egypt, Dimitris Lambros, traveled to the Greek capital for consultations. He took with him leading members of the Greek community organizations of Alexandria and Cairo. The Greek government sent Cairo a message calling for Greeks to be excluded from the legislation. The Athens newspapers criticized the Egyptian government and so did several deputies from all political parties when parliament discussed the issue of the Greeks and Egypt's measures. Within days Greek prime minister Constantinos Karamanlis sent Nasser a letter stressing that the legislation introduced, even though it did not target the Greeks, had created a feeling of panic that could well lead to a mass exodus and requested that Nasser offer some form of reassurance to the Greeks. Karamanlis expressed his concern that conditions in Greece were such that his country would be unable to handle a large influx of Greeks from Egypt. Privately, he was aware that the future movement of Greeks from Egypt to Greece was inevitable but it was important for the Greek government to postpone that event as long as possible. It was only a few years earlier that Greece emerged ruined from a decade of war and it was still experiencing postwar reconstruction, albeit with encouraging results. Not surprisingly, given the close relations between the two states, Nasser responded that his government would do "everything possible to dispel the worries of our brother Greeks . . . for whom I feel the greatest respect and deepest sympathy."

Whether or not it reassured many Greeks in Egypt, it had the intended effect on the Greek Ministry of Foreign Affairs, which expected Egypt's government to introduce favorable measures for the Greeks. That may have been wishful thinking, although Nasser gave an interview to an Athenian daily and said that the Greeks had nothing to be afraid of, and repeated as much when he met with the Greek ambassador to Cairo and affirmed it was not his aim to cause the departure of the Greeks from Egypt. The only real optimism surrounding Nasser's intentions was among part of the left-wing Greeks of Egypt. The Greek–Egyptian Cooperation Committee they had founded during the Suez Crisis came out in support of the Egyptianization measures and the right of a sovereign state to legislate over matters concerning foreign residents. It requested that the Egyptian government guarantee the job situation of those Greeks with residency permits and make the process of acquiring Egyptian citizenship easier. The committee also called upon Nasser to affirm that Egypt still needed the Greeks and if that was not the case they requested the Greeks be granted some time to plan their repatriation to Greece.

Nasser's reassurances notwithstanding, the Egyptianization laws announced in 1957 increased the sense of apprehension among many if not most Greeks. The *Tachydromos* reacted angrily, complaining that the laws implied racial discrimination and stated that the Greeks deserved to be considered as "indigenous" inhabitants of Egypt. In contrast, the *Paroikos*, seeing that the community leaders were calling upon Athens for help, declared it was the wrong strategy and suggested the Greeks had an opportunity to declare themselves on the side of Egypt.[24]

Osgood Caruthers, the *New York Times* correspondent in Egypt, whose coverage of the Suez Crisis was widely praised, conveyed that pervasive sense in his reports in the days after the announcement of the new Egyptianization laws. He described the laws as a definite turning point, "the real beginning of Nasser's revolution." The new laws went beyond replacing one regime with another and signaled Egypt's will to end both poverty and its dependence on "foreign advice, foreign experts and foreign assistance" because "to the Egyptian way of thinking, these foreign influences have served only foreign interests and have failed to benefit the people of Egypt." The consequences of the policies this belief generated were difficult to control, Caruthers pointed out, and the expulsion of the British, French, and Jewish residents "cost Egypt more than their cosmopolitan heritage they had helped establish: their businesses closed down" and that "aggravated the already terrible employment problem caused by the almost complete halt of business in cities along the Suez Canal and the curtailment of activity in Alexandria and Cairo." All this, he went on to say, caused a mass exodus that spread to other foreigners "who have found that after years of residence in Egypt it is no longer possible for them to make a living." Thus, "the big Greek community in Alexandria is rapidly dwindling . . . hundreds of Italians are leaving too."

Even Egyptians with money were affected by the climate of uncertainty and, fearing a continued currency crisis, were buying up the paintings, fine rugs, and antique furniture from the foreigners and Jews leaving the country, while they in turn were buying clothes and whatever other personal items the Egyptian customs authorities would permit them to take with them.[25] The Greek ambassador Dimitris Lambros, who had been born in Alexandria, was well aware of the "panic" among the Greeks that he said would persist "unless the English and French start coming back." Lambros also believed that wealthy Greeks were not doing anything to reassure their compatriots, in the sense they had not positioned them to be better prepared to adapt to the Egyptianization measures.

He organized a two-day meeting in Cairo and invited the leaders of the community organizations and chambers of commerce to discuss how they could confront the "psychosis of disordered flight from Egypt." The left-wing Greek–Egyptian Cooperation Committee was not invited but they echoed the same concerns in a memorandum, identifying the need for Greeks to readjust to new circumstances in Egypt not only in a professional and educational sense but also a psychological one. The Greek government sent a familiar face, Agapitidis, who had drawn up a list of recommendations to address the problems community organizations were facing before the Suez Crisis. He was there yet again to try and prevent emigration to Greece and encourage Greeks leaving Egypt to opt for alternative destinations. Nasser received the conference delegates and Nikolaos Sakellarios, speaking in Arabic, affirmed the loyalty of the Greeks of Egypt, thanked him for exempting the Greek Cypriots with British passports from the Egyptianization measures, and asked for his support in establishing an Arab-Greek association under the auspices of the Greek community organization of Alexandria. The meeting offered Nasser another occasion to allay the fears of the Greeks. He told them that he hoped they felt Egypt was their country and to look to the future with optimism.

Ambassador Lambros passed on an invitation to Nasser to visit Greece, but Egypt's leader refrained from setting a date for the trip because Greece had embraced the Eisenhower Doctrine. Announced in January 1957, the doctrine invited any country to request economic or military aid from the United States if another state was threatening it with armed aggression. The Eisenhower administration's decision to issue this doctrine was motivated in part by its perception that there was an increase in Arab hostility toward the West, and growing Soviet influence in Egypt and Syria following the Suez Crisis. As a member of NATO, Greece naturally endorsed

Eisenhower's initiative and this created a potential Greco–Egyptian rift because Nasser believed, rightly, that the United States wished to split the Arab world by courting states that were not prepared to forge links with the Soviet Union. Concerned about Egypt's reactions, Karamanlis asked to meet Nasser in Cairo to smooth things over and the visit was scheduled for mid-August that year. There was speculation in the press that Karamanlis would try and persuade Nasser to endorse the Eisenhower Doctrine.

The Athens daily *Eleutheria* sent Panos Karavias, an experienced journalist and writer, to cover the visit. Karavias had studied in Paris, served as the correspondent of the Cairo daily *al-Ahram* in Athens between 1934 and 1946, and spent nine years in New York as chief editor of a Greek-language daily. The day before Karamanlis's departure the *Eleutheria* published an interview Nasser gave Karavias in which he dismissed the possibility of Egypt adhering to the Eisenhower Doctrine. The visit, the newspaper editorialized, would be mostly about Greco–Egyptian relations, especially with regard to the unfolding situation in Cyprus, and the status of the Greeks of Egypt. The editorial described the Egyptianization laws as xenophobic and demanded a solution that would alleviate the fears of the Greek community. It pointed out that those leaving were unfairly prevented from repatriating their capital, acquired because of the hard work of several generations who built on the initial investment brought to Egypt. The restrictions imposed on the export of capital from Egypt, according to the Eleutheria, were unethical and also had to be resolved. It was the type of hard-hitting critique of Egyptianization measures that the Greek press in Egypt would not dare publish.[26]

Karamanlis's visit brought nothing concrete aside from the restoration of the close ties between Egypt and Greece. It was an occasion where the two governments and the Greeks of Egypt affirmed the positions everyone had before the Olympic Airways airplane carrying Karamanlis and Evangelos Averoff, the minister for foreign affairs, landed in Cairo at noon on August 17. There was one exception. During his talks with Nasser, Karamanlis requested that Greek firms be excluded from the 1957 laws, something Nasser said he could not do. But he also raised the possibility of Greeks acquiring citizenship, or a status with quasi-citizenship rights that Egypt granted to nationals of other Arab countries. Egypt's short-lived federative experience with Syria under the United Arab Republic demanded new arrangements governing nationality, and a decree issued in Egypt in 1958 enabled any member of the Arab community to become a naturalized

Egyptian with more lenient criteria than those applied to non-Arabs, in a fast-track process that would not entail waiting for five years.[27] Karamanlis's new negotiating tactic was interesting because it put aside the idea that Greeks be exempt from laws affecting foreigners and instead conceived of them becoming more integrated into Egyptian society. Karamanlis was the leader of Greece's conservative party and this proposal was very close to the views of the left-wing Greeks in Egypt. Karamanlis's proposal, the Greek delegation told the press, remained only "at the level of discussions." Nasser listened sympathetically and produced a new round of verbal reassurances about the status of Greeks, how much they were esteemed for their contributions to Egypt, and how close Egyptians felt to Greeks.

Echoing Nasser, the Egyptian weekly *al-Musawar* ran an article praising Greeks for standing by Egyptians during the 1919 uprising. The extensive coverage of the visit by the Cairo press included warm mention of Egypt's Greek residents. The positive atmosphere of the talks—notwithstanding Nasser's refusal to consider pro-Western moves with or without Greece's mediation—prompted Averoff to declare that the Greek side emerged with a sense of optimism, much greater than what they expected to feel prior to the meetings. But he ducked the question about what exactly caused that optimism and went on to talk about the close understanding Greece and Egypt had on the Cyprus issue. The joint communiqué the two governments issued at the conclusion of their talks confirmed that little actual progress had been made on the status of the Greeks of Egypt. It was several paragraphs long and mentioned the Greeks of Egypt only at the very end.

Within a week, Averoff sent a message to all Greek embassies summarizing the outcome of the visit to Egypt. With regard to the status of the Greeks in Egypt he confirmed that there had been no agreement although the Egyptian side had heard the Greek proposals sympathetically. Only after the Egyptian government decided on the status of Arab nationals would it consider the situation of the Greeks, the memorandum explained, concluding with the type of optimism that Averoff had expressed while talking to the press in Cairo.[28]

The Greek leadership in Egypt, community organization leaders, and the press also remained fixed in their approach to the status of the Greeks, in that they saw the visit as an affirmation of the Greek homeland's concern and its role in representing them to the Egyptian government. The day of Karamanlis's arrival the *Tachydromos* came out with a banner headline addressed to Karamanlis and Nasser that read, "Your Excellencies, Save the Greeks of Egypt." The same newspaper gave the most optimistic spin to the outcome of the visit, telling its readers that Nasser did not want the Greeks to leave Egypt—but it did not explain how they would manage to stay. Both Karamanlis and Averoff, aside from the inevitable official schedule that entailed a visit to the Pyramids, the Egyptian Museum, and official dinners, devoted a lot of time during their five-day stay in Egypt to visiting Greek institutions. They visited schools, churches, and other community institutions and had several official lunches and dinners, one of them at the Salvago mansion in the Quartier Grec. The *Tachydromos* saw all this as additional proof that the homeland's government, even if it was the eleventh hour, cared about the Greeks of Egypt and would help them.

Not everyone regarded Athens so positively. The meetings between government officials and the community were an opportunity for several Greek organizations to submit memoranda to the government expressing their views. The Union of Greek Employees of Public (Retail) Stores in Cairo produced an especially hard-hitting critique on how the Greeks had gotten into the crisis they now faced. The union pointed out that the Greek leadership had failed in its responsibility to prepare the community for the upcoming changes by not creating enough vocational schools early on and never really recognizing the importance of teaching Arabic properly in Greek schools. The memorandum then criticized Greece's efforts to redirect Greeks leaving Egypt to countries like Australia, noting how the Greeks of Egypt had stood by their homeland and deserved better if they chose to return to Greece. It ended by demanding a reduction in fees Greek consulates charged Greeks who were returning to Greece and an end to the onerous import taxes on household goods and personal items that Greek customs charged returnees. The memorandum reflected how they envisioned the future, and it was realistic. In terms of substantive progress on the issue of the status of the Greeks there had been little progress. It remained to be seen whether the optimism expressed by Greek government officials would be borne out.

Three years later, when Nasser returned Karamanlis's visit and arrived in Greece for a six-day stay in June 1960, no progress had been made on resolving the issues facing the Greeks of Egypt. Nasser, who brought his family and arrived in Piraeus on his yacht al-Hurriya, was received by the king and queen of Greece, whom he invited to Cairo. He held talks with Karamanlis, went up to the Acropolis, watched a military parade in his honor, visited Delphi and the island of Corfu, and went on to visit President

Tito in neighboring Yugoslavia. Throughout his stay in Greece Nasser was received warmly by the Greek public. A big part of Nasser's popularity was due to his backing of the Greek Cypriot cause in the United Nations during the 1950s and the many other expressions of support, including receiving in Egypt Archbishop Makarios, the Greek Cypriot leader. In his public utterances Nasser mentioned his gratitude for Greece's support during the Suez Crisis and for the services offered by Greek navigation pilots. He spoke of the long friendship of the Egyptian and Greek peoples, and the contributions the Greeks of Egypt had made to Egypt's progress.

Behind closed doors Nasser did not commit to satisfying any of the Greek demands that included a request that the deadline for the Egyptianization of the four Greek-owned banks in Egypt be extended beyond 1962 and easing the procedures for Greeks applying for Egyptian citizenship. Karavias, the Eleutheria journalist who had interviewed Nasser in 1957, believed that despite the goodwill displayed by Nasser, the Greek requests were unlikely to be granted. Ntinos Koutsoumis, who back in 1951 lamented that New Year's wishes in Arabic meant a request for tips, angrily wrote that Greek officials and the Athens media had relegated the demands of the Greeks of Egypt during Nasser's visit, focusing instead mostly on diplomatic relations between Athens and Cairo. It was an accurate assessment of the Greek government's priorities. Greece was the first NATO country Nasser had visited, and this helped create the impression that Greece could act as a bridge between the West and the Arab world. As Karavias had noted, the Greek government's unwillingness to endorse two causes that Nasser was promoting, the return of Palestinian refugees to their homes, and the ongoing struggle for Algerian independence from France, meant that it could not persuade Egypt or the Arab world of its willingness to act as an authentic intermediary. Thus Greece's closeness to Egypt remained mostly confined to well-meaning intentions and rhetoric but little substance—as was the case with Egypt's attitude toward the Greeks of Egypt and their demands.[29]

Flight from Egypt

The Greeks of Egypt were adversely affected by Nasser's refusal to make any concrete concessions within months of his visit to Athens and this finally changed their wait-and-see attitude to Egyptianization. A year earlier the Egyptian government had drawn up a law mandating all foreign residents in Egypt obtain a work permit that had to be renewed every year. Complicating things, the authorities would grant work permits only to those in possession of a residence permit. After the work permit expired it could only be renewed if the holder's country made reciprocal arrangements for Egyptian nationals. There were further restrictions. No business was permitted to have foreign employees comprising more than 15 percent of its staff, and the salaries of foreigners could not make up more than 25 percent of all the salaries the firm paid. The Greek side raised the reciprocity clause during Nasser's visit but nothing specific was agreed. The law duly went into effect at the end of October 1960 and the announcement sent shockwaves through the Greeks in Egypt, who had assumed that somehow they would have been exempted.

While Ambassador Lambros scrambled to persuade Egyptian authorities to make exceptions and concessions that would alleviate the burdens on the Greeks, community organizations held a conference across Egypt. The announcement explained that it would produce a list of demands to present to the Egyptian government separately from those the Greek embassy would be submitting. This was a turning point: the community organizations were no longer ceding the initiative to Greek diplomats but instead were making direct contact with the Egyptian government. The Greek press also changed tone. It critiqued the tactics the Greeks had adopted in the past, namely expecting everything from Greece and not taking steps to adjust to Egyptian reality. It stopped maintaining an optimistic tone, speaking openly of the lack of a sense of security Greeks were experiencing and bitterness at the way they were being treated. The left-wing Greeks, feeling justified in their particular strategies, called upon the leadership to change tactics in order to avert the rising panic among the Greeks of Egypt.

If not actual panic, there was certainly increasing alarm among the Greeks of Egypt in the wake of legislation introduced in late October. When a few weeks later the government made some concessions, it was too late to change many people's minds. It felt like the tightening of the noose, with restrictions steadily becoming more onerous. At that time Egyptian authorities uncovered a Greek spy ring that was monitoring naval movements in the Canal Zone and the Greek consuls of Alexandria, Port Said, and Suez were declared personae non gratae and left Egypt. Twenty-seven Greeks were arrested and deported as well. This damaging news contributed to the growing worries of many Greeks. In December 1960, while hopes for a reprieve from the measures for the Greeks were fading, Egypt nationalized the properties of Belgian nationals, an act of solidarity with the Congolese struggle against Belgian colonialism. Passport applications made to the consulates in Alexandria and Cairo increased and one columnist spoke of ten to fifteen thousand Greeks planning to leave Egypt. All this contributed to the climate of uncertainty, bringing Greeks closer to the decision to leave. The consulates of Alexandria and Cairo reported that the number of persons officially declaring to leave—which was just one indication of the outward trend—increased steadily throughout 1960.

Even when the Egyptian government made some concessions to the Greeks, announcing that workplace quotas on foreign employees would not apply to Greeks born in Egypt before 1932 and those who settled there before 1937 and that Greek institutions would be exempted from hiring quotas, it was too late to stem the tide. More Greeks were leaving. The number of official declarations in March alone had reached 211 in Alexandria and 170 in Cairo. Estimates of Greeks who had either left or were leaving in 1961 were ten thousand, according to one newspaper report in April. Even Greeks who benefited from the exemptions or felt their jobs were safe under the new laws believed that their children faced doubtful opportunities for success given the trend of antiforeign measures.

The Greeks and the Italians did not leave Cairo suddenly, according to one observer; rather, they faded slowly because the economic boom their homelands were experiencing was much more inviting that the uncertain future in Egypt.[30] The red tape involved in securing one's departure was another sign of antiforeign sentiment. There were restrictions on the repatriation of foreign currency. Banks delayed the provision of even the amount allowed and the process of proving the ownership of property in order to sell it was especially complicated. News items about Greeks caught at the border carrying more than the stipulated amount of currency were frequent. Egyptian authorities denied this amounted to xenophobia and was instead a form of protection for their country, which needed funds for its ongoing effort to expand its economy and its industry.[31]

Nasser never expelled the Greeks from Egypt, but the cumulative measures he was taking to enhance Egypt's economic sovereignty and development meant that Greeks who were not or could not become Egyptian citizens in time, because they could not meet the criteria for nationality, were adversely affected. The final straw came with a new set of laws Nasser introduced in July 1961 that were designed to reorient the economy along socialist lines and toward state capitalism. First came the imposition of partial state control over the production of cotton. The symbolism of this move, especially for the Greeks of Egypt, was unmistakable. Cotton was at the core of their wealth and presence in the country. Throughout the 1950s Egypt diversified its economy and reduced its reliance on cotton exports and the Free Officers had abolished large landholdings. Thus it was no coincidence that the Greek cotton barons were increasingly less visible as community leaders and big donors in the 1950s, although Constantine Salvago did serve as vice president of the community organization in Alexandria during that decade until his death in Athens in 1963. He was the last of the 'big three' families—the Benachis, Choremis, and Salvagos—to occupy a leadership position in the major Greek institutions in Alexandria. More measures came, deepening the ongoing expansion of the public sector. The government took control of all imports and exports and closed the Alexandria stock exchange. Other laws called for the distribution of a quarter of company profits to employees. Board member salaries were capped and a new tax bracket favored lower-income earners at the expense of high-income earners. In late July the government nationalized all banks and insurance companies as well as manufacturing companies, some partially, others entirely. The shift toward a socialist economy was well underway.

Unlike Egyptianization laws, the July 1961 laws left little room for the Greeks to maneuver. Community leaders and consular officials rushed to estimate the overall effects on the Greeks, and Foreign Minister Averoff arrived for a five-day visit to Cairo to try and persuade the Egyptian government to soften the blow for Greeks. Calculations of the total effect of the laws on the Greeks varied wildly, from almost LE5 million as far as the Egyptian authorities were concerned to more than double that amount according to community organization figures. Where there was no doubt was that the Alexandria Greeks took a bigger hit than the Greeks of Cairo. The Greek Ministry of Foreign Affairs estimated the market value belonging to Greek citizens that was nationalized totaled over LE6 million. The consulate in Alexandria estimated that thirty-eight Greek firms in the city were affected by nationalizations, whose owners were a who's who of community leaders: Charitatos, Coutarelli, Lagoudakis, Nanopoulos, Pialopoulos, Sarpakis, and Zerbinis. They represented three generations of Greek entrepreneurs: those in banking and export, early investors in manufacturing, and those who established businesses during the industrialization drive of the 1930s. Over one thousand Greeks lost shares they held in companies that were nationalized and a total of 1,325 sought compensation from the Egyptian government.

The loss of jobs was never satisfactorily ascertained. When Averoff arrived, what had become a pattern in Greco–Egyptian contacts was repeated yet again: effusive cordiality at least in public, sincerely stated assurances offered by the Egyptian side with no tangible practical steps taken, and in the end optimistic statements by the Greek side. The two sides agreed that compensation would be paid and Averoff expressed his satisfaction that those Greeks "involved in small businesses" would not have to give up their jobs. That was tantamount to admitting he had not really achieved much, unless what he was really trying to do was raise the expectations of Greeks in order to prevent a massive influx from Egypt. In December 1961 all last-minute negotiations were over, and Greek newspapers published a list of the 866 Greek properties that had been nationalized. Within six months the valuable property foreigners had left behind was being sold in the streets of Alexandria. The nationalization program continued in successive waves through 1962 and 1963 and involved Greek-owned firms ranging from transport companies to beverage and chocolate manufacturers. There was no sign of any preferential treatment of the Greeks. In fact, the Greek ambassador in Cairo, Constantinos Daratzikis, was reduced to compiling lists of the Greek firms that were affected from newspaper reports. He listed thirty-eight Greek firms that had been nationalized by August of 1963.[32]

Even though in theory many Greeks could have remained in their jobs, in practice they faced what they perceived as discriminatory practices that ranged from being overlooked in the case of promotions and raises at work, preferential treatment of job applicants who were Egyptian, the need to complete cumbersome bureaucratic procedures with employers, or government authorities that were especially slow to respond at the workplace, all of which made them feel unwelcome. Faced with this velvet glove treatment, hundreds decided to resign from their positions, take what compensation was still available, and move out of Egypt. Identifying the precise causes of the exodus and invoking a chain of events and a psychological sense of insecurity may sound unsatisfactory. Each foreign community left under specific circumstances, either through expulsion or an accumulation of 'push' factors that were simply too powerful to resist. If we consider that Syrian Greek Catholics, who were Arabs, also chose to leave, we may begin to understand the climate that created the exodus.[33]

The effect of the incremental departures of the Greeks on those who stayed was unmistakable, and often cited in many accounts of this period.

Alexandra Papadimitriou, who recorded her memories of this era decades later, wrote that in Alexandria in 1961 she had to go to a Lebanese tailor for her children's clothes because all the Greek tailors had left. Luckily he came recommended by another Greek and knew French. Later on at a dinner with other Greek families she looked round the table, making a mental note that most if not all were planning their departure from Egypt.³⁴ In the Smouha district of the city, where her family moved, it was evident that many Greek families had already left. The numbers declaring officially they were leaving Alexandria increased steadily from 197 in May to 351 in September 1962. There were fewer departures from Cairo but the numbers peaked to 131 in August. The total number of Greeks who left Alexandria in 1961 was over 2,300 and those who left from Cairo were 1,117. In both cases the numbers departing would increase in 1962, and between 1960 and 1964 the Greek Ministry of Foreign Affairs estimated that almost fourteen thousand Greeks had left from Alexandria and Cairo, the majority headed for Athens. Egypt's official statistics showed that in 1960 the Greeks were just under forty-eight thousand and by 1967 their numbers hovered around seventeen thousand.

In reporting back to Athens Greek diplomats made frequent use of terms such as "panic" or "psychosis" or sometimes settling for "psychological reasons" to explain the decisions many Greeks took to leave Egypt. Those who experienced the events have also adopted that type of explanation. There is also the need to identify who or what was responsible for creating that climate, and here there is a range of interpretations. Some have blamed Nasser's policies or Egypt's unwillingness to confer citizenship to the Greeks. Others have pointed to the inadequate policies of the Greek government. Another target is the Greek leadership for not preparing the community for the changes, choosing to bail out of Egypt and their responsibilities when Egyptianization deepened by the late 1950s. One book-length study on the exodus regards it as a process, a series of responses to Egyptianization and nationalization measures where those factors had a share in the steady outflow in the 1950s, increasing a collective sense of insecurity until it became an 'exodus' in the 1960s.³⁵

The Greek flight from Egypt certainly seems to have had an accumulation of causes, a ripple effect that created an irreversible sense of insecurity, partly based on fact and enhanced by fear, perhaps even panic. Of all the factors that can be listed, Nasser himself cannot be blamed directly because he drove Egypt toward greater independence and economic sovereignty and expansion in ways he believed would achieve those goals. Greater sovereignty excluded the Greeks. The fact that Egypt was reluctant to extend citizenship rights to those who had enjoyed privileges thanks to their foreign citizenship status should be perfectly understandable, even if one believes the Greeks had a special relationship with Egypt. When Nasser turned toward a socialist transformation of the economy, many Greeks who had thrived in a free market economy naturally decided they had no place in Egypt. Up until that point, the making of modern Egypt had unfolded in ways that enabled the presence of the Greeks. The 1960s brought a new era in which the capacity of most Greeks to adapt and to stay relevant in Egypt's development ran out. Only a few thousand Greeks remained because they decided that the new Egypt was still their home.

What has been said about surrealism can also be said, in a sense, about the Greeks in Egypt. It has been argued that the flourishing of surrealism in Egypt through the mid-1950s represents a movement that transcended the ways we think of that country as a terrain in which the West and the non-West, the metropole and the periphery, clashed. Art and Liberty, the group that embodied surrealism in Egypt, represented something in-between those binary categories because it was both Egyptian and European, and produced a unique fusion of modernism.[36] From the time when British control in Egypt began weakening after the First World War, the Greeks displayed the core instincts of all Greek diasporas and tried to adapt to the new circumstances. They strove, some harder than others, to shed their status as privileged foreigners and redefine themselves as an entity that was not only 'in' Egypt but 'of' Egypt. Not quite part of the western metropolis, though also not fully part of the periphery. But in the end, Nasser's vision of not only a sovereign national state but also a nationalized, socialist economy proved too big an obstacle for the vast majority of the Greeks.

8

Memory and Nostalgia

One of the best places serving authentic Egyptian cuisine in Athens is the restaurant in the club of the Association of Greeks of Egypt. Formed in 1933, the association initially served as a way for those who had moved from Egypt to Athens to be able to socialize and offer help to those in need. It still offers those services but just as importantly it is one of several institutions in Greece that works toward keeping alive the history of the Greek presence in Egypt, to showcase their achievements and offer a venue where members can share memories of their lives there. Other institutions play more focused roles. The Greek Literary and Historical Archive, known by its Greek acronym as ELIA, includes extensive records on the history of the Greeks in Egypt.

There are several alumni organizations of the major Greek schools in Egypt that currently exist in Athens: the Ambetios School of Cairo, the Averoff School of Alexandria, the Salvago professional school of Alexandria, and the Greek schools in Mansura. Also in Athens are associations of Greeks from specific cities and towns in Egypt, for example, an association of Greeks from Cairo, another of Greeks from Suez and Port Tawfiq, and another of the Greeks of Ismailiya. There is also a Yachting Club of the Greeks in Egypt, established in 1965, modeled on the Greek Yachting Club of Alexandria, which had been one of the most prestigious Greek clubs in the city. It was located on the water next to the Ras al-Tin Palace overlooking Alexandria's western harbor. Its exclusive membership in the pre-Second World War era had little connection with yatching; "the principal activities were tea and cocktails and being seen, and those not formally dressed were asked to leave."[1] But it also functioned as a sports club and promoted all water sports, including yatching, and boasted the best water polo team in Egypt between 1910 and 1930. In Greece the reconstituted club maintains adult and youth teams in several sports such as sailing, rowing, water polo, canoe-kayak, and table tennis. Its athletes have competed with distinction in domestic and international competitions. The establishment of the club in Greece was not an easy affair, but the Greek government waived its usual bureaucratic objections to such a project because during the Second World War the club in Alexandria had generously turned over its premises to the Greek Navy, which used them as its wartime headquarters. All of these organizations are based in Athens, which was the main destination of Greeks who left Egypt in the late 1950s and 1960s, and who took the initiative in establishing them.

There were of course those who were lucky enough to land on their feet after leaving Egypt. Some used their background as a springboard for an international career, something which was made easier by their experiences in what was left of cosmopolitan Egypt. For example, the singer Demis Roussos's family left Egypt in 1961, when he was fifteen years old, and settled in Athens. A few years later he moved to Paris, where he embarked on a singing career that would make him well known throughout the world. His success has been partially attributed to having two musically-minded parents and also to the fact that in Alexandria "he spent his formative years listening to jazz and to traditional Arab and Greek folk music and began singing in the local Orthodox Church choir."[2] In some cases, such as for the Capsis family who were hoteliers, the younger members of entrepreneurial families managed to continue the family business in Greece.

Arrival in Athens and trying to resettle there was a difficult experience, especially for the middle- and upper-middle-class Greeks of Alexandria and Cairo. Like those Greeks who in earlier times had abandoned cities such as Constantinople (Istanbul), Odessa, or Smyrna (Izmir), not to mention those returning from Chicago or New York, Athens seemed a small, provincial backwater. The Greek capital lacked the tree-lined boulevards, large squares, public spaces, and spacious airy apartment blocks many Alexandrian and Cairene Greeks had taken for granted. Aside from its ancient monuments and the very center of the city, most of Athens was a maze of narrow streets, where the arrival of waves of migrants from the provinces led to old one- and two-story houses giving way to apartment blocks. The need to accommodate this rampant urbanization of the population meant little attention was paid to preserving building codes, public spaces, or anticipating the increase of automobiles. Beyond that, real estate prices in Athens were much higher and available apartments much smaller.

It was not easy to find jobs in a society where connections matter much more than qualifications. Fortunately the ongoing expansion of the Greek tourism industry meant there was demand for those who knew foreign languages, and this was an area where Greeks from Egypt had an incomparable advantage over the local Greeks. The country's airline, Olympic Airways, for example, was one employer that welcomed Greeks from Egypt. The owner, Aristotle Onassis, hired Stelios Papadimitriou as his legal counsel. Papadimitriou was born in Alexandria in 1930 and graduated from the Averoff School. He became closely associated with Onassis, was the executor of his will, and served as president of the Onassis Foundation. There were other areas where Greeks from Egypt made for ideal employees, for example at the Hellenic Shipyards Company, where Greeks who worked on the Suez Canal were able to find jobs. Otherwise, the way to find a job was to rely on networks among the Greeks of Egypt who had settled in and around Athens. Egypt's slow disbursement of the compensation owed to owners whose businesses had been nationalized—Greece claimed the value was over LE29 million, while Egypt agreed to pay just over half that sum—was another hardship many had to endure. When the numbers arriving from Egypt increased beginning in the mid-1950s, the Association of Greeks from Egypt mobilized and became a resource for returnees looking for employment. In the 1960s it persuaded the Greek government to allow returnees to join Greek pension funds, though it took another thirty years for the issue to be satisfactorily resolved. The association also obtained land and helped create a building cooperative that financed an apartment complex in the northern Athens suburb of Kifisiá, known as 'Greeks of Egypt Town.'

Comparisons between life in Egypt and Greece was compounded by the continued erosion of the Greek presence in Egypt in the years after the departures that came in the wake of the nationalization laws. Small businesses, for example in food manufacturing and beverage production, were not affected by the nationalizations and many of their owners decided to stay in Egypt, as did many white-collar professionals and others working in the service sector. But many had already left Egypt and by 1970 the Greek presence in Egypt was confined mainly to Alexandria and Cairo. The departures affected the community organizations, their budgets, and the ability of their institutions to function due to lack of funding and diminishing demand for their services. Throughout the 1960s many Greek institutions in Alexandria, Cairo, and the towns along the canal were closing and their buildings were being sold off, while community organizations in many of the smaller towns had already stopped functioning. The charters of the community organizations stipulated that when they could no longer continue operation, they would be absorbed by one of the bigger organizations. When the larger community organizations ceased to exist or could not hold on to the real estate they would revert to the Greek government, which in most cases sold the property to the Egyptian government.

The Cozzika Hospital in Alexandria, which the community organization had always struggled to administer without a loss, was sold to the Egyptian government in 1967. Alexandria had already witnessed the closure of the Familiades School in 1961; it dated back to the 1920s and had served generations of Greek children whose families lived in or close to the city's Attarin neighborhood. The building was rented out and eventually sold in 1973. The Antoniades old people's home moved to the building that housed the Kaniskeris Orphanage and its building in al-Hadra neighborhood was sold in 1962. In Cairo, the number of students attending Greek schools dropped steadily. In a report to Athens, the Greek ambassador wrote that 2,412 children were starting the 1962–63 school year at the Greek schools in and around Cairo, a decrease of 21 percent from the previous year when 3,024 children attended those schools. This reflected the outflow of Greeks from Egypt, he noted, adding that many of the poorer Greeks were deciding to leave during the school year.[3]

The inevitable prospect that the Greek schools would contract in the near future was prompting many teachers to leave Egypt as well. Two years later, because of a reduced student population and rising costs, the Achilopouleos Girls' School moved from the center of Cairo to the suburb of Heliopolis and into a building that housed the Spetseropouleio Orphanage. In Zagazig, the 1969–70 academic year was the last for the Greek community school. In Kafr al-Zayyat, the Greek School, which had over a hundred students before the Second World War, saw its number drop to twenty in 1962–63. It had five students during its last year, 1965–66. The Ladies Philanthropic Organization had closed in 1963, and the Ermis Cultural Society that dated from 1910 closed in 1965.[4] The 1970s saw further contraction. The Cairo community organization decided it could no longer maintain its sports stadium in the Shubra district and put it up for sale. The vocational schools that had been established in 1950 in Cairo to train Greeks in professions that would enable them to adapt to Egypt's changing economic environment closed in 1978 because of lack of demand. The following year, Cairo's Greek evening schools also closed.

Life in Egypt was much easier and enjoyable than it was in Greece.

The prevailing sense was that the exodus from Egypt had been due to a range of circumstances, not because the Greeks were expelled. What remained in Egypt was growing smaller and smaller, triggering a strong need to preserve the history and memories of the Greek presence in Egypt, something that inevitably became tinged by a strong sense of nostalgia. There was also a wish to stake a place in the Greek national consciousness. Historically, indigenous Greeks have treated Greeks from beyond their borders with suspicion if not contempt, an irony bearing in mind that for about a century Greece's primary foreign policy goal was the Great Idea, the incorporation within its borders of adjacent lands and their peoples that were considered Greek. When the Great Idea collapsed in 1922 and over a million ethnic Greeks from the Ottoman Empire and elsewhere streamed into Greece, the Greeks of Greece saw them as a burden, a threat, and even as bearers of an alien culture. It took several decades for the 'Asia Minor Greeks' to gain full acceptance and recognition both of what they had achieved in the Ottoman Empire and the ways they were contributing to Greece's development.

The Greek Americans who left from Greece's provinces and returned to the homeland were met with contempt and lampooned for their naive 'American' gullibility. The urbanity and cosmopolitanism the returnees from Egypt exuded insulated them from the worst instincts of the indigenous Greeks, but not always. When the Papadimitriou family moved to Athens from Alexandria in the mid-1960s, Alexandra, its matriarch, bitterly observed that while the government welcomed the influx of polyglot Greeks, the locals were antagonized. They called the newcomers "Egyptians," or worse, used the pejorative for Arabs, "Arapáthes," and complained that they took the best-paid jobs. Some of the returnees, she conceded, invited resentment because they boasted about the numbers of servants they had when they lived in Egypt, something which was not common, she added, because many Greeks were employees and small businessmen; that was why the community organizations offered social services.[5]

Resented, misunderstood, or feeling a little insecure in Athens, which remained somewhat provincial throughout the 1960s and early 1970s, certainly by the standards of Alexandria and Cairo, the Greeks of Egypt felt they needed to emphasize and defend their particular background and heritage, which they expressed in a range of views. Many were similar to accounts written by Italians who left Egypt but maintained a strong attachment to their lives there. The Italians' accounts themselves are "less mediated by the often celebratory discourse of harmonious relations between Italy and Egypt," and "convey a more individual expression of the character of a lost cultural milieu and the associated feelings of bereavement in being separated from it."[6] Yet even those Greeks who reflect thoughtfully about their lives in Egypt tend to discount the privileges the Greeks enjoyed.

More recently, this has included public critiques of academic studies that, rightly or wrongly, do not agree with the dominant narrative that the Greeks from Egypt embrace.[7] Sometimes, history and memory do not coincide and this can be upsetting to those who still hold tightly to their Greek-from-Egypt identity.

The preservation of memories from Egypt would take many forms. After all, it meant different things to different people. There was a pining for the easy life in Egypt, but also life among Egyptians and life in the streets of its cities,and their sounds and smells. Many of those born in Egypt had developed a deep relationship with the place. When a young Ilios Yannakakis left Egypt for Greece in 1949, he stood at the stern of the ship watching Egypt's low coastline slowly disappear and realized he did not know "if I was leaving for my country or simply leaving my country."[8] Others, thinking more narrowly, chose to remember Greek life in Egypt and wrote about the achievements of Greeks and the Greek microcosm. Timos Malanos, the literary critic who lived most of his life in twentieth-century Alexandria, concluded a 376-page memoir of his life there by considering whether he would have preferred to live in the United States. He noted, "I am happy I lived in Egypt, both as an ordinary person and a writer, and I am grateful to her a thousand times. And not only for the joys she gifted all of us, but mainly because we were able to return to our land, albeit as refugees, culturally intact. On the one hand our schools, and on the other the religious difference with the locals preserved our Greek identity and prevented our assimilation. We remained Greeks, and that, in my opinion is not insignificant."[9]

The Association of Greeks from Egypt

From the mid-1970s onward, led by its president Anestis Papastephanou, the Association of Greeks from Egypt turned toward cultural activities designed to showcase the history of the Greek presence in Egypt. The initial emphasis was on echoing the continuous presence of the Greeks in Egypt since antiquity and also the literary and artistic works they produced in the modern era, along with the schools and other community institutions that had been established there. By the 1980s the association had moved on to organize historical conferences where presentations covered all aspects of the Greek experience in Egypt. Many of the events focused on remembering the Greek past in Egypt, which created a sense of wistfulness and occasionally struck a melancholic tone. On the whole these were festive occasions, where a great deal of pride for what the Greeks had achieved was on display. Egypt was generally portrayed as a wonderful home that had been regrettably lost, not through the actions of Nasser or anyone else, but as an inevitable consequence of the will of the Egyptian people to regain their dignity and independence.

The 1980s brought the most active and ambitious era of the association's history under the decade-long leadership (1982–92) of President Dimitri Charitatos. Charitatos's ancestors had moved to Alexandria from Cephalonia and he was born in Alexandria in 1910, attending the French school there. He served as a lawyer at the Mixed Courts and later as an executive at the Egyptian Plastics Company, formerly the Jewish-owned Egyptian Plastics and Electrical Industries Company known as "Shafferman Frères."

When the business was nationalized, he moved to Greece and in 1962 became an executive of the Greek subsidiary of the French aluminum manufacturing company Pechiney.[10] A gregarious personality—he was in charge of the company's public relations, among other things—Charitatos had a strong attachment to fellow Greeks of Egypt and he influenced the company's hiring practices. When it began operations in 1966, 11 percent of its employees were Greeks from Egypt.[11] One of the two partners of the advertising agency Charitatos hired was also a Greek from Egypt. Charitatos took on the presidency combining his commitment to the Greeks of Egypt with his skills as a company executive and his boundless energy. He also brought with him a strong sense of the value of history.

A year before leaving Alexandria he had given a talk in French to the Rotary Club on life in the city in the mid-nineteenth century.[12] Charitatos took several initiatives. First came a major exhibit entitled "The Greeks in Egypt—A Four Thousand-year Presence," held in a museum in central Athens in 1982. In the prologue of the exhibit's thick catalog, Charitatos evoked his dynamic view of the identity of the Greeks of Egypt and their ongoing role in Greco–Egyptian relations, noting that the exhibit was not merely a roll call of the names of those who had passed away, a nostalgic reliving of the past, or something honoring the longstanding Greek presence on the banks of the Nile. In addition, the exhibit sought to convey a message of optimism. Despite the difficult years, "we always had friendly bonds with Egypt and those bonds would remain." The catalog included texts by the Patriarch of Alexandria Nikolaos and two well-known writers who were born in Egypt, Manolis Gialourakis and Timos Malanos. The rest of the catalog listed the 733 items that were on show.[13]

The following year there was an exhibition of paintings by Greeks of Egypt between 1860 and 1920 at the National Gallery of Greece as well as a conference on Cavafy at the French Institute in Athens. In 1984 in Athens the association, with government support, held a World Conference of Greeks of Egypt. There were participants from associations in Australia and the United States and individuals from other countries as well. All those events were major occasions with representatives of the Greek and Egyptian governments in attendance and extensive coverage in the Greek media. Charitatos also cajoled his fellow Greeks of Egypt to contribute money to enable the association to acquire its own spacious premises in downtown Athens. He established several committees including one dedicated to promoting the organization's activities among its younger members. From 1985 onward the association began producing its own magazine, the *Panegyptia*, which is still being published. The journal covers the association's activities, carries news from Greek organizations in Egypt, includes articles on the history of Greeks in Egypt, and mentions members' news, including obituaries. It is a venue preserving the spirit of the Greeks of Egypt, forging ties among them, and preserving their identity and memories of Egypt.

History Preservation and Writing

The Greek Literary and Historical Archive (ELIA), which among its wide-ranging holdings includes a Greeks in Egypt archive of documents and photographs, was a major resource the association could draw upon for those events. Charitatos's son Manos, who had been born in Alexandria in 1944 and moved to Athens at a young age, established the archive along with a friend, Dimitris Portolos, a historian and an executive of a mining company. Manos inherited his father's interest in collecting and became an avid collector of old books, newspapers, prints, photographs, artifacts, and everything connected with the presence of the Greeks in Egypt. In the 1980s the ELIA acquired and refurbished an old neoclassical building in the Plaka district of Athens, which became the home of the archive. Displaying an urbanity and openness that was true to his Alexandrian upbringing, Manos encouraged visitors, shattering the norms of Greek archival practices that guarded the contents jealously from the prying eyes of researchers.

Researchers flocked to the ELIA and many individuals or organizations brought their own records to be deposited there, and as a result the ELIA expanded its holdings on subjects relating to the Greeks of Egypt. It began with Dimitri Charitatos's extensive collection of Greek books and journals published in Egypt as well as books in other languages on Egypt's history and culture, which his son Manos steadily expanded. With the help of Efthymios Souloyannis, an Alexandrian Greek and a historical researcher, the ELIA acquired the records of the Greek community organization of Alexandria and the Greek Orthodox Patriarchate of Alexandria, which were brought over from Egypt. It also acquired the personal papers of a number of prominent Greeks of Egypt, including the author Stratis Tsirkas and literary critic Timos Malanos. The Greeks in Egypt archive of the ELIA also houses the records of the community organization of Mansura, as well as Greek books and journals published in Egypt (roughly 70 percent of the total collection), the core of which are publications collected by the Charitatos family.

Even before the ELIA's Greeks in Egypt archive began functioning as a resource, Greeks of Egypt who settled in Athens, especially those who were writers or journalists, began producing articles and books on the history of the Greek experience in Egypt. The earliest of those publications focused on Greek literary works published in Egypt, a large part of those devoted to Cavafy. The poet was already widely recognized in Greece. His reputation grew in the post-Second World War era and his fellow Greeks from Egypt played a significant role in disseminating his life and work to the Greek public. Even before they left Egypt, Tsirkas and Malanos had a running feud over the significance of Cavafy's homosexuality, which Malanos regarded as the key to understanding his verses. Tsirkas responded with a blockbuster study of Cavafy "and his era," which was a well researched account of Cavafy's family and the poet's life set against the background of Egypt's unfolding history.

Tsirkas's purpose was to demonstrate that Cavafy was a "social" and "political" poet whose verses reflected the times. For example, Tsirkas argued that one of Cavafy's poems was inspired by his disgust at the harsh punishments suffered by Egyptian villagers at the hands of British authorities in 1906, an event known as the Denshawai incident. Tsirkas's study appeared in 1958 and a few years later, Manolis Gialourakis, a journalist at

Alexandria's *Tachydromos*, published an overview of Greek literary production in Egypt. Dimitris Charitatos encouraged Gialourakis, who settled in Athens permanently in 1965, to write an overall history of the Greeks in Egypt. He produced a seven hundred-page volume entitled *The Egypt of the Greeks* that appeared in 1967 and covered all aspects of Greek activities in Egypt, from antiquity to the exodus. Charitatos bought hundreds of copies and proudly began distributing them to relatives, friends, and business associates.

In the mid-1970s, following the collapse of the military dictatorship that had ruled Greece since 1967 and amid widespread introspection about Greece's evolution, academic historiography singled out Greece's economic dependence on its merchant diaspora communities in the Mediterranean and the Black Sea in the nineteenth century. While investments and donations flowed in from abroad, the thinking went, Greece acquired a dependency on the whims of merchant capitalists. The absence of a strong domestic bourgeoisie along with the presence of a bloated state sector prevented Greece from focusing on manufacturing and industrialization, which would have allowed the country to enjoy greater financial independence and be less dependent on foreign capital.[14]

This yielded more analyses, studies, and monographs of the Greek role in Egypt and the relationship of the Greeks of Egypt with Greece. Among the main studies of the Greek diaspora phenomenon was one by Nikos Psyroukis, who was born in Ismailiya in 1926, became involved in left-wing politics, and in the 1940s, made his way to Czechoslovakia where he studied history. He returned to Egypt in the 1950s to work for the newspaper *Paroikos* and in 1961 moved to Greece. In the mid-1970s the public rehabilitation of the communist movement that had been proscribed since the civil war in the late 1940s brought with it renewed interest in the role of the Left during the 1940s. Among the topics attracting attention were the events surrounding the left-wing movement that developed among the Greek military units stationed in Egypt and elsewhere in the Middle East.

This brought increased interest in Stratis Tsikas's three-part novel *Drifting Cities* (the Greek title is Ακυβέρνητες Πολιτείες) that was set in Jerusalem, Cairo, and Alexandria, a fictional account of the Greek left-wing movement that closely followed actual events. The three novels were published in Athens between 1961 and 1965, just before Tsirkas left Egypt because the company he worked for was nationalized. The caricature-like depiction of a Stalinist apparatchik who dominated the first of the three novels led to Tsirkas's dismissal from the Greek communist organization in Alexandria.

After 1974 the Greek public augmented its knowledge of the "movement in the Middle East" as it was known, thanks to the reissue of other protagonists' accounts, including several Greeks of Egypt, such as Ambetios schoolteacher Giorgios Athanasiadis and publisher Lambis Rappas, who had lived in Egypt for a decade and returned to Greece after the war.

The 1990s and the early 2000s witnessed ongoing activity related to the study of the Greeks of Egypt. The need to continue the genre of chronicling and showcasing the positive role of the Greeks in Egypt that Gialourakis had begun was taken up by historian and researcher Efthymios Souloyannis, who succeeded Charitatos as president of the Association of the Greeks from Egypt in 1992. From the 1980s, when his first publications appeared, until his death in 2015, Souloyannis produced several books and over a hundred articles published in a wide number of journals in Greece and elsewhere, many of them publications of organizations of the Greeks of Egypt, especially the association's *Panegyptia*. Souloyannis covered every topic conceivable, from the evolution of the community organizations, their institutions, the history of the Patriarchate of Alexandria, the status of the Greeks in Egypt, their ties to Greece and Egypt, and presentations of the lives and achievements of many prominent Greek men and women who lived in Egypt.

A public conference on the exodus of the Greeks from Egypt held in Athens in 2008 succeeded in bringing together both academics and the Association of the Greeks of Egypt in a demonstration of how scholarly research and interest in preserving the memories of the Greek experiences in Egypt could coexist and reinforce each other. Matoula Tomara-Sideris, a professor at Panteion University in Athens, organized the conference and her own work on the subject straddled that particular divide. She had published glossy volumes on wealthy Greek families and Greeks in the cotton trade, which cast the Greek role as a contribution to Egypt's development. Yet she also examined the philanthropic contributions of the Greeks through an academic lens and discussed their motivations. Most of the papers submitted at the conference were published in article form in a scholarly journal based in the United States. The editors noted, "the focus of the conference, the exodus of the Greeks from Egypt in the 1950s and early 1960s, inaugurated a new chapter in the study of the Greek diaspora and it also gave many Greeks from Egypt—known as Egyptiot–Greeks or more commonly as *Egyptiotes*—who are now settled in Athens an opportunity to learn and reflect on the final phase of the more than century-long significant and demographically extensive Greek presence in Egypt. It was also an occasion that enabled all participants to recall what is generally considered a long-standing amicable relationship between Egypt and Greece and one which withstood the strains of the Greek exodus."[15]

Aside from the more conventional academic presentations, anthropologist Irene Chrysocheri, who was born in Alexandria and moved to Greece, screened excerpts of interviews she had filmed with Alexandrian Greeks living in Athens, who spoke of their memories of life in Alexandria. Her work took place under the auspices of the Alexandrian and Mediterranean Research Centre of the Bibliotheca Alexandrina from 2004–07. It was part of a bigger project entitled "Mediterranean Voices: Oral History and Cultural Practice in Mediterranean Cities," funded by a Euro-Mediterranean program (Euromed Heritage II) and conducted in cooperation with London Metropolitan University and thirteen Mediterranean cities. The main purpose of the research was to study the cultural heritage of these cities and create an audiovisual database of oral history consisting of photographs and excerpts from oral interviews. The Bibliotheca Alexandrina was commissioned to integrate Alexandria into the programme in 2002. It focused its research on the city's twentieth-century cosmopolitan character and broadened the scope of interviews to include former Alexandrians who resided in Greece. The journal that published the conference papers included three contributions by Greeks of Egypt. Veteran journalists Sophianos Chryssostomidis, who had worked at the left-wing *Paroikos* newspaper in the 1950s, spoke about the multiple causes of the Greek exodus. Historian and writer Harry Tzalas shared passages of his writing on Alexandria "in which nostalgia is the predominant feeling." Another writer, Panagiotis Karmatzos, who in 1972 locked shut the doors of the Salvago Commerical School for the last time, spoke about his sense of loss and concluded by stating, "Egypt gave us, along with the benefits of its cosmopolitanism, the ability to hold on to our Hellenic character, our language, and our religion." He added that the Greeks left worried about their future, but "who can blame a people fighting for their independence and the right to rule over their own country?" which nicely summed up the conventional wisdom among most Greeks of Egypt who settled in Athens.[16]

Memorialization in Egypt

The association's activities strengthened the ties of the returnees with Egypt, but there was a sense that Alexandria and Cairo should experience the past richness of Greek cultural events that had been so common in the decades prior to the exodus. The combined initiative of three persons, the Greek general consul in Alexandria Panayotis Valassopoulos, Alkistis Soulogianni, who worked at the Greek Ministry of Culture, and Takis Alexiou, an Alexandrian artist and painter who moved to Greece, produced the "Cavafia." This event named after and focusing on Cavafy intended to reintroduce the Egyptian public to Greek culture before the exodus of the Greeks. It was also a way of strengthening ties between Greece and Egypt, and it received official support from Melina Mercouri, Greece's minister of culture. The first Cavafia took place in 1983, the fiftieth anniversary of the poet's death, and the roster of participants included one of the foremost authorities on Cavafy, literary critic and Harvard professor G.P. Savvides. The Cavafia began growing steadily following its inaugural event, including activities in Cairo. It encompassed literature, music, and art and began covering other Greek literary figures, beginning with Stratis Tsirkas as well as Greek writers and poets who had not lived in Egypt.

A major transformation came thanks to the efforts of historian and public intellectual Kostis Moskoff, who was appointed Greek cultural attaché in Egypt. Beginning in 1990 Moskoff transformed the Cavafia into an international literary conference that was held regularly until his death in 1998, and revived a few years later. Moskoff also succeeded in creating a museum in the apartment that Cavafy lived in during the last decades of his life. The organizers of the Cavafia had placed a commemorative plaque outside the building but the indefatigable Moskoff had intervened and what had been formerly the "Pension Amr" became the "Cavafy House" in 1992. The name of the street, Sharm al-Sheikh (it had been called Lepsius in Cavafy's time) was renamed C.P. Cavafy.[17]

The scope of the Cavafia notwithstanding, as a commemorative event it had a limited impact on the Greeks of Egypt, both the few thousands that remained in the country and all those who had moved to Greece. The Cavafia involved Greek and Egyptian intellectuals concerned with the poet's legacy and the literary traditions of pre-1952 Alexandria. Instead what captured the imagination of the Greeks who remained in Alexandria was a photographic exhibit on the history of the Greeks in the city, curated by Irene Chrysocheri as part of her work toward a doctorate in visual anthropology at Goldsmith's College, University of London. Leaders of the community organization of Alexandria at first did not see the value of such an exhibit, an attitude that contrasted sharply with the practices of the Association of Greeks of Egypt in Greece. But the exhibit was eventually mounted and opened with great fanfare in 2012 on the premises of the Greek consulate of Alexandria (in the old building of the Benachi Orphanage). Its popularity was such that the exhibit was extended and in fact became permanent. It has become the first stop for all dignitaries visiting Alexandria from mainland Greece because it offers community leaders an opportunity to recount the history of the Greek presence visually. From a display that was assumed would have a short life, the "Traveling to the Then and Now" exhibit has now become a site of memory, according to Chrysocheri.[18]

Nostalgia on Film

In 2012, the same year the exhibition opened in Alexandria, the wish of the Greeks of Egypt to memorialize their past found its expression in an hour-long documentary film entitled "Egypt: The Other Homeland." It was commissioned by the media organization Al Jazeera Arabic and directed by an accomplished Greek filmmaker, Yorgos Avgeropoulos. It took six months to plan and prepare (Chrysocheri was one of the historical researchers) with two weeks of filming in Egypt.[19]

The documentary featured the return to Egypt of several Greeks who reminisced nostalgically about their past and how they felt at home in Egypt, showing no bitterness at having to leave in the 1960s. There was an obligatory opening with a reference to a poem by Cavafy, followed by a discussion of the ties between Egypt and Greece during antiquity featuring archaeologist and writer Harry Tzalas. The film then moves on to the modern era and outlines the important role the Greeks played in Egypt's cotton economy and the country's development. Micky Capaitzis, who grew up in both Alexandria and Cairo, talks about his uncle's Papatheologos Brothers cigarette manufacturing company and the close relations between the Greeks and the Egyptians. Two cousins, Stathis Athanasoglou and Georgios Sideris, grew up in Alexandria where their family began as door-to-door cloth merchants and then built the Salon Vert, one of the biggest retail stores in Cairo and Alexandria, which used to close its doors to customers when members of the visiting Saudi royal family went to the store to choose fabrics. Sideris is filmed visiting the Salon Vert and being welcomed there by the staff.

Another person featured in the film is Penelope "Popi" Deligeorgi, who was a medical student in Port Said during the Suez Crisis and volunteered for one of the civilian defense militias. She appeared on the cover of a magazine at the time, with the caption describing a young Egyptian woman ready to defend her country. Deligeorgi, speaking on camera, describes Egypt as a homeland. She acknowledges a bitterness when she was leaving her apartment in Port Said for good in the early 1960s and recalls when she was about to lock the door, the neighbor told her not to bother because he was going to move in immediately. In a sequence that restores the positive feelings of Egyptians toward the Greeks, the documentary shows the encounter of Capaitzis with an old friend, Muhammad Awad, a renaissance man who is a practicing architect, historian, lecturer at Alexandria University, and founder of the Alexandria Preservation Trust.

The Alexandria Preservation Trust is a private organization founded for the general purpose of promoting awareness and preservation of Alexandria's cultural heritage, ancient and modern, with a special emphasis on the city's architecture. On film, Awad mentions that his mother was Greek Orthodox and risked excommunication from the Patriarch of Alexandria because she wanted to marry a Muslim—Awad's Egyptian father. He then takes Capaitzis through one of the permanent exhibits at the Bibliotheca Alexandrina, the modern library Egypt built to rekindle the spirit of the city's famous library lost in antiquity. The items are all from his personal collection. Entitled *Impressions of Alexandria*, it consists of original engravings, lithographs, and maps that reveal artists' and travelers' impressions of Alexandria from the fifteenth to the nineteenth centuries. It also includes rare photographs of the city from the early nineteenth century to the mid-twentieth century, and highlights the cultural life in the cosmopolitan city as portrayed by its prominent writers and artists.[20] On camera, Awad shows Capaitzis a photograph of the old Casulli family mansion in Alexandria.

The Awad collection, and its owner's passion to preserve the architectural legacy of the old cosmopolitan Alexandria, shows how the wish of the Greeks of Egypt to keep alive the memories of their lives in Egypt is reinforced by contemporary Egypt's own sense that its pre-1952 past has value. Before Awad's initiative there were several examples of Egyptians remembering the Greeks, through novels, films, and newspaper articles. The treatments—in works such as Naguib Mahfouz's novels or films that may gently satirize Greeks but treats them with a sense of wistful nostalgia—matches what the Greeks from Egypt nourish across the Mediterranean.[21]

The best example of how the recent emphasis on Alexandria's cosmopolitan past has drawn in both the Greeks who remain in Egypt and those abroad in Greece came when the Greek community organization in Alexandria presented the city with a statue of Alexander the Great. The statue's installation proved extremely controversial because many in the city felt that the authorities ought to be doing more to honor Egyptian historical figures—after all, Alexander was not only the founder of the city but also its conqueror. The new sense of cosmopolitanism is subject to fierce debate and its critics appear to be resisting "a belated act by the dwindling Egyptian Greek community to inscribe itself on the public face of the city."[22] We should note, however, that the old views of Alexandria as being a "Greek" city are no longer proposed by the city's Greeks—they have adapted to the new circumstances.

In early 2018 the Egyptian government announced a project aimed at inviting former foreign residents—which it described as second- and third- generation Egyptians living abroad—to come to Egypt to visit its tourist sites. Described as the "Nostos initiative," the project was "part of the diaspora program signed between Egypt, Cyprus and Greece, which aims to gather Cypriots and Greeks or their descendants in Alexandria for a return trip to the place where they or their ancestors once lived."[23] This is more than a move to jump-start the country's tourist economy; it is tied to the officially sanctioned but controversial revival of cosmopolitanism.

The announcement came just over two centuries after Muhammad Ali invited Greeks to Egypt to help him in his modernization project. Now they will come as tourists, with a less ambitious agenda than their ancestors, but their presence suggests that the Greeks might still have a small part to play in the making of modern Egypt.

Notes

Notes to Introduction

1 Alexander Kitroeff, *The Greeks in Egypt 1919-1937: Ethnicity and Class* (London: Ithaca Press, 1989).

2 Karl Baedeker, *Egypt: Handbook for Travellers* (Leipzig: Baedeker, 1898), 31.

3 Alexander Kazamias, "Between Language, Land and Empire: Humanist and Orientalist Perspectives on Egyptian Greek Identity," in *Greek Diaspora and Migration since 1700: Society, Politics and Culture*, ed. Dimitris Tziovas (Farnham: Ashgate, 2009), 179–91.

4 Joel Beinin and Zachary Lockman, *Workers on the Nile: Nationalism, Communism, Islam and the Egyptian Working Class, 1882–1954* (Cairo: American University in Cairo Press, 1998), 51.

5 André Aciman, *Out of Egypt* (New York: Picador, 2007), 151.

6 Francesca Biancani, "Let Down the Curtains around Us: Sex Work in Colonial Cairo, 1882–1952" (PhD diss., London School of Economics, 2012), 134.

7 Kitroeff, *The Greeks in Egypt*, 16–18.

8 Anthony Gorman, "The Italians of Egypt: Return to Diaspora," in *Diasporas of the Modern Middle East: Contextualising Community*, eds. Anthony Gorman and Sossie Kasbaian (Edinburgh: Edinburgh University Press, 2015), 13.

9 Stefanos Tamvakis, "Ο Αιγυπτιώτης Ελληνισμός σήμερα. Το αύριο" [The Greeks of Egypt Today. The Future?], February 2016, www.tamvakis.com

Notes to Chapter 1

1 Cited in Efthymios Souloyannis, *Η Θέση των Ελλήνων στην Αίγυπτο* [The Status of the Greeks in Egypt] (Athens: Municipality of Athens, 1999), 51.

2 *Elpis*, November 11, 1873.

3 Athanasios Politis, *Ο Ελληνισμός και η Νεωτέρα Αίγυπτος* [Hellenism and Modern Egypt], vols. 1 and 2 (Alexandria: Grammata, 1928).

215

4   Dimitrios Callimachos, Οι Έλληνες εν Αιγύπτω κατα την Γαλλικήν Κατοχήν
     1798–1801 [The Greeks in Egypt during the French Occupation,
     1798–1801] (Cairo: n.p., 1912); Politis, Hellenism, 81–150.
5   Afaf Lutfi al-Sayyid Marsot, Egypt in the Reign of Muhammad Ali
     (Cambridge: Cambridge University Press, 1984), 30–31.
6   Kenneth M. Cuno, "The Origins of Private Ownership of Land in
     Egypt: A Reappraisal," in The Modern Middle East: A Reader, eds.
     Albert Hourani, Phillip S. Khoury, and Mary C. Wilson (Berkeley:
     University of California Press, 1994), 212.
7   George Yannoulopoulos, "Beyond the Frontiers: The Greek
     Diaspora," in The Greeks: Classical, Byzantine and Modern, ed. Robert
     Browning (New York: Portland House, 1985), 287–98.
8   G.B. Dertilis, Ιστορία του Ελληνικού Κράτους 1830–1920 [History of
     the Greek State, 1830–1920] (Iraklio: University of Crete Press,
     2016), 81–103.
9   Alexander Kitroeff, "The Greek Diaspora in the Mediterranean
     and the Black Sea 18th–19th Centuries: Seen by American Eyes," in
     The Greeks and the Sea, ed. Speros Vryonis Jr. (New York: Caratzas,
     1993), 153–71.
10   Ioannis Gikas, Πενήντα Χρόνια Δάσκαλος [Fifty Years as a Teacher]
     (Alexandria: Phacos, 1950), 39–45.
11   Dertilis, History of the Greek State, 32–34.
12   Politis, Hellenism, 160–70.
13   Henry Dodwell, The Founder of Modern Egypt: A Study of Muhammad
     'Ali (Cambridge: Cambridge University Press, 1931), 71.
14   Politis, Hellenism, 172–98.
15   John Bowring, Report on Egypt and Candia (London: Clowes and
     Sons, 1840), 116–17.
16   Bowring, Report on Egypt, 10.
17   Andrew Archibald Paton, A History of the Egyptian Revolution from
     the Period of the Mamlukes to the Death of Mohammed Ali (London:
     n.p., 1870), 251, 288.
18   Edward Roger John Owen, Cotton and the Egyptian Economy 1820–
     1914 (Oxford: Oxford University Press, 1969), 54–55.
19   Owen, Cotton and the Egyptian Economy, 55.
20   Bowring, Report on Egypt, 80–81.
21   Ioannis Karaminas, Ο Ιερός Ναός του Ευαγγελισμού της Ελληνικής εν
     Αλεξανδρεία Κοινότητος [The Holy Church of the Annunciation
     of the Greek Community of Alexandria] (Alexandria: Kasimatis,
     1937), 11–54.
22   Radamanthis Radopoulos, Εισαγωγή εις την Ιστορίαν της Ελληνικής
     Κοινότητος Αλεξανδρείας 1830–1927 [An Introduction to the History

of the Greek Community of Alexandria, 1830–1927] (Alexandria: Kasimatis, 1928), 31–38.

23 Constantine N. Livanos, *John Sakellaridis and Egyptian Cotton* (Alexandria: Procaccia, 1939), 27.

24 "Egyptian Cotton, Its Modern Origin and Importance of the Supply," *New York Times*, June 26, 1864.

25 Ioannis Diakofotakis, Ιστορία της Ελληνικής Παροικίας Καφρ-Ελ-Ζαγιατ *1865–1972* [History of the Greek Community of Kafr al-Zayyat, 1865–1972] (Alexandria: n.p., 1973), 10–11, 17–20.

26 Stratis Tsirkas, Ο Καβάφης και η Εποχή του [Cavafy and His Era], 12th edition (Athens: Kedros, 1983), 55.

27 Tsirkas, *Cavafy*, 57–64.

28 Georgios K. Typaldos, Ανατολικαί Επιστολαί Σμύρνη Αύγυπτος Παλαιστίνη [Letters from the East: Smyrna, Egypt, Palestine] (Athens: n.p., 1859), 35.

29 David Landes, *Bankers and Pashas: International Finance and Economic Imperialism in Egypt* (New York: Harper & Row, 1969), 25.

30 Owen, *Cotton and the Egyptian Economy*, 68–70.

31 Joseph E. Nourse, *Maritime Canal of Suez: Brief Memoir* (Washington City: Philp & Solomons, 1869), 27; Politis, *Hellenism*, 71–78.

32 Typaldos, *Letters from the East*, 82.

33 Manolis Gialourakis, Η Αίγυπτος των Ελλήνων Συνοπτική Ιστορία του Ελληνισμού της Αιγύπτου [The Egypt of the Greeks: A Concise History of Hellenism in Egypt] (Athens: Mitropolis, 1967), 143.

34 Christos Hadziiosif, "La Colonie Grecque en Egypte 1833–1856" (PhD thesis, Ecole Pratique des Hautes Etudes, Paris, Université de Paris-Sorbonne), 1980.

35 Landes, *Bankers and Pashas*, 27.

36 Landes, *Bankers and Pashas*, 322.

37 Georgios I. Kipiadis, Έλληνες εν Αιγύπτω: Η Συγχρόνου Ελληνισμού Εγκατάστασης [Greeks in Egypt: The Establishment of Modern Hellenism] (Alexandria: n.p., 1892), 14.

38 Typaldos, *Letters from the East*, 11, 76–78.

39 Typaldos, *Letters from the East*, 12.

40 Juan Cole, *Colonialism and Revolution in the Middle East: Social and Cultural Origins of Egypt's 'Urabi Movement* (Cairo: American University in Cairo Press, 1999), 193.

41 Cole, *Colonialism and Revolution*, 203.

Notes to Chapter 2

1 Donald Malcolm Reid, *Whose Pharaohs? Archaeology, Museums, and Egyptian National Identity from Napoleon to World War I* (Oakland:

University of California Press, 2003), 150.

2   Alfred Milner, *England in Egypt* (London: Edward Arnold, 1894), 28.

3   Alexander Kazamias, "Cromer's Assault on 'Internationalism':
British Colonialism and the Greeks of Egypt, 1882–1907," in *The
Long 1890s in Egypt: Colonial Quiescence, Subterranean Resistance*, eds.
Marilyn Booth and Anthony P. Gorman (Edinburgh: Edinburgh
University Press, 2014), 261.

4   *Paliggenesia*, May 13, 1882.

5   *Paliggenesia*, June 3, 1882.

6   Tsirkas, *Cavafy*, 99–100; Kazamias, "Cromer's Assault," 261–62.

7   Charles Royle, *The Egyptian Campaigns 1882 to 1885 and the Events
that Led to Them*, vol. 1 (London: Hurst and Blackett, 1886), 44.

8   Tsirkas, *Cavafy*, 99–100; Cole, *Colonialism and Revolution*, 254–55.

9   Royle, *The Egyptian Campaigns 1882 to 1885*, 114.

10   *Paliggenesia*, May 28, June 1, 1882, 3, 11, 14, 16, 18, 22–28.

11   Penelope S. Delta, Πρώτες Ενθυμήσεις [First Memories], ed. P.L.
Zannas (Athens: Ermis, 2008), 50–54.

12   Kazamias, *Cromer's Assault*, 262.

13   Tsirkas, *Cavafy*, 186–94.

14   Politis, *Hellenism*, vol. 2, 173–76.

15   Kazamias, *Cromer's Assault*, 256–59.

16   Henry Hamilton Johnston, "Lord Cromer's 'Modern Egypt,'"
Journal of the Royal African Society 7, no. 27 (April 1908): 239–48.

17   The Earl of Cromer, *Modern Egypt*, vol. 2 (London: Macmillan,
1908), 250–52; Kazamias, *Cromer's Assault*, 257.

18   Omar Foda, "The Pyramid and the Crown: The Egyptian Beer
Industry from 1897 to 1963," *International Journal of Middle East
Studies* 46 (2014): 144.

19   Russell Pasha, *Egyptian Service 1902–1946* (London: John Murray,
1949), 244–48.

20   Milner, *England in Egypt*, 48–51.

21   Cromer, *Modern Egypt*, 439–42.

22   Kazamias, *Cromer's Assault*, 258.

23   Kazamias, *Cromer's Assault*, 259.

24   Foreign Office, Correspondence Egypt and the Sudan No. 130, Sir E.
Baring to the Marquis of Salisbury No. 119, Cairo, February 23, 1889.

25   Foreign Office, Correspondence Egypt and the Sudan No. 17,
Memorandum by Mr. Rennell Rodd, November 13, 1889.

26   Foreign Office, Correspondence Egypt and the Sudan No. 43, Sir
E. Baring to the Marquis of Salisbury No. 37, February 6, 1890.

27   Will Hanley, *Identifying with Nationality: Europeans, Ottomans, and
Egyptians in Alexandria* (New York: Columbia University Press, 1917);

Shane Minkin, "Documenting Death: Inquests, Governance and Belonging in 1890s Alexandria," in *The Long 1890s in Egypt: Colonial Quiescence, Subterranean Resistance*, eds. Marilyn Booth and Anthony P. Gorman (Edinburgh: Edinburgh University Press, 2014), 31–56.

28 Pandelis Kerkinos, *Η Ελληνική Ιθαγένεια εν Αιγύπτω* [Greek Nationality in Egypt] (Alexandria: Grammata, 1930), 28–75.

29 Foreign Office, Correspondence Egypt and the Sudan No. 38, Mr. Rodd to the Earl of Kimberley No. 108, July 19, 1894.

30 Kitroeff, *The Greeks in Egypt*, 98–100; Kazamias, "Cromer's Assault"; Relli Schecter, "Selling Luxury: The Rise of the Egyptian Cigarette and the Transformation of the Egyptian Tobacco Market, 1850–1914," *International Journal of Middle East Studies* 35, 1 (2003): 55–56; *Omonoia*, August 24/September 5, 1885, cited in Tsirkas, *Cavafy*, 167.

31 Shechter, "Selling Luxury," 56–57.

32 Politis, *Hellenism*, vol. 2, 185.

33 Robert Tignor, "The Egyptian Revolution of 1919: New Directions in the Egyptian Economy," in *The Middle Eastern Economy: Studies in Economics and Economic History*, ed. Elie Kedourie (New York: Routlege, 2014), 61.

34 Georgios E. Partheniadis, *Ελληνικά Νοσοκομεία της Αλεξάνδρειας* [Greek Hospitals of Alexandria] (Alexandria: Typografio Emporiou, 1960), 48–57.

35 Matoula Tomara-Sideris, *Αλεξανδρινές Οικογένειες Χωρέμη-Μπενάκη-Σαλβάγου* [Alexandrian Families Choremi-Benachi-Salvago] (Athens: Kerkyra, 2013), 66.

36 Livanos, *John Sakellaridis*, 33, 36–38.

37 Livanos, *John Sakellaridis*, 50–56; Owen, *Cotton and the Egyptian Economy*, 222.

38 Pandelis Glavanis, "Aspects of the Economic and Social History of the Greek Community in Alexandria During the Nineteenth Century" (PhD diss., University of Hull, 1989), 86.

39 Delta, *First Memories*, 114–15.

40 Michael Haag, *Alexandria: City of Memory* (New Haven: Yale University Press, 2004), 132.

41 Politis, *Hellenism*, vol. 2, 52–61.

42 Politis, *Hellenism*, vol. 2, 184–85.

43 Politis, *Hellenism*, vol. 2, 317–22.

44 Tsirkas, *Cavafy*, 286.

45 Politis, *Hellenism*, vol. 1, 264.

46 Delta, *First Memories*, 67–68.

47 Kazamias, *"Cromer's Assault,"* 271–75.

48   *Omonoia*, January 19, 1914.

Notes to Chapter 3

1   Jasper Yeates Brinton, *The Mixed Courts of Egypt* (New Haven: Yale University Press, 1968), 186–87.
2   Kitroeff, *The Greeks in Egypt*, 38–41.
3   Kitroeff, *The Greeks in Egypt*, 41–42; Curzon to Granville, May 28, 1920, No. 238 E S212/509/16 FO 371/4999; Hurst to Granville, May 28, 1920, unnumbered E512/504/16 FO 371/4999; Granville to Curzon, June 15, 1920, No. 152 E6738/509/16 FO 371/4999; Curzon to Granville, June 23, 1920, No. 96 E6738/509/16 FO 371/4999.
4   Gialourakis, *The Egypt of the Greeks*, 174–77.
5   Alexander Kitroeff, "The Greek State and the Diaspora: Venizelism Abroad, 1910-1932," in *Historical Poetics in Nineteenth and Twentieth Century Greece: Essays in Honor of Lily Macrakis*, ed. Stamatia Dova (Cambridge: Center for Hellenic Studies, Harvard University), https://chs.harvard.edu/CHS/article/display/4883
6   Kitroeff, *The Greeks in Egypt*, 42–44.
7   Kitroeff, *The Greeks in Egypt*, 44–47.
8   Kitroeff, *The Greeks in Egypt*, 57–60.
9   Kitroeff, *The Greeks in Egypt*, 61–63; Lord Lloyd, *Egypt Since Cromer*, vol. 2, reprinted from 1934 edition (New York: AMS Press, 1970), 185–222.
10   Yunan Labib Rizk, "The Fall of Lord Lloyd," *al-Ahram Weekly*, July 18–24, 2002, http://weekly.ahram.org.eg/Archive/2002/595/chrncls.htm
11   J.B. Milne, "Trade Treaties and Capitulations in Morocco," *Journal of the British Institute of International Affairs* 5, 1 (January 1926): 32–43.
12   Kitroeff, *The Greeks in Egypt*, 65–66.
13   Kitroeff, *The Greeks in Egypt*, 66–68.
14   Radamanthis Radopoulos, Ο Βασιλεύς Φουάτ ο Αος και η Αναγενωμμένη Αίγυπτος [King Fu'ad I and Egypt Reborn] (Alexandria: Kasimatis, 1930). See also Manolis Marangoulis, «Καιρός να Συγχρονισθώμεν» Η Αιγυπτος και η Αιγυπτιώτικη Διανόηση (1919–1939) ["A Time to Modernize": Egypt and the Greek Egyptian Intellectuals (1919–1939)] (Athens: University of Cyprus and Gutenberg Press, 2011), 95 and 324–29.
15   The French edition is Athanasios Politis, *L'Hellénisme et l'Égypte Moderne* (Paris: Alcan, 1929–30).
16   Christophoros II, Τα Απαντα [Collected Works], 2 vols. (Alexandria:

Patriarchate of Alexandria, 1960).

17   Evgenios Michaelides, *Ο Αιγυπτιωτης Ελληνισμός και το Μέλλον του* [The Greeks of Egypt and Their Future] (Alexandria: Grammata, 1927); Marangoulis, "A Time to Modernize," 137–45.
18   Marangoulis, "A Time to Modernize," 332–42.
19   Kitroeff, *The Greeks in Egypt*, 68.
20   Archimandrite Anthimos Siskos, *Η Διοικητική Οργάνωσις της Εκκλησίας της Αλεξανδρείας τ. 1ος Η Νομική και Κανονική Θέσις της Εκκλησίας Αλεξανδρείας Εναντι της Αιγυπτιακής Επικράτειας* [The Administrative Governance of the Church of Alexandria, vol. 1, The Legal and Canonical Position of the Church of Alexandria in Relation to the Egyptian State] (Alexandria: Typografion Emporiou, 1937).
21   Gudrun Krämer, *The Jews in Modern Egypt 1914–1952* (London: I.B.Tauris, 1989), 73.
22   Kitroeff, *The Greeks in Egypt*, 69–70.
23   Angelos Dalachanis, *The Greek Exodus from Egypt: Diaspora Politics and Emigration 1937–1962* (New York: Berghan, 2017), 16–18.
24   Najat Abdulhaq, *Jewish and Greek Communities in Egypt: Entrepreneurship and Business Before Nasser* (New York: I.B.Tauris, 2016), 116–22, 145–47.
25   Cleomenis Nicolaou, *Το Παρελθόν, το παρόν και το μέλλον της Κοινότητος Ιμπραημίας* [The Past, Present, and Future of the Community Organization of al-Ibrahimiya] (Alexandria: n.p., 1942).
26   Dalachanis, *The Greek Exodus*, 25–29.
27   Dalachanis, *The Greek Exodus*, 25.
28   Dalachanis, *The Greek Exodus*, 29.
29   Dalachanis, *The Greek Exodus*, 29–30.
30   "Το Κείμενον των Συνθηκών Εγκαταστάσεων εν Αιγύπτω" [The Text of the Treaties of Establishment in Egypt], August 4, 1949.
31   "Η Χθεσινή Τελευταία Συνεδρίασις των Μικτών Δικαστηρίων Καΐρου" [Yesterday's Last Session of the Mixed Courts in Cairo], *Tachydromos*, October 12, 1949, 4.
32   "Egypt Ends Foreigners' Courts," *New York Times*, October 16, 1949, 2; "Το Τέλος των Μικτών Δικαστηρίων" [The End of the Mixed Courts], *Tachydromos*, October 14, 1949, 1.
33   Dalachanis, *The Greek Exodus*, 30–31.

Notes to Chapter 4

1   Abdulhaq, *Jewish and Greek Communities*, 128.
2   Robert Mabro and Samir Radwan, *The Industrialization of Egypt 1939–1973: Policy and Performance* (Oxford: Oxford University Press, 1976), 27.

3   Robert Vitalis, *When Capitalists Collide: Business Conflict and the End of Empire in Egypt* (Berkeley: University of California Press, 1995), 34.

4   Tignor, *State, Private Enterprise*, 190–94.

5   Kitroeff, *The Greeks in Egypt*, 80–81; Elie I. Politi, *Annuaire des Sociétés Égyptiennes par Actions* (Alexandria: Procaccia, 1938), 720.

6   Kitroeff, *The Greeks in Egypt*, 82–85; *Cinquante Ans de Labeur 1894– 1944, The Kafr-El-Zayat Cotton Co. Ltd.*, n.p., n.d.

7   Kitroeff, *The Greeks in Egypt*, 85–88.

8   Kitroeff, *Greeks in Egypt*, 101–109; Shechter, *Smoking, Culture and Economy*, 88–95.

9   Kitroeff, *Greeks in Egypt*, 108–111; Shechter, *Smoking, Culture and Economy*, 96–113; Gialourakis, *The Egypt of the Greeks*, 500–501.

10   Tasos Paleologos, *Ο Αιγυπτιώτης Ελληνισμός Ιστορία και Δράσις 753 πχ – 1953* [The Greeks of Egypt: History and Activities 753 bc–1953] (Alexandria: n.p., 1953), 83–85.

11   Kitroeff, *The Greeks in Egypt*, 114–18.

12   Kitroeff, *The Greeks in Egypt*, 90–91.

13   Kitroeff, *The Greeks in Egypt*, 117–18; Christopher Aidan Long, "Theodore Polychronis Cozzika Family Group Sheet," www.christopherlong.co.uk/gen/choremigen/fg08/fg08_279.html

14   Nikos Nikitaridis, *Αιγυπτιώτικες Προσωπικότητες του Χθες* [Eminent Greeks of Egypt of Yesteryear] (Athens: Aggelaki, 2017), 386–88.

15   Paleologos, *The Greeks of Egypt*, 162–64.

16   Paleologos, *The Greeks of Egypt*, 172–73.

17   Dalachanis, *The Greek Exodus*, 79–89.

18   Floreska Karanasou, "Egyptianisation: The 1947 Company Law and the Foreign Communities in Egypt" (DPhil diss., Oxford University, 1992), 19–23, 32–34, 40.

19   Karanasou, "Egyptianisation," 4–45.

20   Kitroeff, *The Greeks in Egypt*, 176–77.

21   Kitroeff, *The Greeks in Egypt*, 173–76; Pantelis Lekkou, *Το Αβερώφειο Γυμνάσιο Αλεξανδρείας απο της Ιδρύσεως του έως το 1960* [The Averoff High School of Alexandria from Its Establishment until 1960] (Thessaloniki: Zitis, 2004), 87–98.

22   Artemis Cooper, *Cairo in the War: 1939–45* (London: John Murray, 1913), 250.

23   Marzia Borsoi, "Alexandria and Cairo: the 'Balad' or 'Terra Nostra' of the Italians in Egypt 1860-1956" (MA thesis, University of North Carolina Wilmington, 2010), 102–107.

24   Dalachanis, *The Greek Exodus*, 90–92; Karanasou, "Egyptianisation," 50–55.

25   Gianluca P. Parolin, *Citizenship in the Arab World: Kin, Religion and*

Nation-State (Amsterdam: Amsterdam University Press, 2009), 81.

26   Karanasou, "Egyptianisation," 85–86; *Tachydromos,* June 21, 1947, 1, and June 24, 1947, 2.

27   Tignor, *State, Private Enterprise,* 180–81.

28   Karanasou, "Egyptianization," 102–10; *Tachydromos,* January 7, 1947, 1.

Notes to Chapter 5

1   Souloyannis, *The Status of the Greeks,* 164–67.

2   E.M. Forster, *Two Cheers for Democracy* (London: Edward Arnold, 1951), 237.

3   Giorgis Athanasiades, *Η Πρώτη Πράξη της Ελληνικής Τραγωδίας Μέση Ανατολή 1941–44* [The First Act of the Greek Tragedy, Middle East 1941–44] (Athens: Planitis, 1975), 14.

4   Alekos Lidorikis, *Η Προπολεμική Αίγύπτος και οι Έλληνες* [Prewar Egypt and the Greeks] (Athens: Kastaniotis, 2005), 57.

5   Kitroeff, *The Greeks in Egypt,* 145.

6   Demetrios J. Constantelos, *Byzantine Philanthropy and Social Welfare* (New Brunswick: Rutgers University Press, 1968); Matoula Tomara-Sideris, *Ευεργετισμός και Προσωπικότητα Ευεργέτες Έλληνες του Καΐρου* [Giving and Personality: Greek Benefactors of Cairo], vols. 1 and 2 (Athens: Papazis, 2002); Matoula Tomara-Sideris, *Benefaction in Modern Greece: Theory and Practice* (Athens: Economic Publishing, 2017).

7   Kitroeff, *The Greeks in Egypt,* 149.

8   Efthymios Souloyannis, *Η Ελληνική Κοινότητα Αλεξάνδρειας 1843–1993* [The Greek Community of Alexandria 1843–1993] (Athens: ELIA, 2005), 90–91; Kitroeff, *The Greeks in Egypt,* 149–51.

9   Christina Pallini, "Geographic Theaters, Port Landscapes and Architecture in the Eastern Mediterranean," in *Cities of the Mediterranean from the Ottomans to the Present Day,* eds. Biray Kolluoglu and Meltem Toksöz (London: I.B.Tauris, 2010), 61–77; Souloyannis, *The Greek Community of Alexandria,* 218–19.

10   Kitroeff, *The Greeks in Egypt,* 149–54.

11   Giota Papadimitriou, "Ο Μαθητικός Τύπος ως Άτυπο Σχολικό Αρχείο: Η περίπτωση του μαθητικού περιοδικού Γλαύξ (1931–1957)" [Student Magazines as Informal School Archives: The Case of the School Magazine Glaux (1931–1957) in *Προγράμματα Σπουδών – Σχολικά Εγχειρίδια: απο το παρελθόν στο παρόν και στο μέλλον Πρακτικά Συνεδρίου τ. Γ'* [Curricula–School Manuals: From the Past to the Present and Future, Conference Proceedings, vol. 3], eds. S. Grosdos (Athens: Mouseio Scholikis Zois and Ekpaideysis, Pedagogiki Eteria Ellados, Pierce, American College of Greece, 2016).

12   Panagiota Papadimitriou, "Η εκπαίδευση στις ελληνικές παροικίες της Αιγύπτου. Το παράδειγμα των Ελληνικών Εκπαιδευτηρίων Μανσούρας" [Education in the Greek Communities of Egypt: The Case of the Greek Schools in Mansura] (PhD diss., University of Athens, 2003), and Giota Papadimitriou, "Εκπαιδευτικός Ομιλος Αιγύπτου – Η ιδρυση του και η Δράση του κατά το 1919" [The Educational Society of Egypt: Its Establishment and Activities in 1919] (proceedings of the Third International Conference on the History of Education, University of Patra, 2004); Ekaterini Trimi-Kirou, "Kinotis Grecque d'Alexandrie: Sa politique éducative (1843–1932)" (PhD thesis, Université des Sciences Humaines de Strasbourg), 1996.

13   Souloyannis, *The Greek Community of Alexandria*, 179–92.

14   Papadimitriou, "Education in the Greek Communities of Egypt," 306–10.

15   Edmund Keeley, *Cavafy's Alexandria: Study of a Myth in Progress* (Cambridge: Harvard University Press, 1976), 7–8.

16   Christopher Montague Woodhouse, *The Apple of Discord* (London: Hutchinson, 1948), 41–42.

17   *Ο Αιγυπτιώτης Ελληνισμός στας Επάλξεις* [The Greeks of Egypt on the Battlements] (Alexandria: n.p., 1946), 16.

18   Stratis Tsirkas, "Η Πνευματική Αντίσταση στη Μέση Ανατολή" [The Intellectual Resistance in the Middle East] *Epitheorise Technes* [Review of Art] no. 87–88 (1962): 480.

19   Foreign Office Minutes, Sir Orme Sargent, September 19, 1941 R8505/254/19 FO 371/29850.

20   *The Greeks of Egypt on the Battlements*, 79–81; Athanasiades, *The First Act*, 51; Partheniadis, *Greek Hospitals*, 123–26.

21   Minister of State to Christopher II, Letter, June 16, 1942 FO 371/3316; Christopher II to Minister of State, Letter, June 20, 1942 FO 371/3316.

22   Tsouderos to Dixon, Note, January 10, 1942 and attached Patriarch's text FO R3015/112/19.

23   *Pantainos* 7, March 1, 1942, 1.

24   Panayotis Canellopoulos, *Ημερολόγιο Κατοχής 31 Μαρτίου 1942 – 4 Ιανουαρίου 1945* [Diary of the Occupation, March 31, 1942–January 4, 1945] (Athens: Estia, 2003), 72–75, 134–45.

25   Tsirkas, *Drifting Cities*, 341.

26   Krämer, *The Jews in Modern Egypt*, 175–78.

27   Brock to Dixon, Letter, June 15, 1943 and enclosure "Greek Communists" R4896/1/19 FO 371/37197.

28   Alexander Kitroeff, "Η Ελληνική Παροικία στην Αίγυπτο και ο Δεύτερος Παγκόσμιος Πόλεμος Η Περίπτωση του Εθνικού Απελευθερωτικού

Συνδέσμου" [The Greek Community in Egypt and the Second World War: The Case of the National Liberation Association] *Mnemon* 9 (1981): 1–32.

29   Minister of State (Cairo) to Foreign Office, telegrams #724, March 24, 1943 R2660/1/19 and #107, March 29, 1943 R3092/194/19 FO 371/37216.

30   Georgios Seferis, Πολιτικό Ημερολόγιο A' *1935–1944* [Political Diary, vol. 1, 1935–1944] (Athens: Ikaros, 1992), 178.

31   Petros Rousos, H Μεγάλη Πενταετία [The Great Five Years] (Athens: Sinchroni Epochi, 1976), 400.

32   Kitroeff, "The Greek Community in Egypt," 19–23.

33   Haag, *Alexandria*, 220.

34   Ntinos Koutsoumis, *4 Χρόνια Αγνωστη Ιστορία* [4 Years' Unknown History] (Alexandria: n.p., 1946); Athanasiades, *The First Act*, 170–74; Leeper to FO #17, March 26, 1944 R5297/59/19 FO 371 43705.

35   Foreign Office to Leeper #146, April 14, 1944 R6027/9/19 FO 371/43701.

36   *Tachydromos*, January 6, 1945, 2.

Notes to Chapter 6

1   Delta, *First Memories*, 78.

2   Eugène Gellion-Danglar, *Letters sur L'Égypte Contemporaine (1865–1875)* (Paris: Sandoz et Fischbacher, 1876), 6–7.

3   *A Few Lines about Alexandria* (Alexandria: n.p., 1911), 32.

4   Lawrence Durrell, *The Alexandria Quartet* (New York: E.P. Dutton, 1962), 17.

5   Will Hanley, "Cosmopolitan Cursing in Late Nineteenth-Century Alexandria," in *Cosmopolitanisms in Muslim Contexts: Perspectives from the Past*, eds. Derryl N. MacLean and Sikeena Karmali Ahmed (Edinburgh: Edinburgh University Press, 2012), 10.

6   Khaled Fahmy, "Towards a Social History of Modern Alexandria," in *Alexandria, Real and Imagined*, eds. Anthony Hirst and Michael Silk (Burlington: Ashgate, 2004), 282.

7   Deborah Starr, *Remembering Cosmopolitan Egypt: Literature, Culture, and Empire* (New York: Routledge, 2009), 19–23.

8   Robert Ilbert, "A Certain Sense of Citizenship" in *Alexandria 1860–1960: The Brief Life of a Cosmopolitan Community*, eds. Robert Ilbert and Ilios Yannakakis with Jacques Hassoun (Alexandria: Harpocrates, 1997), 18–34.

9   Robert Mabro, "Alexandria 1860–1960: The Cosmopolitan Identity," in *Alexandria, Real and Imagined*, eds. by Anthony Hirst

and Michael Silk (Burlington: Ashgate, 2004), 261.

10   Katerina Trimi and Ilios Yannakakis, "The Greeks: The Parikia of Alexandria," in *Alexandria 1860–1960: The Brief Life of a Cosmopolitan Community*, eds. Robert Ilbert and Ilios Yannakakis with Jacques Hassoun (Alexandria: Harpocrates, 1977), 65–71.

11   Nancy Y. Reynolds, *A City Consumed: Urban Commerce, the Cairo Fire, and the Politics of Decolonization in Egypt* (Stanford: Stanford University Press, 2012), 27.

12   Martin S. Briggs, *Through Egypt in Wartime* (London: Fisher Unwin, 1918), 17.

13   Briggs, *Through Egypt*, 18.

14   Tsirkas, *Drifting Cities*, 439, 464–65.

15   Arnold Wright, *Twentieth Century Impressions of Egypt* (London: Lloyd's, 1909), 433; Gabriel Baer, "The Beginnings of Municipal Government in Egypt," *Middle East Studies* vol. 4 (1968): 131.

16   E.M. Forster, *Pharos and Pharillon* (Richmond: Hogarth Press, 1923), 98.

17   Kitroeff, *The Greeks in Egypt*, 59.

18   Jean Marc Oppenheim, "Twilight of a Colonial Ethos: The Alexandria Sporting Club, 1890–1956" (PhD diss., Columbia University, 1991), 7–8.

19   Haag, *Alexandria*, 28.

20   Philip Mansel, *Levant: Splendour and Catastrophe on the Mediterranean* (New Haven: Yale University Press, 2010), 133.

21   Max Rodenbeck, *Cairo: The City Victorious* (New York: Vintage, 1999), 137.

22   Briggs, *Through Egypt*, 37–38.

23   Rodenbeck, *Cairo*, 145.

24   Edward Said, *Out of Place: A Memoir* (New York: Vintage, 2012), 196.

25   Briggs, *Through Egypt*, 82.

26   Valeska Huber, *Channelling Mobilities: Migration and Globalization in the Suez Canal Region and Beyond, 1869–1914* (New York: Cambridge University Press, 2013), 48.

27   Huber, *Chanelling Mobilities*, 300.

28   Personal communication from Nick Markettos, January 2018.

29   George M. Cotzas, *Memories from Egypt* (Athens: privately published, 2015), 77–78.

30   Rodenbeck, *Cairo*, 138.

31   Durrell, *Alexandria Quartet*, 56–57.

32   Hanley, "Cosmopolitan Cursing," 95.

33   Albert Hourani, *Minorities in the Arab World* (Oxford: Oxford University Press, 1947), 25.

34   Robert Tignor, "The Economic Activities of Foreigners in Egypt, 1920–1950: From Millet to Haute Bourgeoisie," *Comparative Studies in Society and History* 22, no. 3 (July 1980): 433.
35   Tignor, "The Economic Activities of Foreigners in Egypt," 432.
36   Politi, *Annuaire des Sociétés Égyptiennes Par Actions*, 237–808.
37   Tignor, "The Economic Activities of Foreigners in Egypt," 433–40.
38   Sahar Hamouda and Colin Clement, *Victoria College: A History Revealed* (Cairo: American University in Cairo Press, 2005), 85.
39   Hamouda and Clement, *Victoria College*, 23.
40   Said, *Out of Place*, 34.
41   Said, *Out of Place*, 177, 188.
42   Haag, *Alexandria*, 44.
43   Ilios Yannakakis, "Farewell Alexandria," in *Alexandria 1860–1960: The Brief Life of a Cosmopolitan Community*, eds. Robert Ilbert and Ilios Yannakakis with Jacques Hassoun (Alexandria: Harpocrates, 1977), 108.
44   Tsirkas, *Drifting Cities*, 271.
45   Kitroeff, *The Greeks in Egypt*, 136–37; Beinin and Lockman, *Workers on the Nile*, 50–52, 106–10.
46   Kitroeff, *The Greeks in Egypt*, 137–40; Tareq Y. Ismael and Rifa'at El-Sa'id, *The Communist Movement in Egypt*, 1920–1988 (Syracuse: Syracuse University Press, 1990), 12–22.
47   For an account of the early phase of surrealism in Egypt see Sam Bardaouil, *Surrealism in Egypt: Modernism and the Art and Liberty Group* (New York: I.B. Tauris, 2007), Chapter 1.
48   Maria Adamantidou, Ελληνικός Αθλητισμός στο Κάϊρο του 20ού αιώνα [Greek Sports in Cairo in the 20th century] (Athens: Greek Community of Cairo, 2005), 23–132; Nikos Nikitaridis, Τα Ελληνικα Σωματεία στην Αιγυπτο [Greek Associations in Egypt] (Athens: Aggelaki, 2015), 93–118, 337–51.
49   Egyptian Olympic Committee, www.egyptianolympic.org/history.html; Wilson Chacko Jacob, *Working Out Egypt: Effendi Masculinity and Subject Formation in Colonial Modernity 1870–1940* (Durham: Duke University Press, 2011), 127–40.
50   *Tachydromos*, January 2, 1928, 2.
51   *Tachydromos*, October 5, 1951, 2.
52   Christophoros Nomikos, Εισαγωγή στην Ιστορία των Αράβων [Introduction to the History of the Arabs] (Alexandria: Grammata, 1927), 10.
53   Marangoulis, "Time to Modernize," 243–46, 291–94.
54   *Tachydromos*, March 30, 1925, cited in Marangoulis, "Time to Modernize," 330.

55 *Tachydromos*, January 3–March 1, 1928, 1.
56 *Tachydromos*, January 10, 1928, 1.
57 *Tachydromos*, January 12, 1928, 1.
58 Marangoulis, "Time to Modernize," 408–21.
59 Marangoulis, "Time to Modernize," 356–65, 371–78.
60 Thomas Phillip, *The Syrians in Egypt 1725–1975* (Stuttgart: Franz Steiner Verlag, 1985), 146.
61 Stratis Tsirkas, "Αναμνήσεις απο την Ανω Αίγύπτο" [Memories from Upper Egypt] *E Lexi* 27 (September 1983): 786–87.
62 Dalachanis, *The Greek Exodus*, 33.
63 Evgenios Michaelides, Βιβλιογραφία των Ελλήνων Αιγυπτιωτών [Bibliography of the Greeks of Egypt] (Alexandria: n.p., 1965–66), 207–11.
64 Eleni I. Kontaxi, "Κωστας Τσανγκαράδας: ένας Πηλειορείτης Λόγιος στην Αιγυπτο" [Kostas Tsangaradas: A Man of Letters from Mount Pelion in Egypt] (PhD diss., University of Thessaly, 2006), 50–445.
65 Adamantidou, *Greek Sports*, 260–72.
66 Nikos Tsaravopoulos, *Η Εγκατάσταση των Ελλήνων στην Αίγύπτο* [The Establishment of the Greeks in Egypt] (Cairo: Tsouma, 1948), 40.
67 Interview with Aris Tsaravopoulos, Athens, January 4, 2018.

Notes to Chapter 7

1 Anthony P. Gorman, "Egypt's Forgotten Communists: The Postwar Greek Left," *Journal of Modern Greek Studies* 20, no. 1 (May 2002): 21.
2 Ntinos Koutsoumis, "Koulou Sana," *Tachydromos*, January 1, 1951, 1.
3 *Tachydromos*, January 14, 1951, 1.
4 Reynolds, *A City Consumed*, 188, 193–94.
5 Rodenbeck, *Cairo*, 157.
6 Dalachanis, *The Greek Exodus*, 33–37, 159.
7 *Tachydromos*, July 26, 1952, 1, and November 10, 1952, 1.
8 Karanasou, "Egyptianization," 306–16, 230–31.
9 Dalachanis, *The Greek Exodus*, 163–69, 181–84.
10 George N. Sfeir, "The Abolition of Confessional Jurisdiction in Egypt: The Non-Muslim Courts," *Middle East Journal* 5, no. 3 (summer 1956): 248–56.
11 Villy N. Politi, *Ελληνική Κοινότητα 100 Χρόνια Σφραγίδα στο Καϊρο* [Greek Community: A One Hundred-year Seal on Cairo] (Cairo: Greek Community of Cairo, 2006), 80–83.
12 Cléobule Tsourkas, *Les Hellènes dans l'intérieur de l'Égypte* (Thessaloniki: Society of Macedonian Studies, 1957), 20.
13 Souloyannis, *The Status of the Greeks*, 220–24; Souloyannis, *The Greek Community of Alexandria*, 311–15.

14 Leonidas G. Markantonatos, Τα Εν Αιγύπτω Ελληνικά Εκπαιδευτήρια [The Greek Schools in Egypt] (Thessaloniki: Society of Macedonian Studies, 1957).

15 Sam Pope Brewer, "Egyptians Awaiting Nasser Counter-Blow," *New York Times*, September 16, 1956, E5.

16 Osgood Caruthers, "Cairo Issues Threat of Canal Priorities," *New York Times*, August 23, 1956, 1.

17 Sam Pope Brewer, "U.S. Invokes Curb on Pilots in Suez," *New York Times*, September 26, 1956, 5; "Ships Plying Canal; Egyptians Confident," *New York Times*, September 16, 1956, 1.

18 al-Sayyid Marsot, *A Short History of Egypt*, 115–16.

19 Joel Beinin, *The Dispersion of Egyptian Jewry* (Cairo: American University in Cairo Press, 2005), 87.

20 Robert C. Doty, "Port Said Leader Puts Dead at 3,000," *New York Times*, November 25, 1956, 27.

21 Robert C. Doty, "1,500 Europeans to Quit Port Said," *New York Times*, December 7, 1956, 6.

22 Osgood Caruthers, "Egypt Takes Over Assets of Banks of British, French," *New York Times*, January 16, 1957, 1; Osgood Caruthers, "Nasser Rebuked in 2 Cairo Papers," New York Times, February 6, 1956, 6; Dalachanis, *The Greek Exodus*, 61–63.

23 John Sakkas, "Greece and the Mass Exodus of the Egyptian Greeks," *Journal of the Hellenic Diaspora* 35, no. 2 (2009): 102–105.

24 Constantinos Daratzikis, Διπλωματικές Σημειώσεις απο την Αίγυπτο 1955-1976 [Diplomatic Notes from Egypt, 1955-1976] (Athens: Golema, 2000), 66–70, 90–96.

25 Osgood Caruthers, "Nasser's Egypt: A Nation in Suspense," *New York Times*, February 10, 1957, 210.

26 *Eleutheria*, August 17, 1957, 1, 6, and August 18, 1957, 1, 6.

27 Parolin, *Citizenship*, 82.

28 Dalachanis, *The Greek Exodus*, 67–69; *Tachydromos*, August 17, 1957, 1–2; August 18, 1–6; August 19, 1–4; August 20, 1–3; August 21, 1; August 22, 1–4; August 23, 1–4.

29 *Eleutheria*, August 10, 1960, 1, 5; August 11, 1, 6; August 14, 6; August 15, 1, 6; August 16, 1, 6; *Tachydromos*, August 9–17, 1960.

30 Rodenbeck, *Cairo*, 158.

31 Jay Walz, "Cairo Laws Spur Flight of Greeks," *New York Times*, April 16, 1961, 23.

32 Takis D. Psarakis, Ανθολογιο Αλεξάνδρειας [An Anthology of Alexandria] (Athens: Nea Sinora Livanis, 1992), 67–70; Daratzikis, *Diplomatic Notes*, 215–16.

33 Philipp, *The Syrians*, 146–58.

34   Alexandra Papadimitriou, Αλεξάνδρεια-Αθήνα [Alexandria–Athens] (Athens: Kastaniotis, 2010), 76.

35   Dalachanis, *The Greek Exodus*; Anthony Gorman, "The Failures of Readjustment (*Αναπροσαρμογή*): The Post-War Greek Egyptian Experience," *Journal of the Hellenic Diaspora* 35.2 (2009): 45–60; Sophianos Chryssostomidis, "The Left, Nasser, and the Exodus of the Greeks from Egypt," *Journal of the Hellenic Diaspora*, 35.2 (2009): 155–60; Alexander Kazamias, "The 'Purge of the Greeks' from Nasserite Egypt: Myths and Realities," *Journal of the Hellenic Diaspora* 35.2 (2009): 13–34; Nikos Sideris, "The Greek Settlers' Flight from Egypt: The Psychological Aspects," *Journal of the Hellenic Diaspora* 35.2 (2009): 145–54.

36   Bardaouil, *Surrealism in Egypt*, Conclusion.

Notes to Chapter 8

1   Michael Haag, *Vintage Alexandria: Photographs of the City, 1860–1960* (Cairo: American University in Cairo Press, 2008), 113.

2   Niki Kitsantonis, "Demis Roussos Dies at 68; Greek Singer Was Internationally Known," *New York Times*, January 30, 2015, A24.

3   Photini Tomai, "Η Εξοδος των Ελλήνων απο την Αίγύπτο" [The Exodus of the Greeks from Egypt], *To Vima*, May 8, 2007, http://www.tovima.gr/relatedarticles/article/?aid=182739

4   Tomai, *The Exodus of the Greeks from Egypt*.

5   Papadimitriou, *Alexandria–Athens*, 300.

6   Gorman, *The Italians*, 157.

7   See, for example, the 'Letters to the Editor' section in the Athens-based newspaper *Kathimerini*, November 9, 2016, http://www.kathimerini.gr/874268/opinion/epikairothta/politikh/grammata-anagnwstwn

8   Yannakakis, "Farewell Alexandria," 212.

9   Timos Malanos, Αναμνήσεις ενός Αλεξανδρινού [Memories of an Alexandrian] (Athens: Boukoumanis, 1971), 375–76.

10   Communication from Petros Charitatos, February 9, 2018; Paleologos, *The Greeks of Egypt*, 185, 391.

11   Ivan Griberg and Phillipe Mioche, *Aluminium de Grèce: l'usine aux trois rivages* (Grenoble: Presses Universitaires de Grenoble, 1996), 79–82.

12   Dimitri P. Caritato, *Alexandrie, Il y a une Centaine d'Années (1850–1870)* (Alexandria: Société de Pulications Egyptiennes, 1961).

13   Dimitris Charitatos, Prologue in Οι Ελληνες στην Αιγυπτο 4,000 Χρόνια Παρουσία [The Greeks in Egypt: A Four Thousand-year Presence] (Athens: Association of Greeks from Egypt, 1982), 1–3.

14   Kostis Moskoff, *Η Εθνική και Κοινωνική Συνείδηση στην Ελλάδα
      1830-1909 Ιδεολογία του Μεταπρατικού Χώρου* [National and Social
      Consciouness in Greece, 1830–1909: Ideology of a Comprador
      Space] (Athens: Synchroni Epochi, 1974, 3rd edition);
      Constantinos Tsoucalas, *Εξάρτηση και Αναπαραγωγή Ο Κοινωνικός Ρόλος
      των Εκπαιδευτικών Μηχανισμών στην Ελλάδα* (1830-1922) [Dependency
      and Reproduction: The Social Role of Educational Mechanisms in
      Greece (1830–1922)] (Athens: Themelio, 1977).
15   Dan Georgakas, Alexander Kitroeff, and Matoula Tomara-Sideris,
      "Introduction," *Journal of the Hellenic Diaspora* 35.2 (2009): 5–10.
16   Irini Chrysocheri, "Recording Oral History: Memories of
      Alexandrians," 133–36; Chryssostomidis, "The Left, Nasser, and
      the Exodus of the Greeks from Egypt," 155–60; Harry Tzalas,
      "Literary Alexandria and Nostalgic Alexandrian Literature," *Journal
      of the Hellenic Diaspora* 35.2 (2009): 169–74; Panagiotis Karmatzos,
      "The Book of Nostos and the Big Decision," *Journal of the Hellenic
      Diaspora* 35.2 (2009): 161–68.
17   Hala Halim, "Rooted in the Mediterranean," *al-Ahram Weekly*, July
      9–15, 1998, http://weekly.ahram.org.eg/Archive/1998/385/eg7.
      htm; *Patris*, October 29, 2005, 1.
18   Conversation with Irini Chrysocheri, Athens, January 23, 2018.
19   Communication from Yorgos Avgeropoulos, February 13, 2018.
20   Bibliotheca Alexandrina, "Impressions of Alexandria: The
      Awad Collection," www.bibalex.org/en/center/details/
      ImpressionsofAlexandria
21   Azza Kararah, "Egyptian Literary Images of Alexandria," in
      Alexandria, Real and Imagined, eds. Anthony Hirst and Michael
      Silk (Burlington: Ashgate, 2004), 307–21; Joel Gordon, "*Hasan and
      Marika*: Screen Shots from a Vanishing Egypt," *Journal of Levantine
      Studies* 7, no. 1 (summer 2017): 35–56.
22   Starr, *Remembering Cosmopolitan Egypt*, 34.
23   Omnia Osama, "Nostos initiative to return Greek tourists to Egypt,"
      Egypt Today, January 31, 2018, www.egypttoday.com/Article/9/41511/
      Nostos-initiative-to-return-Greek-tourists-to-Egypt

Bibliography

Official Publications
Cinquante Ans de Labeur 1894–1944, The Kafr-El-Zayat Cotton Co. Ltd., n.p., n.d.
A Few Lines about Alexandria. Alexandria: n.p., 1911.
Foreign Office Documents on Egypt, FO/371 1889, 1890, 1894, 1940, 1941, 1942.
"Το Κείμενον των Συνθηκών Εγκαταστάσεων εν Αιγύπτω" [The Text of the Treaties of Establishment in Egypt], Greek Ministry of Foreign Affairs, August 4, 1949.

Newspapers and Magazines
Chronos-Phos (Cairo)
Egyptiotis Ellin (later *Ellin*) (Alexandria)
Eleutheria (Athens)
Elpis (Alexandria)
Images (Cairo)
Kathimerini (Athens)
La Réforme Illustrée (Cairo?)
Le Canal (Port Said?)
New York Times (New York)
Omonoia (Alexandria)
Paliggenesia (Athens)
Pantainos (Alexandria)
Paroikos (Alexandria)
Patris (Pyrgos)
Tachydromos (Alexandria)

Websites
Bibliotheca Alexandrina. "Impressions of Alexandria: The Awad Collection,"

www.bibalex.org/en/center/details/ImpressionsofAlexandria

Egyptian Olympic Committee. "History," www.egyptianolympic.org/history.html

Long, Christopher Aidan. "Theodore Polychronis Cozzika Family Group Sheet," www.christopherlong.co.uk/gen/choremigen/fg08/fg08_279.html

Books, Dissertations, and Journal Articles

Abdulhaq, Najat. *Jewish and Greek Communities in Egypt: Entrepreneurship and Business Before Nasser.* New York: I.B.Tauris, 2016.

Aciman, André. *Out of Egypt.* New York: Picador, 2007.

Adamantidou, Maria. *Ελληνικός Αθλητισμός στο Κάϊρο του 20ου αιωνα* [Greek Sports in Twentieth-century Cairo]. Athens: Greek Community of Cairo, 2005.

———. *Κόριννα (1946-1949) Ενα Ξεχωριστό Περιοδικό του Αχιλλοπουλείου Παρθεναγωγείου της Ελληνικής Κοινότητας Καΐρου* [Korina (1946–1949): An Exceptional Magazine of the Achillopoulos Girls' School of the Greek Community Organization of Cairo]. Athens: Ekdoseis, 2017.

Athanasiades, Giorgis. *Η Πρώτη Πράξη της Ελληνικής Τραγωδίας Μέση Ανατολή 1941–44* [The First Act of the Greek Tragedy, Middle East 1941–44]. Athens: Planitis, 1975.

Awad, Mohamed, and Shaha Hamouda, eds. *Voices from Cosmopolitan Alexandria.* Vol. 1. Alexandria: Bibliotheca Alexandrina, 2012.

Baedeker, Karl. *Egypt: Handbook for Travellers.* Leipzig: Baedeker, 1898.

Baer, Gabriel. "The Beginnings of Municipal Government in Egypt." *Middle East Studies* 4 (1968): 118–40.

Bardaouil, Sam. *Surrealism in Egypt: Modernism and the Art and Liberty Group.* New York: I.B. Tauris, 2007.

Beinin, Joel. *The Dispersion of Egyptian Jewry.* Cairo: American University in Cairo Press, 2005.

Beinin, Joel, and Zachary Lockman. *Workers on the Nile: Nationalism, Communism, Islam, and the Egyptian Working Class, 1882–1954.* Cairo: American University in Cairo Press, 1998.

Biancani, Francesca. "Let Down the Curtains around Us: Sex Work in Colonial Cairo, 1882–1952." PhD diss., London School of Economics, 2012.

Borsoi, Marzia. "Alexandria and Cairo: the 'Balad' or 'Terra Nostra' of the Italians in Egypt 1860-1956." MA thesis, University of North Carolina Wilmington, 2010.

Bowring, John. *Report on Egypt and Candia*. London: Clowes and Sons, 1840.

Briggs, Martin S. *Through Egypt in Wartime*. London: Fisher Unwin, 1918.

Brinton, Jasper Yeates. *The Mixed Courts of Egypt*. New Haven: Yale University Press, 1968.

Callimachos, Dimitrios. *Οι Έλληνες εν Αιγύπτω κατα την Γαλλικήν Κατοχήν 1798–1801* [The Greeks in Egypt during the French Occupation 1798–1801]. Cairo: n.p., 1912.

Canellopoulos, Panayotis. *Ημερολόγιο Κατοχής 31 Μαρτίου 1942 – 4 Ιανουαρίου 1945* [Diary of the Occupation, March 31, 1942–January 4, 1945]. Athens: Estia, 2003.

Caritato, Dimitri P. *Alexandrie, Il y a une Centaine d'Années (1850–1870)*. Alexandria: Société de Publications Egyptiennes, 1961.

Charitatos, Dimitris. Prologue in *Οι Έλληνες στην Αιγυπτο 4,000 Χρόνια Παρουσία* [The Greeks in Egypt: A Four Thousand-year Presence]. Athens: Association of Greeks from Egypt, 1982.

Christophoros II. *Τα Απαντα* [Collected Works], 2 vols. Alexandria: Patriarchate of Alexandria, 1960.

Chrysocheri, Irini. "Recording Oral History: Memories of Alexandrians." *Journal of the Hellenic Diaspora* 35.2 (2009): 133–36.

Chryssostomidis, Sophianos. "The Left, Nasser, and the Exodus of the Greeks from Egypt." *Journal of the Hellenic Diaspora* 35.2 (2009): 155–60.

Cole, Juan. *Colonialism and Revolution in the Middle East: Social and Cultural Origins of Egypt's 'Urabi Movement*. Cairo: American University in Cairo Press, 1999.

Constantelos, Demetrios J. *Byzantine Philanthropy and Social Welfare*. New Brunswick: Rutgers University Press, 1968.

Cooper, Artemis. *Cairo in the War: 1939–45*. London: John Murray, 1913.

Cotzas, George M. *Memories from Egypt*. Athens: privately published, 2015.

Cromer. *The Earl of Modern Egypt*, vols. 1 and 2. London: Macmillan, 1908.

Cuno, Kenneth M. "The Origins of Private Ownership of Land in Egypt: A Reappraisal." In *The Modern Middle East: A Reader*, edited by Albert Hourani, Phillip S. Khoury, and Mary C. Wilson, 195–227. Berkeley: University of California Press, 1994.

Dalachanis, Angelos. *The Greek Exodus from Egypt: Diaspora Politics and Emigration 1937–1962*. New York: Berghan, 2017.

Daratzikis, Constantinos. *Διπλωματικές Σημειώσεις απο την Αίγυπτο 1955-1976* [Diplomatic Notes from Egypt, 1955–1976]. Athens: Golema, 2000.

Delta, Penelope S. Πρώτες Ενθυμήσεις [First Memories]. Edited by P.L. Zannas. Athens: Ermis, 2008.

Dertilis, Giorgos B. Ιστορία του Ελληνικού Κράτους 1830–1920 [History of the Greek State, 1830–1920]. Iraklio: University of Crete Press, 2016.

Diakofotakis, Ioannis. Ιστορία της Ελληνικής Παροικίας Καφρ-Ελ-Ζαγιατ 1865–1972 [History of the Greek Community of Kafr al-Zayyat, 1865–1972]. Alexandria: n.p., 1973.

Dodwell, Henry. The Founder of Modern Egypt: A Study of Muhammad 'Ali. Cambridge: Cambridge University Press, 1931.

Durrell, Lawrence. The Alexandria Quartet. New York: E.P. Dutton, 1962.

Fahmy, Khaled. "For Cavafy, with Love and Squalor: Some Critical Notes on the History and Historiography of Modern Alexandria." In Alexandria, Real and Imagined, edited by Anthony Hirst and Michael Silk, 263–80. Burlington: Ashgate, 2004.

———. "Towards a Social History of Modern Alexandria." In Alexandria, Real and Imagined, edited by Anthony Hirst and Michael Silk, 281–306. Burlington: Ashgate, 2004.

Foda, Omar. "The Pyramid and the Crown: The Egyptian Beer Industry from 1897 to 1963." International Journal of Middle East Studies 46 (2014): 139–58.

Forster, E.M. Pharos and Pharillon. Richmond: Hogarth Press, 1923.

———. Two Cheers for Democracy. London: Edward Arnold, 1951.

Gellion-Danglar, Eugène. Letters sur L'Égypte Contemporaine (1865–1875). Paris: Sandoz et Fischbacher, 1876.

Georgakas, Dan, Alexander Kitroeff, and Matoula Tomara-Sideris. "Introduction." Journal of the Hellenic Diaspora 35.2 (2009): 5–10.

Gialourakis, Manolis. Η Αίγυπτος των Ελλήνων Συνοπτική Ιστορία του Ελληνισμου της Αιγύπτου [The Egypt of the Greeks: A Concise History of Hellenism in Egypt]. Athens: Mitropolis, 1967.

Gikas, Ioannis. Πενήντα Χρόνια Δάσκαλος [Fifty Years as a Teacher]. Alexandria: Phacos, 1950.

Glavanis, Pandelis. "Aspects of the Economic and Social History of the Greek Community in Alexandria during the Nineteenth Century." PhD diss., University of Hull, 1989.

Gordon, Joel. "Hasan and Marika: Screen Shots from a Vanishing Egypt." Journal of Levantine Studies 7, no. 1 (summer 2017): 35–56.

Gorman, Anthony P. "Egypt's Forgotten Communists: The Postwar Greek Left." Journal of Modern Greek Studies 20, no. 1 (May 2002): 1–27.

————. "The Failures of Readjustment (Αναπροσαρμογή): The Post-War Greek Egyptian Experience." *Journal of the Hellenic Diaspora* 35.2 (2009): 45–60.

————. "The Italians of Egypt: Return to Diaspora." In *Diasporas of the Modern Middle East: Contextualising Community*, edited by Anthony Gorman and Sossie Kasbarian, 138–70. Edinburgh: Edinburgh University Press, 2015.

Griberg, Ivan, and Phillipe Mioche. *Aluminium de Grèce: l'usine aux trois rivages* [Aluminium of Greece: the Factory on the Three Shores]. Grenoble: Presses Universitaires de Grenoble, 1996.

Haag, Michael. *Alexandria: City of Memory*. New Haven: Yale University Press, 2004.

————. *Vintage Alexandria: Photographs of the City, 1860–1960*. Cairo: American University in Cairo Press, 2008.

Halim, Hala. "Rooted in the Mediterranean," *al-Ahram Weekly*, July 9–15, 1998, http://weekly.ahram.org.eg/Archive/1998/385/eg7.htm

Hadzifotis, Ioannis M. *Αλεξάνδρεια: οι Δύο Αιώνες του Νεώτερου Ελληνισμού (1905-2005)* [Alexandria: The Two Centuries of Modern Hellenism, Ninteenth to the Twentieth Centuries]. Athens: Ellinika Grammata, 1999.

Hadziiosif, Christos. "La Colonie Grecque en Egypte 1833–1856." Phd Diss, Ecole Pratique des Hautes Etudes, Paris, 1980.

Hamouda, Sahar, and Colin Clement. *Victoria College: A History Revealed*. Cairo: American University in Cairo Press, 2005.

Hanley, Will. "Cosmopolitan Cursing in Late Nineteenth-Century Alexandria." In *Cosmopolitanisms in Muslim Contexts: Perspectives from the Past*, edited by Derryl N. MacLean and Sikeena Karmali Ahmed, 92–104. Edinburgh: Edinburgh University Press, 2012.

————. *Identifying with Nationality: Europeans, Ottomans, and Egyptians in Alexandria*. New York: Columbia University Press, 2017.

Hourani, Albert. *Minorities in the Arab World*. Oxford: Oxford University Press, 1947.

Huber, Valeska. *Channelling Mobilities: Migration and Globalization in the Suez Canal Region and Beyond, 1869–1914*. New York: Cambridge University Press, 2013.

Ilbert, Robert. "A Certain Sense of Citizenship." In *Alexandria 1860–1960: The Brief Life of a Cosmopolitan Community*, edited by Robert Ilbert and Ilios Yannakakis with Jacques Hassoun, 18–34. Alexandria: Harpocrates, 1997.

Ilbert, Robert, and Ilios Yannakakis, with Jacques Hassoun, eds. *Alexandria*

1860–1960: The Brief Life of a Cosmopolitan Community. Alexandria: Harpocrates, 1997.

Ismael, Tareq Y., and Rifa'at El-Sa'id. The Communist Movement in Egypt, 1920–1988. Syracuse: Syracuse University Press, 1990.

Jacob, Wilson Chacko. Working Out Egypt: Effendi Masculinity and Subject Formation in Colonial Modernity 1870–1940. Durham: Duke University Press, 2011.

Johnston, Henry Hamilton. "Lord Cromer's 'Modern Egypt.'" Journal of the Royal African Society 7, no. 27 (April 1908): 239–48.

Karaminas, Ioannis. Ο Ιερός Ναός του Ευαγγελισμού της Ελληνικής εν Αλεξανδρεία Κοινότητος [The Holy Church of the Annunciation of the Greek Community of Alexandria]. Alexandria: Kasimatis, 1937.

Karanasou, Floreska. "Egyptianisation: The 1947 Company Law and the Foreign Communities in Egypt." DPhil diss., Oxford University, 1992.

Kararah, Azza. "Egyptian Literary Images of Alexandria." In Alexandria, Real and Imagined, edited by Anthony Hirst and Michael Silk, 307–21. Burlington: Ashgate, 2004.

Karmatzos, Panagiotis. "The Book of Nostos and the Big Decision." Journal of the Hellenic Diaspora 35.2 (2009): 161–68.

Kazamias, Alexander. "The 'Purge of the Greeks' from Nasserite Egypt: Myths and Realities." Journal of the Hellenic Diaspora 35.2 (2009): 13–34.

———. "Between Language, Land and Empire: Humanist and Orientalist Perspectives on Egyptian Greek Identity." In Greek Diaspora and Migration since 1700: Society, Politics and Culture, edited by Dimitris Tziovas, 179–91. Farnham: Ashgate, 2009.

———. "Cromer's Assault on 'Internationalism': British Colonialism and the Greeks of Egypt, 1882–1907." In The Long 1890s in Egypt: Colonial Quiescence, Subterranean Resistance, edited by Marilyn Booth and Anthony P. Gorman, 253–83. Edinburgh: Edinburgh University Press, 2014.

Keeley, Edmund. Cavafy's Alexandria: Study of a Myth in Progress. Cambridge: Harvard University Press, 1976.

Kerkinos, Pantelis. Η Ελληνική Ιθαγένεια εν Αιγύπτω [Greek Nationality in Egypt]. Alexandria: Grammata, 1930.

Kipiadis, Georgios I. Έλληνες εν Αιγύπτω: Η Συγχρόνου Ελληνισμού Εγκατάστασης [Greeks in Egypt: The Establishment of Modern Hellenism]. Alexandria: n.p., 1892.

Kitroeff, Alexander. "Η Ελληνική Παροικία στην Αίγυπτο και ο Δεύτερος Παγκόσμιος Πόλεμος Η Περίπτωση του Εθνικού Απελευθερωτικού Συνδέσμου" [The

Greek Community in Egypt and the Second World War: The Case of the National Liberation Association]. *Mnemon* 9 (1981): 1–32.

———. "The Greek Diaspora in the Mediterranean and the Black Sea 18th–19th Centuries: Seen by American Eyes." In *The Greeks and the Sea*, edited by Speros Vryonis Jr, 153–71. New York: Caratzas, 1993.

———. *The Greeks in Egypt 1919–1937: Ethnicity and Class*. London: St. Antony's College and Ithaca Press, 1989.

———. "The Greeks of Egypt in the United States." *Journal of the Hellenic Diaspora* 35.2 (2009): 117–30.

———. "The Greek State and the Diaspora: Venizelism Abroad, 1910-1932." In *Historical Poetics in Nineteenth and Twentieth Century Greece: Essays in Honor of Lily Macrakis*, edited by Stamatia Dova. Cambridge: Center for Hellenic Studies, Harvard University, 2012, https://chs.harvard.edu/CHS/article/display/

———. "The International Dimension of the Interim Olympics in Athens 1906." In *The Interim Olympics in Athens, Greece, 1906*, edited by Christina Koulouri, 377–93. Athens: Hellenic Olympic Committee, 2004.

Kitsantonis, Niki. "Demis Roussos Dies at 68; Greek Singer Was Internationally Known," *New York Times*, January 29, 2015.

———. "The Greek State and the Diaspora: Venizelist Abroad, 1910–1932." In *Historical Poetics in Nineteenth and Twentieth Century Greece: Essays in Honor of Lily Macrakis*, edited by Stamatia Dova. Cambridge: Center for Hellenic Studies, Harvard University, 2015, https://chs.harvard.edu/CHS/article/display/4883

Konstantinidou, Anna I. *Ο Ρόλος Της Ελληνικής Παροικίας στην Αίγυπτο – Η Εξοδος και το Αιγυπτιακό Ζήτημα* [The Role of the Greeks in Egypt: The Exodus and the Egyptian Question]. Thessaloniki: Stamouli, 2017.

Kontaxi, Eleni I. "Κωστας Τσαγκαράδας: ένας Πηλειορείτης Λόγιος στην Αιγυπτο" [Kostas Tsangaradas: A Man of Letters from Mount Pelion in Egypt]. PhD diss., University of Thessaly, 2006.

Koutsoumis, Ntinos. *4 Χρόνια Αγνωστη Ιστορία* [4 Years' Unknown History]. Alexandria: n.p., 1946.

———. *Πως και Γιατί Διαλύθηκε η Παροικια της Αιγύπτου* [How and Why the Settlement in Egypt Was Dissolved]. Athens: n.p., 1992.

Krämer, Gudrun. *The Jews in Modern Egypt 1914–1952*. London: I.B.Tauris, 1989.

Landes, David. *Bankers and Pashas: International Finance and Economic Imperialism in Egypt*. New York: Harper & Row, 1969.

Books, Dissertations, and Journal Articles   239

Lekkou, Pantelis. *Το Αβερώφειο Γυμνάσιο Αλεξανδρείας απο της Ιδρύσεως του έως το 1960* [The Averoff High School of Alexandria from Its Establishment until 1960]. Thessaloniki: Zitis, 2004.

Liddel, Robert. *Cavafy: A Critical Biography*. London: Duckworth, 1974.

Lidorikis, Alekos. *Η Προπολεμική Αίγυπτος και οι Ελληνες* [Prewar Egypt and the Greeks]. Athens: Kastaniotis, 2005.

Livanos, Constantine N. *John Sakellaridis and Egyptian Cotton*. Alexandria: Procaccia, 1939.

Lloyd, Lord. *Egypt Since Cromer*, vol. 2, reprinted from 1934 edition. New York: AMS Press, 1970.

Mabro, Robert. *The Egyptian Economy 1952–1972*. Oxford: Clarendon Press, 1974.

———. "Alexandria 1860–1960: The Cosmopolitan Identity." In *Alexandria, Real and Imagined*, edited by Anthony Hirst and Michael Silk, 247–62. Burlington: Ashgate, 2004.

Mabro, Robert, and Samir Radwan. *The Industrialization of Egypt 1939–1973: Policy and Performance*. Oxford: Oxford University Press, 1976.

Malanos, Timos. *Αναμνήσεις ενός Αλεξανδρινού* [Memories of an Alexandrian]. Athens: Boukoumanis, 1971.

Mamlouk, Michel Antoine. *Memoirs of an Ottoman Mamlouk of Egypt*. Bloomington: Xlibris Corporation, 2010.

Mansel, Philip. *Levant: Splendour and Catastrophe on the Mediterranean*. New Haven: Yale University Press, 2010.

Marangoulis, Manolis. *«Καιρός να Συγχρονισθώμεν» Η Αιγυπτος και η Αιγυπτιώτικη Διανόηση (1919–1939)* ["A Time to Modernize": Egypt and Greek-Egyptian Intellectuals (1919–1939)]. Athens: University of Cyprus and Gutenberg Press, 2011.

Markantonatos, Leonidas G. *Τα Εν Αιγύπτω Ελληνικά Εκπαιδευτήρια* [The Greek Schools in Egypt]. Thessaloniki: Society of Macedonian Studies, 1957.

Michaelides, Evgenios. *Ο Αιγυπτιώτης Ελληνισμός και το Μέλλον του* [The Greeks of Egypt and their Future]. Alexandria: Grammata, 1927.

———. *Βιβλιογραφία των Ελλήνων Αιγυπτιωτών* [Bibliography of the Greeks of Egypt]. Alexandria: n.p., 1965–66.

———. *Πανόραμα: Εικονογραφημένη Ιστορία του Δημοσιογραφικού Περιοδικού Τύπου της Αιγύπτου υπό Αιγυπτιωτών Ελλήνων (1862–1972)* [Panorama: Illustrated History of the Magazines of the Greeks of Egypt in Egypt (1862–1972)]. Alexandria: Center for Greek Studies, 1972.

Milne, M.B. "Trade Treaties and Capitulations in Morocco." *Journal of the British Institute of International Affairs* 5, 1 (January 1926): 32–43.

Milner, Alfred. *England in Egypt*. London: Edward Arnold, 1894.

Minkin, Shane. "Documenting Death: Inquests, Governance and Belonging in 1890s Alexandria." In *The Long 1890s in Egypt: Colonial Quiescence, Subterranean Resistance*, edited by Marilyn Booth and Anthony P. Gorman, 31–56. Edinburgh: Edinburgh University Press, 2014.

Moskoff, Kostis. *Η Εθνική και Κοινωνική Συνείδηση στην Ελλάδα 1830-1909 Ιδεολογία του Μεταπρατικού Χώρου* [National and Social Consciouness in Greece, 1830–1909: Ideology of a Comprador Space]. 3rd edition. Athens: Synchroni Epochi, 1974.

Nicolaou, Cleomenis. *Το Παρελθον, το παρόν και το μέλλον της Κοινότητος Ιμπραημίας* [The Past, Present, and Future of the Community Organization of al-Ibrahimiya]. Alexandria: n.p., 1942.

Nikitaridis, Nikos. *Τα Ελληνικά Σωματεία στην Αίγυπτο* [Greek Associations in Egypt]. Athens: Aggelaki, 2015.

———. *Αιγυπτιώτικες Προσωπικότητες του Χθές* [Eminent Greeks of Egypt of Yesterday]. Athens: Aggelakis, 2017.

Nomikos, Christophoros. *Εισαγωγή στην Ιστορία των Αράβων* [Introduction to the History of the Arabs]. Alexandria: Grammata, 1927.

Nourse, Joseph Everett. *Maritime Canal of Suez: Brief Memoir*. Washington City: Philp & Solomons, 1869.

———. *Ο Αιγυπτιώτης Ελληνισμός στας Επάλξεις* [The Greeks of Egypt on the Battlements]. Alexandria: n.p., 1946.

Oppenheim, Jean Marc. "Twilight of a Colonial Ethos: The Alexandria Sporting Club, 1890–1956." PhD diss., Columbia University, 1991.

Osama, Omnia. "Nostos initiative to return Greek tourists to Egypt," *Egypt Today*, January 31, 2018, www.egypttoday.com/Article/9/41511/Nostos-initiative-to-return-Greek-tourists-to-Egypt

Owen, Edward Roger John. *Cotton and the Egyptian Economy 1820–1914*. Oxford: Oxford University Press, 1969.

Paleologos, Tasos. *Ο Αιγυπτιώτης Ελληνισμός Ιστορία και Δράσις 753 πχ – 1953* [The Greeks of Egypt: History and Activities 753 BC–1953]. Alexandria: n.p., 1953.

Pallini, Christina. "Geographic Theaters, Port Landscapes and Architecture in the Eastern Mediterranean." In *Cities of the Mediterranean from the Ottomans to the Present Day*, edited by Biray Kolluoglu and Meltem Toksöz, 61–77. London: I.B.Tauris, 2010.

Papadimitriou, Alexandra. *Αλεξάνδρεια-Αθήνα* [Alexandria–Athens]. Athens: Kastaniotis, 2010.

Papadimitriou, Giota. "Εκπαιδευτικός Όμιλος Αιγύπτου – Η ιδρυση του και η Δράση του κατά το 1919" [The Educational Society of Egypt: Its Establishment and Activities in 1919]. Proceedings of the 3rd International Conference on the History of Education, University of Patra, 2004.

————. "Ο Μαθητικός Τύπος ως Ατυπο Σχολικό Αρχείο: Η περίπτωση του μαθητικού περιοδικού Γλαύξ (1931–1957)" [Student Magazines as Informal School Archives: The Case of the School Magazine Glaux (1931–1957)]. In *Προγράμματα Σπουδών – Σχολικά Εγχειρίδια: απο το παρελθόν στο παρόν και στο μέλλον Πρακτικά Συνεδρίου τ. Γ* [Curricula–School Manuals: From the Past to the Present and the Future, Conference Proceedings, vol. 3]. Edited by S. Grosdos. Athens: Mouseio Scholikis Zois and Ekpaideysis, Pedagogiki Eteria Ellados, Pierce, American College of Greece, 2016.

Papadimitriou, Panagiota. "Η εκπαίδευση στις ελληνικές παροικίες της Αιγύπτου. Το παράδειγμα των Ελληνικών Εκπαιδευτηρίων Μανσούρας" [Education in the Greek Communities of Egypt: The Case of the Greek Schools in Mansura]. PhD diss., University of Athens, 2003.

Papakyriacou, Marios. "Formulation and Definitions of the Greek National Ideology in Colonial Egypt (1856–1919)." PhD diss., Berlin University, 2014.

Parolin, Gianluca P. *Citizenship in the Arab World: Kin, Religion and Nation-State*. Amsterdam: Amsterdam University Press, 2009.

Partheniadis, Georgios E. *Ελληνικά Νοσοκομεία Αλεξανδρείας* [Greek Hospitals of Alexandria]. Alexandria: Typografio Emporiou, 1960.

Paton, Andrew Archibald. *A History of the Egyptian Revolution from the Period of the Mamlukes to the Death of Mohammed Ali*. London: n.p., 1870.

Petridis, Ioannis. *Αίγυπτος-Ελλάς 1800–1933* [Egypt–Greece 1800–1933]. Athens: Ermis, 1933.

Phillip, Thomas. *The Syrians in Egypt 1725–1975*. Stuttgart: Franz Steiner Verlag, 1985.

Politi, Elie I. *Annuaire des Sociétés Égyptiennes Par Actions*. Alexandria: Procaccia, 1938.

Politi, Villy N. *Ελληνική Κοινότητα 100 Χρόνια Σφραγίδα στο Κάιρο* [Greek Community: A One Hundred-year Seal on Cairo]. Cairo: Greek Community of Cairo, 2006.

Politis, Athanasios. *Ο Ελληνισμός και η Νεωτέρα Αίγυπτος* [Hellenism and

Modern Egypt], vols. 1 and 2. Alexandria: Grammata, 1928.

———. *L'Hellénisme et l'Egypte Moderne*. Paris: Alcan, 1929–1930.

Psarakis, Takis D. *Ανθολογιο Αλεξάνδρειας* [An Anthology of Alexandria]. Athens: Nea Sinora Livanis, 1992.

Radopoulos, Radamanthis. *Εισαγωγή εις την Ιστορίαν της Ελληνικής Κοινότητος Αλεξανδρείας 1830–1927* [An Introduction to the History of the Greek Community of Alexandria, 1830–1927]. Alexandria: Kasimatis, 1928.

———. *Ο Βασιλεύς Φουάτ ο Αος και η Αναγενωμμένη Αίγυπτος* [King Fu'ad I and Egypt Reborn]. Alexandria: Kasimatis, 1930.

Reid, Donald Malcolm. *Whose Pharaohs? Archaeology, Museums, and Egyptian National Identity from Napoleon to World War I*. Oakland: University of California Press, 2003.

Reynolds, Nancy Y. *A City Consumed: Urban Commerce, the Cairo Fire, and the Politics of Decolonization in Egypt*. Stanford: Stanford University Press, 2012.

Rizk, Yunan Labib. "The Fall of Lord Lloyd," *al-Ahram Weekly*, July 18–24, 2002, http://weekly.ahram.org.eg/Archive/2002/595/chrncls.htm

Rodenbeck, Max. *Cairo: The City Victorious*. New York: Vintage, 1999.

Rota, Maria. "Το Περιοδικό Γράμματα της Αλεξάνδρειας" [The Journal *Grammata* of Alexandria, 1911–1919]. PhD diss., University of Athens, 1994.

Rousos, Petros. Η *Μεγάλη Πενταετία* [The Great Five Years]. Athens: Sinchroni Epochi, 1976, 400.

Royle, Charles. *The Egyptian Campaigns 1882 to 1885 and the Events that Led to Them, vol. 1*. London: Hurst and Blackett, 1886.

Russell Pasha, *Egyptian Service 1902–1946*. London: John Murray, 1949.

Said, Edward. *Out of Place: A Memoir*. New York: Vintage, 2012.

Sakkas, John. "Greece and the Mass Exodus of the Egyptian Greeks." *Journal of the Hellenic Diaspora* 35, 2 (2009): 102–105.

al-Sayyid Marsot, Afaf Lutfi. *Egypt in the Reign of Muhammad Ali*. Cambridge: Cambridge University Press, 1984.

Schecter, Relli. "Selling Luxury: The Rise of the Egyptian Cigarette and the Transformation of the Egyptian Tobacco Market, 1850–1914." *International Journal of Middle East Studies* 35, 1 (2003): 51–75.

———. *Smoking, Culture, and Economy in the Middle East: The Egyptian Tobacco Market 1850–2000*. New York: I.B.Tauris, 2006.

Seferis, Georgios. *Πολιτικό Ημερολόγιο Α' 1935–1944* [Political Diary, vol. 1, 1935–1944]. Athens: Ikaros, 1992.

Sfeir, George N. "The Abolition of Confessional Jurisdiction in Egypt: The Non-Muslim Courts." *Middle East Journal* 5, no. 3 (summer 1956): 248–56.

Sideris, Nikos. "The Greek Settlers' Flight from Egypt: the Psychological Aspects." *Journal of the Hellenic Diaspora* 35.2 (2009): 145–54.

Siskos, Archimandrite Anthimos. *Η Διοικητική Οργάνωσις της Εκκλησίας της Αλεξανδρείας τ. ιος Η Νομική και Κανονική Θέσις της Εκκλησίας Αλεξανδρείας Έναντι της Αιγυπτιακής Επικράτειας* [The Administrative Governance of the Church of Alexandria, vol. 1, The Legal and Canonical Position of the Church of Alexandria in Relation to the Egyptian State]. Alexandria: Typografion Emporiou, 1937.

Soliman, Amany. "The Rise of Egyptian Nationalism and the Perception of Foreigners in Egypt 1914–1923." In *The First World War and its Aftermath: the Spacing of the Middle East*, edited by T.G. Fraser, 19–39. London: Gingko Press, 2015.

Souloyannis, Efthymios. *Αντώνης Εμμανουήλ Μπενάκης 1873-1954 Ο ευπατρίδης, ο διανοούμενος, ο ανθρωπιστής* [Antonis Emmanuil Benachi 1873–1954: Nobleman, Intellectual, Humanist]. Athens: Kastaniotis - Benaki Museum, 2004.

———. *Η Θέση των Ελλήνων στην Αίγυπτο* [The Status of the Greeks in Egypt]. Athens: Municipality of Athens, 1999.

———. *Η Ελληνική Κοινότητα του Καΐρου* [The Greek Community of Cairo]. Athens: Kotinos, 2001.

———. *Η Ελληνική Κοινότητα Αλεξάνδρειας 1843–1993* [The Greek Community of Alexandria 1843–1993]. Athens: ELIA, 2005.

Starr, Deborah. *Remembering Cosmopolitan Egypt: Literature, Culture, and Empire*. New York: Routledge, 2009.

Tamvakis, Stefanos. "Ο Αιγυπτιώτης Ελληνισμός σήμερα. Το αύριο" [The Greeks of Egypt Today. The Future?], February 2016, www.tamvakis.com

Tignor, Robert. "The Economic Activities of Foreigners in Egypt, 1920–1950: From Millet to Haute Bourgeoisie." *Comparative Studies in Society and History* 22, no. 3 (July 1980): 416–49.

———. *Egypt: A Short History*. Princeton: Princeton University Press, 2010.

———. "The Egyptian Revolution of 1919: New Directions in the Egyptian Economy." In *The Middle Eastern Economy: Studies in Economics and Economic History*, edited by Elie Kedourie. New York: Routlege, 2014.

———. *Egyptian Textiles and British Capital 1930–1956*. Cairo: American University of Cairo Press, 1989.

————. "Nationalism, Economic Planning, and Development Projects in Interwar Egypt." *The International Journal of African Historical Studies* 10, no. 2 (1977): 185–208.

————. *State, Private Enterprise and Economic Change in Egypt, 1918–1952.* Princeton: Princeton University Press, 1984.

Tomai, Photini. "Η Εξοδος των Ελλήνων απο την Αίγύπτο" [The Exodus of the Greeks from Egypt], *Tò Vima*, May 8, 2007.

Tomara-Sideris, Matoula. *Αλεξανδρινές Οικογένειες Χωρέμη-Μπενάκη-Σαλβάγου* [Alexandrian Families Choremi-Benachi-Salvago]. 3rd edition. Athens: Kerkyra, 2013.

————. *Ευεργετισμός και Προσωπικότητα Ευεργέτες Έλληνες του Καΐρου* [Benefaction and Personality: Greek Benefactors of Cairo], vols. 1 and 2. Athens: Papazis, 2002.

————. *Ο Αιγυπτιωτης Ελληνισμός στους Δρόμους του Μπαμπακιού* [The Greeks in Egypt on the Cotton Roads]. Athens: Kerkyra, 2011.

————. *Benefaction in Modern Greece: Theory and Practice.* Athens: Economic Publishing, 2017.

Trimi, Katerina, and Ilios Yannakakis. "The Greeks: The *Parikia* of Alexandria." In *Alexandria 1860–1960: the Brief Life of a Cosmopolitan Community*, edited by Robert Ilbert and Ilios Yannakakis with Jacques Hassoun, 65–71. Alexandria: Harpocrates, 1977.

Trimi-Kirou, Ekaterini. "Kinotis Grecque d'Alexandrie: Sa politique éducative (1843–1932)." PhD diss., Université des Sciences Humaines de Strasbourg, 1996.

Tsaravopoulos, Nikos. *Η Εγκατάσταση των Ελλήνων στην Αίγύπτο* [The Establishment of the Greeks in Egypt]. Cairo: Tsouma, 1948.

Tselika, Valentini. Πηνελόπη Δέλτα Αφήγηση Ζωής [Penelope Delta: A Life Story]. Athens: Olkos - Banaki Museum, 2004.

Tsirkas, Stratis. "Η Πνευματική Αντίσταση στη Μέση Ανατολή" [The Intellectual Resistance in the Middle East]. *Epitheorise Technes Review of Art* no. 87–88 (1962): 480.

————. *Drifting Cities.* Translated by Kay Cicellis. New York: Knopf, 1974.

————. *Ο Καβάφης και η Εποχή του* [Cavafy and His Era], 12th edition. Athens: Kedros, 1983.

————. "Αναμνήσεις απο την Ανω Αίγύπτο" [Memories from Upper Egypt]. *E Lexi* 27 (September 1983): 786–87.

Tsoucalas, Constantinos. *Εξάρτηση και Αναπαραγωγή Ο Κοινωνικός Ρόλος των Εκπαιδευτικών Μηχανισμών στην Ελλάδα (1830-1922)* [Dependency and

Reproduction: The Social Role of Educational Mechanisms in Greece (1830–1922)]. Athens: Themelio, 1977.

Tsourkas, Cléobule. *Les Hellènes dans l'intérieur de l'Égypte.* Thessaloniki: Society of Macedonian Studies, 1957.

Typaldos, Georgios K. *Ανατολικαί Επιστολαί Σμύρνη Αύγυπτος Παλαιστίνη* [Letters from the East: Smyrna, Egypt, Palestine]. Athens: n.p., 1859.

Tzalas, Harry. *Farewell to Alexandria: Eleven Short Stories.* Cairo: American University in Cairo Press, 2004.

———. "Literary Alexandria and Nostalgic Alexandrian Literature." *Journal of the Hellenic Diaspora* 35.2 (2009): 169–74.

Vatikiotis, Panayotis Jerasimos. *Nasser and his Generation.* London: Croom Helm, 1978.

Vitalis, Robert. "The End of Third Worldism in Egyptian Studies." In *The Arab Studies Journal* 4, no. 1 (Spring 1996): 13–32.

———. *When Capitalists Collide: Business Conflict and the End of Empire in Egypt.* Berkeley: University of California Press, 1995.

Woodhouse, Christopher Montague. *The Apple of Discord.* London: Hutchinson, 1948.

Wright, Arnold. *Twentieth Century Impressions of Egypt.* London: Lloyd's, 1909.

Yannakakis, Ilios. "Farewell Alexandria." In *Alexandria 1860–1960: The Brief Life of a Cosmopolitan Community,* edited by Robert Ilbert and Ilios Yannakakis with Jacques Hassoun, 106–22. Alexandria: Harpocrates, 1977.

Yannoulopoulos, George. "Beyond the Frontiers: The Greek Diaspora." In *The Greeks: Classical, Byzantine and Modern,* edited by Robert Browning, 287–98. New York: Portland House, 1985.

Index

Agapitidis, Sotirios 179, 180, 188
Alexandria: architecture 149–50;
  bombardment of, 1882 49–54, 107;
  Chatby 71, 143, 151; foreign residents
  and anti-foreign incidents 23, 47,
  51–55, 59, 78–80, 83, 96, 146–51, 153;
  General Produce Association 64; Greek
  Chamber of Commerce 109, 117–18,
  184; Greek community organization
  37, 39–40, 68–71, 94, 178–79; Greek
  Consular authorities 25, 33, 51, 70,
  79–81, 85, 98, 177, 194, 211–12;
  Municipal Council 149–50; Quartier
  Grec neighborhood 67, 135, 149, 162,
  191; Sporting Club 151–52
Ambetios Greek School, Cairo 167, 170,
  199, 209
d'Anastasi, Ioannis 31, 36–38, 45, 49
Anglo-Egyptian Bank 48, 54, 71, 107
Anglo-Egyptian Treaty 82–83, 96, 173, 174
Antifasistiki Protoporia 143, 171
Antoniades, Ioannis 49, 54, 70, 202
Armenians in Egypt 27–28, 34, 44, 79, 116,
  156, 158, 160
Arvanitakis, Georgios 88
Association of Greeks of Egypt 199, 201,
  204–206
Asyut 40, 166–69
Averoff, Evangelos 189–91, 195–96
Averoff, Georgios 69–72
Averoff High School in Alexandria 70–71,
  114–15, 205, 201
Australia 177–79, 191, 206

Benachi: Antonis 53, 67, 123, 162;
  Emmanuel 53, 64, 65, 69, 71–73,
  108, 123, 149, 162; family and family
  members 53, 67, 102, 149, 154, 195;
  Penelope (Delta) 53, 67, 72, 145
Bibliotheca Alexandrina 210, 213
Bolanachi, Angelo 160–61
Briggs, Martin 148–49, 152, 157

Britain: Alexandria, bombardment of,
  1882 49–52; business community
  and residents 77, 83, 183–84, 187;
  Capitulations, attitude towards 55, 58,
  75–77, 80–85, 89–92; Greeks in Egypt,
  attitude towards 60–67; maritime
  presence in the Mediterranean 29–30;
  occupation and rule over Egypt 1882–
  1914 24, 49–50, 53–60; relations with
  Greece 47, 95, 143–44; Suez Crisis and
  presence in the Canal Zone 173–77,
  181–83; World War II policies towards
  Egypt and Greeks in Egypt 93–94,
  115–16, 133–42

Cairo: architecture 151–52; "Black Saturday"
  Fire, 1952 173–74; cosmopolitanism
  147–48, 152, 156–57; foreign residents
  and anti-foreign incidents 35, 47,
  52, 96, 153, 156; Greek community
  organization 39–40, 72, 79, 108, 134,
  136, 169, 173, 178, 184, 186, 202;
  Greek population and professions 26,
  32, 35, 43, 46, 59, 69, 110, 115, 142;
  Greek schools 40, 72, 122, 130, 138,
  170, 199, 202
Canellopoulos, Panayotis 137–39
Capitulations 25, 39, 49, 50, 55, 58–59,
  75–78, 81–86, 88–95, 117, 119, 125
Casulli family and family members 31, 41,
  49, 65, 102, 213
Cavafy, Constantine P. 42, 54–55, 121–22,
  130–33, 151, 157–58, 168, 206–207,
  211–12
Charitatos, Dimitri 195, 205–209
Chios 28, 43, 67, 124
Choremi, Benachi & Company 65, 67, 102,
  154
Choremi: family and family members 65,
  102, 111, 149, 172, 195; Ioannis 41, 65
Christophoros, Patriarch of Alexandria 87,
  90, 136, 143

247

Ismail, Khedive 24, 45, 48–49, 55, 68, 107, 152
Israel 116, 178, 181–82, 185
Italian language 23, 38, 84, 114, 146, 161
Italians in Egypt 27, 47, 57, 80, 84–85, 92, 116, 146, 148–53, 156, 158–60, 174, 183–84, 187, 194, 203
Italy 48, 77, 91–93, 107, 116, 134, 136, 139, 142, 149, 159, 161, 184, 204

Jews: in the Ottoman Empire 27–28, 31; in Egypt 34, 84, 93, 116, 138, 149, 151, 153, 156, 160, 178, 183–84, 188

Kafr al-Zayyat 41–42, 78, 102, 107–108, 130, 132, 155, 179, 202
Karamanlis, Constantinos 186, 189–91

labor unions and strikes 104, 113–14, 141–42, 158, 191
Levantines 34, 148, 151–52, 154
Lloyd, Lord 82–84

Malanos, Timos 159, 204, 206–207
Malta and Maltese in Egypt 31, 34, 52, 146, 149, 153, 156
Mansura 41–42, 129–30, 160, 174, 199, 207
Metaxas, Ioannis 89, 92, 125, 133–37
Michaelides, Evgenios 87–88, 163
Michalakopoulos, Andreas 85–86, 125
Milner, Alfred 50, 58, 76, 80
Modinos, Polys 95, 97
Muhammad Ali 24–28, 30–37, 40, 45, 47, 49, 86, 88, 149, 160, 214

Naguib, Muhammad 175, 177
al-Nahhas, Mustafa 91–92
Nasser, Gamal Abd al- 175, 177, 181–94, 197–98, 205
Nicolaou, Nikolaos 68, 81, 150
Nile Delta 23, 41–43, 65, 72, 79, 87, 103, 174
Nomikos, Christophoros 162–63

Ottoman Empire 24–29, 31–33, 37, 39, 43, 47, 50–51, 57–58, 60, 63–64, 72–73, 75–76, 79, 85, 107, 113, 119, 121–22, 124, 130, 147–48, 178, 203

Papadimitriou, Alexandra 197, 203
Petridis, Georgios 164–65, 168
Pialopoulos, Symeon 109–11, 195
Politis, Athanasios 25, 84–88, 90, 159
Politis, Nikolaos 90–92
Port Said 45, 47, 130, 132, 152–53, 159–60, 172, 181–84, 193, 212–13

Ralli Family and Ralli & Company 40–41, 64, 69, 154, 156

Ramla 32, 53, 67, 123, 149
Roussos, Georgios 85, 91, 134, 139, 141–42

Said, Edward 152, 154, 156–57
Sakellarios, Nikolaos 174–75, 188
Salvago: family 71, 128, 149, 154, 191, 195; Constantine 70–72; Mikés 67, 71, 80, 92, 94, 100, 110, 126–28, 141, 143–44
Seferis, Georgios 139–41
Sinadino family and members 48, 51, 65, 69, 78, 102, 156
Smyrna (Izmir) 77, 130, 154, 200
Suez: Canal 44–45, 72, 78, 89, 148, 152, 158, 171, 173–74, 177, 181–83, 185, 187, 193; Canal Company 158, 176, 181, 201, 212; crisis 178, 181–88, 192; Greeks 44–45; town 40, 45, 47, 136, 152–53, 193, 199
Syrians in Egypt 40, 42, 46, 62, 100, 146, 149, 155–56, 166, 196

Tewfik, Khedive 49–50, 63–64
Tossizza: family 31, 37; Michael 33, 36–40, 49, 69
Trikoupis, Charilaos 51–60
Tsangardas, Kostas 166–67, 169
Tsirkas, Stratis 42, 54–55, 69, 138, 149, 158, 167–68, 207–208, 211
Tsouderos, Emmanuel 134–35, 137, 139–42

Upper Egypt 40, 43, 66, 72, 79, 103, 122, 130, 166–67, 169
'Urabi, Ahmad 50–51, 54, 145

Vatimbellas, Nikolaos 85, 91
Venizelos, Eleftherios 73, 77, 78, 85, 89, 124–25, 139
Victoria College 151, 156, 158

Wafd party 79, 82, 97, 150, 166

Xenakion School, Cairo 122, 135, 138

Yalourakis, Manolis 206–209

Zagazig 42, 87, 130, 132, 136, 174, 202
Zaghlul, Sa'd 76, 81–82
Zerbinis, Dimitris and Stratis 103, 107, 142, 174, 195
Zervoudachi family and family members 42, 54, 68–71, 149, 151, 154, 172
Ziwar, Ahmed Pasha 81, 102, 107
Zizinia, Stephanos 31–32, 36–39, 45, 49, 54–55, 149